AF477782

THE SIMPLE ART
OF VOTING

THE SIMPLE ART OF VOTING

The Cognitive Shortcuts of Italian Voters

Delia Baldassarri

TRANSLATED BY NICHOLAS CROTTY

OXFORD
UNIVERSITY PRESS

OXFORD
UNIVERSITY PRESS

Oxford University Press is a department of the University of Oxford.
It furthers the University's objective of excellence in research,
scholarship, and education by publishing worldwide.

Oxford   New York

Auckland   Cape Town   Dar es Salaam   Hong Kong   Karachi
Kuala Lumpur   Madrid   Melbourne   Mexico City   Nairobi
New Delhi   Shanghai   Taipei   Toronto

With offices in

Argentina   Austria   Brazil   Chile   Czech Republic   France   Greece
Guatemala   Hungary   Italy   Japan   Poland   Portugal   Singapore
South Korea   Switzerland   Thailand   Turkey   Ukraine   Vietnam

Oxford is a registered trademark of Oxford University Press in the UK and certain other countries.

Published in the United States of America by Oxford University Press
198 Madison Avenue, New York, NY 10016

Originally published as *La Semplice Arte di Votare* © Il Mulino, 2005

Library of Congress Cataloging-in-Publication Data
Baldassarri, Delia.
[Semplice arte di votare. English.]
The simple art of voting : the cognitive shortcuts of voters / Delia Baldassarri.
p.   cm.
Originally published in Italian in 2005 as: La semplice arte di votare.
Includes bibliographical references and index.
ISBN 978-0-19-982824-1 (hardcover : alk. paper)
1. Voting—Italy. 2. Elections—Italy. 3. Italy—Politics and government—1994– I. Title.
JN5611.B2713   2012
324.945—dc23   2012009572

1 3 5 7 9 8 6 4 2

Printed in the United States of America
on acid-free paper

CONTENTS

Preface to the English Edition | ix

Introduction | 3

PART ONE Choosing and Voting

1. Voting: An Individual and Reasoned Choice | 15
   What Electoral "Rationale"? | 15
   Voting as a Nonrandom yet Nondetermined Choice | 16
   Voting as an Individual Choice | 22
   Voting as a Reasoned Choice | 26

2. Human Decision Making and Heuristics of Judgment | 32
   The Study of Human Decision Making | 32
   The Rational Choice Approach to Decision Making | 34
   Heuristics and Biases Program | 37
   Fast and Frugal Heuristics and Ecological Rationality | 46

3. Political Cognition, Sophistication, and Heuristics | 57
   The Political Cognition Approach | 57
   The Concept of Political Sophistication | 59
   The Heterogeneity of Cognitive Processes | 63

Voting Heuristics | 67
The Art of Making It Simple: Heuristics
 in the Social Sciences | 73

PART TWO The Cognitive Shortcuts
of Italian Voters

4. The Heuristics of Italian Voters | 79

Theoretical Framework and Research Hypotheses | 79
The "Ecology" of the Italian Political System | 85
Toward a Classification of Italian Voters | 91
Utilius: The Spatial Voter | 95
Amicus: The Sympathetic Voter | 105
Aliens: The Voter "Innocent of Ideology" | 112
The Typology of Political Heuristics | 117

5. Who are *Utilius, Amicus, Aliens,* and *Medians?* | 122

Heuristics and Political Sophistication:
 a Cognitive Profile | 123
Heuristics and Social-Contextual Factors:
 A Sociodemographic Profile | 133
Voting Heuristics Rooted in Cognition and
 Political Culture | 142

6. Systematic and Effective Voting Heuristics | 157

Ideological Coherence in Issue Preferences | 159
Ideological Coherence in Organizing Future
 Voting Preferences | 166
Univocal Evaluations of Governmental Capacity | 172
The Effectiveness of the Voting Typology | 177

7. Heterogeneity of the Decision-Making Processes | 185

The Organization of the Elements of Choice | 186
Utilius vs *Aliens*: Ideology *Versus* the
  "TV Remote" Effect | 194
Amicus/Hostis: A Zero-Sum Game | 200

8. Conclusions | 209

Results | 211
Outlines for Future Research | 216
FAQ: "Who Do They Vote For in the End?" | 223

REFERENCES | 229

INDEX | 249

This book is a revised version of *La Semplice Arte di Votare*, which was originally published in Italian by Il Mulino in 2005. I started this line of research in my undergraduate years: As a student in sociology and political science, I believed in the possibility of making sense of Italian voters. I also believed that this could be done more effectively by looking at how people make up their minds instead of by focusing on their actual voting choices. This was in sharp contrast with the popular zeitgeist. By the end of the 1990s, most accounts of Italian politics were already dominated by the exceptional and polarizing figure of Silvio Berlusconi. Experts and pundits came to see Berlusconi as an agent of either extraordinary change, absolute evil, or both, and to describe those who voted for him accordingly. The left-wing intelligentsia tended to depict Berlusconi voters as rich tax-evaders; ignorant, television-fed housewives and retirees; or corrupted members of the southern political machine. Right-wing supporters, by contrast, presented themselves as hard-working professionals; self-made business entrepreneurs; and 'homegrown' yuppies. To avoid the perils of stereotyping, I decided to study voters' decision-making strategies, adopting a perspective that considers who people vote for as secondary to the process through which they actually come to a decision. Instead of engaging in endless debates about the rationality or goodness of people's voting choices, I started from the assumption that any political choice is the byproduct of some reflective process and set out to identify these reasoning processes themselves, and the cognitive and contextual conditions that determine their adoption. The classification of Italian voters presented in this book is the outcome of this effort.

By the time the opportunity to revise and translate the book came about, I had realized that there was a second, more fundamental reason that guided my research. Although a few theories of action have been advanced, most sociologists show little interest in the actual decision-making processes that lead people to act as they do. They often dismiss rational choice theory as inadequate because of its assumption of a selfish actor and its reliance on optimization strategies that are cognitively implausible, but they have failed to provide a real alternative. This book documents my journey into political cognition and decision science in search of the building blocks of a theory of adaptive decision making that is sensitive to the cognitive and contextual constraints that limit and enable human action. I hope that the theoretical framework that emerges, and the analytical strategy I have adopted, might be of some use to other people in the discipline.

The book could not be possible without the close collaboration with Hans Schadee, who introduced me to the research on political psychology and has been a constant source of inspiration through the earlier years of my career. Some of the results presented in this book have appeared elsewhere in a joint publication (see D. Baldassarri, H. Schadee "Voter Heuristics and Political Cognition in Italy: An Empirical Typology," *Electoral Studies*, 2006). I am also extremely grateful to Mario Diani and Piergiorgio Corbetta for their precious support and to the members of the Italian National Election Studies (ITANES) for offering the invaluable professional opportunity of working with them. I thank the Italian Political Science Association for awarding *La Semplice Arte di Votare* the prize for the best Political Science book published by a young scholar (2005–2006), and the Societá Italiana di Studi Elettorali for the "Celso

Ghini" National Prize for the best dissertation on political and electoral studies (2002–2003).

I am grateful to colleagues Alejandro Portes, Paul DiMaggio, Peter Bearman, and Jeff Manza for encouraging the book translation; the Department of Sociology at Princeton University and the Russell Sage Foundation for providing an ideal environment to work on the revisions; Nicholas Crotty for translating the book; and editorial assistant Rebecca Clark and editor James Cook at Oxford University Press for working with me to substantially improve the quality of the manuscript.

As I finish revising the manuscript, Berlusconi's government has been forced to resign. *Sic transit gloria mundi.*

New York, November 2011

THE SIMPLE ART
OF VOTING

Introduction

Voting is an art: the art of rendering simple an exercise in decision making that in many regards is complex. The information that arises out of political debate is often contradictory and redundant. How can we select from it? What should we focus on? Parties, coalitions, leaders, and issues form an entangled mass of stimuli that thrust themselves on electorates day after day. How is it possible to unravel them all? With what cognitive strategies? In other words, how do voters perceive, judge, and organize the various objects that fill the political landscape?

Politics is a bit like sport. For some it is entertainment, for others just a pointless expenditure of time and energy. Some citizens—very few—are interested, well-informed, and engaged, fans of a particular party or candidate; others—a great many—are uninterested, distracted, or even bored by the spectacle and willing only to take an occasional glance at the game or perhaps just the final score. Even these people, however, have an opinion; even they vote. And perhaps these same people experience emotions as well: perhaps they too are happy or disappointed about someone winning or losing.

On the one hand, then, voting is a choice of a complex nature, one which necessarily entails a substantial effort to understand and simplify; on the other, citizens are extremely varied in terms of the degree of interest, emotional investment, and involvement they have in politics. How is it possible, then, from a scientific point of view, to provide a comprehensive account both of the complexity of the choice and the heterogeneity of the actors involved? In other words, how is it possible to account for the way in which citizens, with different levels of political sophistication, confront the decision of who to vote for?

This book suggests the following solution: to perform the common task of selecting a party, voters make use of various cognitive shortcuts—heuristics—in accordance with the type of information and the level of cognitive sophistication that they have at their disposal. Voters absorb and interpret political debate in a range of ways that are qualitatively different, in that they use different types of information and different criteria of judgment, and adopt different decision-making strategies to determine their voting preference. And it is precisely through the use of different strategies of reasoning that voters with varying degrees of interest and types of information are able to reduce the complex task of evaluating many political options to a manageable form and reach a satisfactory decision.

The heuristics people use are domain-specific. In the context of politics they rely on the political environment to furnish the elements—ideology, parties, leaders, and issues—upon which judgment processes are based. Heuristics are all the more effective when they succeed in reproducing the information structure of the political context and, moreover, exploit its peculiar composition. For instance, the categories of left and right are at the core of an efficient form of heuristic reasoning because they facilitate the organization of political information on various political objects: parties, leaders, and issues can all be placed on the ideological left-right continuum.

In more general terms, this book deals with the problem of human decision making under conditions of uncertainty and limited information. Most theories of action in sociology dismiss rational choice theory as inadequate for its assumption of a selfish actor and for its reliance on optimization strategies that are cognitively implausible. However, so far sociologists have failed to provide a real alternative. Most scholars either do not spell out how decisions are made, or rely on decision-making processes that still include some sort of utility maximization. In contrast, research programs in cognitive psychology and decision science have developed computational models of adaptive decision making that rely on fast and frugal heuristics, a set of "satisficing" strategies that do not require a large amount of information (frugal) and rely on reasoning algorithms that are very simple and rapid (fast). At the core of this approach stands Simon's concept of ecological rationality, according to which individuals achieve satisficing choices drawing on their cognitive capacities and the structure of information in the context in which the decision making takes place.

Instead of engaging in the endless debate over the rationality of human action, its definition, and its scope conditions, we will start from the pragmatic assumption that any political choice is the byproduct of some reflective process and aim at the identification of these reasoning processes, and the cognitive and contextual conditions that determine their adoption. In Simon's own words "human rational behavior . . . is shaped by a scissor whose two blades are the structure of task environments and the computational capabilities of the actor" (1990, 7). While most research in cognitive psychology has focused on the constraints of the human mind, often stripping context away in laboratory settings, the analysis presented in this book will begin from the context in which the decision-making task takes place, and will show how the cognitive shortcuts of Italian voters are forged by the combination of the political context and their cognitive and affective dispositions.

In particular, the Italian national general elections of the 1990s are an ideal setting for understanding the role of contextual and institutional factors, due to the novelty and complexity of the political offering. Following the collapse of the entire political system of the First Republic, Italian voters had to quickly get acquainted with a new electoral law, a mixed system that combined a majoritarian and proportional component, and a new political landscape, which was populated by almost a dozen major parties, most of which were new, a largely renovated political leadership, and two prominent party coalitions. When compared to the "minimalist" American two-party system, the set of options provided by the Italian political landscape is larger, thus opening up to a few possible decision-making strategies.

In our perspective, the electoral choice is a phenomenon of interest in terms of how that decision comes about. The focus is on the actual *process* of making the choice, rather than its aggregate *outcome*. In the latter case, the object of inquiry is the citizen as voter for a particular party or coalition and the research question concerns the factors that influence voting preferences. In contrast, when studying the process that leads to the formation of political preferences and party choice, the object is the voter as decision-maker and attention centers on the procedures for making choices—specifically, on the way in which political belief systems are organized; on the judgment criteria used; and on the way in which political knowledge and institutional factors combine to determine the heuristic adopted.

Most academic research on public opinion and voting behavior accounts for the outcome of voters' decision making by concentrating on the extent to which certain sociodemographic and attitudinal factors (social class, gender, race, age, level of education, geopolitical area of residence, religiosity, etc.) contribute to the victory of one or other party. By contrast, this study investigates the structuration of political preferences starting out from the way citizens perceive and understand the political debate. Voters are not distinguished in terms of the party they vote for, but on the basis of the cognitive shortcuts they use to determine their particular voting preferences. These voting *heuristics* are hypothesized as pathways that can be freely pursued by individuals regardless of their ethical frameworks and distinct aspirations and, for this reason, open to voters of different parties and coalitions.

As voters differ in their level of political interest and information, it is not plausible to assume that they all deploy the same decision-making strategy. Yet, most empirical analyses of public opinion surveys make precisely this assumption by modeling the electoral choice of all voters using a single set of independent variables. In contrast, this book is based on the assumption of *political heterogeneity*, starting from the premise that reasoning voters use various cognitive shortcuts—*heuristics*—to arrive at decisions, and adopts a strategy of data analysis sensitive to the fact that citizens might reason in qualitatively different ways, evaluate according to different criteria, and use different types of information.

By using a parsimonious set of variables present in nearly all election surveys, it is possible to identify four types of voters. The first type, *utilius*, understands politics using the ideological categories of "left" and "right" and defines his own voting preference following a principle of spatial proximity. The second type of voter, *amicus*, conceives of politics as a dichotomy; she tends to reduce reality to a dualism: the competition between party coalitions (and between their leaders). Although less demanding from a cognitive and information perspective, this way of reasoning allows voters to construct a map of the political landscape that is almost as effective as that of the *utilius* voters. A third type, *aliens*, is driven by an active rejection of politics and is unwilling or unable to represent the political debate through traditional ideological categories; he carefully keeps his distance from the political debate and maintains a general feeling of distrust toward politics. Nonetheless, he/she too makes choices, in some cases selecting the parties of the right and in others those of the left. This voter does not rely on any systematic voting strategy, and is easy prey for television broadcasters. The last type, *medians*, constitutes a residual category, including all those cases that do not belong to the previous categories. This type of voter is placed in an intermediary position along a path between *utilius* and *amicus*, on the one hand, and *aliens*, on the other, and has the role of a category of comparison *vis-à-vis* the other three.

In general, by distinguishing voters according to their actual knowledge and style of political reasoning, we identify classification criteria that are both able to grasp actual differences in the level of political cognition and sophistication, and suggest what kinds of information are pertinent for each type of voter. It is evident that people follow multiple strategies and rely selectively on different kinds of available information. It follows that parties, leaders, coalitions, and media affect voter behavior, but they have different leverage on different types of voters. A proper account of voting behavior needs to incorporate the different mechanisms through which voters perceive, represent, and evaluate politics.

Roadmap of the Book

To better understand the *rationale* that guides human decision making, and electoral choice in particular, we have, first, to come to terms with the fact that in sociology the debate on the rationality of human action has for a considerable time been at a dead end. The only way to escape from this impasse is by turning the focus of inquiry away from the analysis of "what rational behavior is" toward an analysis of the actual procedures of rational thinking. In this regard, considerable help has come from two related areas of scientific research: the recent achievements of studies on human decision making and the application of cognitive psychology to the study of political behavior. The first part of this book offers an account of these developments.

Chapter 1 draws a profile of the voter as decision maker, the protagonist of a choice. Voting is argued to be a nonrandom yet not-determined, individual, and reasoned choice. The chapter confronts the more general problem of the rationality of human action, arguing that recent attempts to extend the concept of rationality to incorporate the cognitive limitations and contextual constraints of human decision making have led to a blurred distinction between rational and nonrational action. These considerations form the base of two important aspects of the book. First, the research investigates the reasoning that leads to a particular choice, not the rationality or correctness of that choice. Second, since the rationality of human action can only be defined in relation to the context and the actual capacities of the actor, different individuals might employ diverse decision-making strategies.

Chapter 2 introduces the conceptual developments of the research on human decision making, an important instrument for understanding how individuals make choices in complex situations characterized by uncertainty, incomplete information, and limited time. In particular, we will focus on two different approaches to heuristics, Kahneman and Tversky's "Heuristics and Biases" research program and Gigerenzer and the ABC Research Group's "Fast and Frugal Heuristics." Each is a set of decision-making strategies based on the use of a limited amount of information and simple and quick reasoning algorithms. While both approaches constitute a plausible alternative to rational choice models of decision making, the "Heuristic and Biases" approach relies on a "right answer," and is therefore difficult to apply to the study of political decisions. In deciding whom to vote for, whom to marry, or where to relocate, there is no right answer. The "Fast and Frugal Heuristics" approach, with its focus on *satisficing* choice rather than *best* choice, is better suited for the study of this type of decision making.

Chapter 3 presents the key features of the political cognition approach and illustrates its contribution to the understanding of political behavior. Specifically, the chapter discusses political sophistication, the problems involved in its definition and measurement, the heterogeneity of cognitive processes, and the use of heuristics in the field of politics.

This combination of concepts derived from studies on human decision making and the political cognition approach form the basis of our novel interpretative framework. This framework is based on assumptions that are distinct from and much more realistic than those pertaining to the rational choice approach and it aspires to accounting for the cognitive mechanisms of a large and heterogeneous part of the electorate, given the capacity of the human mind and the constraints of the social environment in which individuals operate. The second part of the book deploys this framework in an empirical investigation of the judgment processes that Italian citizens use when making up their minds about politics.

Chapter 4 enters directly into the heart of the book. First, it provides a summary of the theoretical framework and outlines our major research hypotheses. Second, it describes the Italian political system of the 1990s and highlights its most salient characteristics, thus setting the basis for our classification of Italian citizens. Finally, it describes the classification criteria used to assign our respondents to the *utilius*, *amicus*, *aliens*, and *medians* categories, which form the previously described typology of voters. The analysis is based on two nationally representative public opinion surveys carried out by the Itanes (Italian National Election Studies) research group.

The validity of our typology of voting heuristics should not be judged only with respect to the criteria that inspired its construction but also according to its capacity to differentiate between groups of voters with respect to their levels of political sophistication, political participation, and certain sociodemographic characteristics. Accordingly, Chapter 5 describes the profile of each type of voter along these dimensions and confirms the validity of our typological partition. *Utilius* and *amicus* are more educated, informed, and interested in politics than is any other type of voter, while *aliens* voters have instead minimal levels of political sophistication. Similarly, *utilius*, and, to a lesser extent, *amicus* voters, tend to discuss politics with others quite frequently, are engaged in associations, are politically active, and are consistent in their voting patterns, while, in contrast, *aliens* voters are the least likely to actively participate to political and associational life and to engage in political conversations. Finally, the sociodemographic profile of *utilius* and *amicus* voters presents many traits of social centrality: they tend to be male, hold stable jobs, and live in the industrial areas of the North and Center-North. In contrast, *aliens* voters tend to live in the southern regions, and are overrepresented among women, unemployed individuals, and housewives. Taken together, these factors combine to determine the type of decision-making strategy a voter adopts. In particular, the level of political sophistication and variables relating to political participation mediate the influence exerted by social and environmental factors.

Chapter 6 examines the effectiveness of the cognitive shortcuts and the consistency of their use, and shows that the judgment strategies used by *utilius*, *amicus*, and *aliens* are deployed not just in determining their voting behavior but also in other decision-making tasks they undertake. In particular, we show that *utilius* voters rely on the left-right ideological dimension even when they judge policy issues, or their future voting preferences, and that *amicus* voters use their simplified vision of politics in which the political competition is limited to the two major coalitions both in their judgment of political leaders and the performance of the government. The effectiveness of these heuristics is proved by the fact that *utilius* and *amicus* voters show levels of coherence in the organization of their opinions that are higher than those of the most interested and educated individuals. On the contrary, the *aliens* type, who does not follow the decision-making mechanisms employed by *utilius* and *amicus*, is much less capable of using the left-right dimension to manage the organization of the parties and his/her issue opinions even compared to the least educated and interested voters. However, even the *aliens* voter is not privy of an organizing principle. Indeed, he is guided by a cynic realism, or pessimism, that leads to systematically negative evaluations of every party, coalition, and political leader.

Chapter 7 brings the analytic component of the book to a conclusion, providing further evidence that *utilius*, *amicus*, and *aliens* are guided by distinct heuristics. To a considerable extent, the typology overrides the effect that political factors have in influencing the decision-making process. Specifically, the left-right ideology, candidates for the office of prime minister, and media partisanship do influence voting behavior, but not in the same way for all individuals.

Each of these factors has an effect on the vote that varies according to the type of decision-making strategy in question. Ideological considerations mostly drive *utilius*, while *amicus* focus their attention on the candidates. Only marginally affected by political factors, *aliens* mainly rely on occasional cues gathered from their favorite television network.

Chapter 8 summarizes our various findings and discusses them in relation to the debate over the measurement of political sophistication and the more general issue of the low political literacy of citizens in democratic societies. In general, the Italian population is described as divided between citizens who are highly capable of handling the political debate either through classical ideological categories—the *utilius*—or through an effective simplification of the political competition—the *amicus*—, and citizens who are peripheral to politics, and do not possess the instruments necessary for making sense of it—the *aliens*. The strategy used to build the typology of voting heuristics is offered as a general interpretive framework for analyzing decision-making strategies in political environments characterized by a multiplicity of parties and a mixed electoral system. This approach offers new bases for estimating levels of political competence, and for measuring the political sophistication of the mass public. Finally, a number of ideas are put forward as to how experimental research might advance the study of cognitive processes.

PART ONE

Choosing and Voting

Chapter 1

Voting

An Individual and Reasoned Choice

Usus habitum in voluntate hominis consistit

—THOMAS AQUINAS

What Electoral "Rationale"?

Voting is a choice. The ritual through which it is performed leaves no room for doubt. One has the choice of going or not going to the polling booth, the ballot paper gives a range of options, and there is even the possibility of not choosing any of them.

Voting is, moreover, a nonrandom choice. Voters divide up, so far as their political preferences are concerned, based on socially significant commonalities—be they socioeconomic, geographic, or religious, among others. Considered at an aggregate level, voting is the expression of the preferences of a collectivity determining winners and losers among the contending parties. At the same time, voting is a nondetermined choice. Although political identities or previous behaviors can predict voting choice, they do not constitute, per se, a sufficient motivating force for it.

Voting is also an individual choice. It is a right recognized *ad personam*, safeguarded by the complete secrecy in which it occurs. This characteristic of individuality does not rule out the fact that the choice is influenced by factors external to the individual, i.e., through mechanisms of interpersonal or social influence and imitation;

15

rather, it simply means that any possible conditioning operates at the level of the individual voter.[1]

Finally, voting is a reasoned choice. This assumption, whose validity will be motivated at length in the next chapters, initially arises from a commonsense consideration. It would be extremely difficult to explain how democratic societies manage to enjoy a significant degree of stability and equilibrium if one were to assume that the political structure on which they hinge is the product of irrational individual choices. We start instead, then, from an image of society made up of individuals who, though deprived of complete and exhaustive information, are nonetheless able to choose in a "reasonable" way the men and women who govern them. By assuming a bounded rationality framework, we take into account both the cognitive limitations and contextual constraints that affect individuals, and presuppose that every political choice is characterized by some form of reasoning. Our research does not aim at assessing the normative validity, rationality, or correctness of the choice; rather, our goal is to study the process behind it.

These three assumptions—that voting choice is nonrandom, individual, and reasoned—are the basis of our investigation of the cognitive shortcuts of Italian voters, and will be discussed in greater detail in the following pages.

Voting as a Nonrandom yet Nondetermined Choice

Studying the act of voting through the lens of decision making only makes sense if voting is a decision over which people in fact deliberate. This implies arguing both (a) that voting does not happen "at random," and (b) that it is not fully determined ex ante, as a habit, or a mere consequence of party identification or social identity.

---

1. This, however, does not mean that voting is a free choice. Such a conceptual category is meaningless for descriptive purposes, and ambiguous at a normative level.

A convincing proof of voting choice not being random is the fact that all three major interpretative paradigms of voting behavior have identified "explanatory" variables that account for voting choice. These variables range from individuals' socioeconomic status or demographic characteristics to socio-psychological factors. The first paradigm, which lies at the basis of modern studies of voting behavior, is the so-called "Columbia approach" and has its roots in the Lazarsfeld and Berelson research on the US presidential elections of the 1940s. Also known as "the sociological approach," this paradigm traces political preferences back to the sociodemographic characteristics of voters in general and to their socioeconomic status and ethnicity in particular (Berelson, Lazarsfeld, and McPhee 1954). This approach holds that the relationship between voter and party is not based purely on the correspondence between the individual's interests and the parties' policy proposals. Instead, the voter-party relationship is mediated by the beliefs that the voter forms about the party itself. Parties, the sociological approach argues, maintain their support not only by systematically pursuing the interests of the social groups they represent, but also by creating and relying on their supporters' sense of belonging to a social base.

Further elaborations on this theme led to the second interpretive paradigm, the "Michigan approach," which started with Campbell, Converse, Miller, and Stokes's *The American Voter* (1960), and was built around the concept of party identification. Also referred to as the "psychological approach," it argues that party identification stems from psychological mechanisms activated during an individual's political socialization, in particular from family ties and from the influence of the social groups to which he belongs. Party identification influences voting both directly, through the affective bond that ties a voter to his or her party, and indirectly, by inducing individuals to absorb political information selectively, preventing them from forming attitudes that contradict their party allegiance (Campbell et al. 1960; Budge, Crewe, and Farlie 1976). Initially, party identification was used to account for the relative stability of voting behavior.

Subsequently, however, largely on account of the significant increase in electoral volatility in American politics over the course of the 1970s, the concept of party identification was reexamined to acknowledge the growing importance of independent voters, and their focus on short-term factors, like leaders and issues.

The application of the rational choice approach to the interpretation of political behavior gave rise to a third explanatory model. Originating with Anthony Downs's *An Economic Theory of Democracy* (1957), the "economic approach" was conceived as a deductive and positive model of the workings of the political system. Downs's model integrates the action strategies of the government and other principle political actors (political parties, citizens, and interest groups) into Walras's theory of general equilibrium. Each actor, the model posits, operates with economic rationality, oriented toward maximizing primarily egoistic interests. Voters and parties move within the same ideological space, and the rational voter makes use of the criterion of spatial proximity to identify the party that is best able to safeguard his own interests.

This brief excursion should suffice to support our claim that, since the inception of the studies on political behavior, a series of "determinants" of voting behavior have been identified, be they sociodemographic and economic characteristics, party identification, or the pursuit of egoistic interests, confirming the assumption that the creation of political preferences is not a process that can be ascribed merely to chance, or to the idiosyncrasies of the individual. However, the extent to which voting behavior is determined *ex ante* instead of being an actual choice remains to be ascertained. A first, very convincing argument is that the predictive capacity of the variables previously mentioned is not particularly high, and fluctuates over time and across countries. For instance, in Italy the predictive capacity of socioeconomic variables, such as income and class, as well as interest-based or issue voting models of party choice has always been very weak (Bellucci and Segatti 2010). Second, comparative research on voting behavior has consistently pointed to the increased "individualization" of voting choice, as classical forms of political and group identification (i.e., class, religion, ethnicity, etc.) become less relevant in modern, or postmaterialist societies (Franklin, Makie, and Valen 1992, Dalton and Wattenberg 2000; LeDuc, Niemi, and Norris 2002).

Both arguments suggest we should exclude the possibility that external constraints or individual biography directly determine voting behavior. However, voting might also be considered a determined choice in the sense that its outcome can be taken for granted. Either because it is the expression of deep-rooted partisan identifications, or simply a habitudinal action, any given voting choice might simply replicate previous choices, or be perceived as a ritual, a confirmation of one's identity, more than the actual evaluation of competing parties and their leaders. This concern is particularly relevant in the context of Italian politics, due to the tradition of political subcultures and partisan identification that has characterized the political history of the country for decades. To address this concern, we will first put forward some general considerations, and then discuss in further detail why the study of the Italian case offers an excellent opportunity to study voting as a decision-making process.

In general, reducing voting behavior to a habit, or to the mere expression of group membership or party identification, can serve the goal of predicting voting outcomes quite well, but does not add per se to our understanding of the motivations behind the choices in question. In fact, if used to account for motivations, such conceptual categories merely reduce explanation to a tautology. Saying that people vote for a certain party because they identify with it, or that people vote for a party because they belong to a group or community whose members favor said party, are lines of reasoning that have patently little real substance.

Identification and membership are factors that can powerfully describe the voting phenomenon at the aggregate level, but they do not establish the reasons behind it or, more precisely, the motivating forces that animate individual choices. They should not, therefore, be considered constitutive elements of the decision-making process itself, even though they can be effective in describing the profile of the electorate.

A similar argument can be advanced in relation to the idea that voting behavior is a habit, in the Weberian sense of a traditional action dictated by beliefs not subjected to scrutiny (Weber 1922). One can argue, for instance, that voting consistency—the fact that voters tend to vote for the same party, or candidate, over time—is indeed an indicator of customary and habitual behavior. However, voting consistency is a phenomenon that presupposes the act of voting itself and can only be observed *ex post*. Moreover, it would be completely arbitrary to argue that an individual votes out of habit just because she always votes for the same party (Brody 1991, 179–181). In fact, reconfirming support for a party that one has voted for in the past should be considered a choice, since a significant number of individuals, on the contrary, modify their voting behavior from one election to the next.

Moreover, there is no type of identity or habit—with the possible exception of cheering for a soccer team—that is never put in question. Even the most heartfelt forms of identification are subject in certain situations to rational judgments. Very often the result of such examinations is a reconfirmation of the membership, buttressed now by newly acquired, reasoned supports (Aronson, Wilson, and Akert 1999). It is not tenable, however, to assume a priori that such an outcome is inevitable. In any case it would still be necessary to understand the bases, whether instrumental or symbolic, of the membership and even more so the modes in which an attitude of loyalty is structured (Hirschmann 1970).

Moving on to considering the Italian case specifically the most successful interpretative model of voting behavior, up until the beginning of the 1990s, was based on the role of territorial subcultures in the process of the political socialization of Italian citizens (Galli, Capecchi, Cioni-Polacchini, and Sivini 1968; Corbetta, Parisi, and

Schadee 1988).[2] This interpretative framework takes its inspiration from Seymour Lipset and Stein Rokkan's (1967) description of the "freezing" of the political alternatives in the party systems in Europe and is built on the concept of a locality-based political subculture. Drawing on this basic idea, researchers from the Istituto Cattaneo concluded that

> the substantial stability of the Italian electorate can be explained for the most part by the existence of very deep-rooted subcultural traditions in certain areas of the country, one of the consequences of which is a particular orientation in voting choice (Galli *et al.* 1968, 320).

Namely, the North-East regions of the country—the "White" zone—were heavily dominated by the Christian Democratic party, while the Center-North regions—the "Red" zone—were largely controlled by the Communist Party. In each of these geopolitical areas, Italian citizens were rooted in extremely homogeneous and pervasive "membership networks," so much so that "the attitude towards voting" seemed "like an acquired and non-modifiable one (. . .)" (*ibidem*, 320). The "socialist and Catholic cultures, along with their distinctive political components" gave rise to regional subcultures and crystallized, over the years, into a politico-territorial cleavage (*ibidem*, 322).

While the pervasiveness of these political subcultures was undeniable throughout the First Republic, by the time our study takes place, their importance had already declined substantially as a consequence of the total collapse of the established party system that

---

2. Not that there have not been a number of other interpretative paradigms. In fact, over the years the research on voting behavior in Italy has been characterized by some methodological heterogeneity (Poggi 1968; Sani 1973; Sani and Sartori 1978). However, the model of regional subcultures has been an irreplaceable point of reference for all subsequent studies. Moreover, the results achieved using other analytical approaches have very often confirmed its explanatory capacity (Corbetta, Parisi, and Schadee 1988; Mannheimer 1989; Venturino 2000).

occurred at the beginning of the 1990s. In this book we will consider the first few years of the Second Republic and will focus on the national general elections of 1996 and 2001, which took place in a political context of profound transformation and great uncertainty. As we will discuss in greater detail in Chapter 4, following widespread investigations of political corruption in 1992, the political system experienced dramatic changes: all the major parties underwent an astonishing renewal, or were replaced by new ones, and a new electoral law that changed the terms of the electoral competition was introduced. In this climate, political actors had to cope with a new political landscape and new rules. For the first time in many years, voters had to make up their minds almost from scratch: they could not rely on the experience of previous decades or on their preexisting political identities. They had to evaluate and decide in a new political environment, in which identification with the parties of the First Republic was of little help in navigating the agitated waters of the overhauled political system.

It seems therefore reasonable to assume, at least in the context of the present study, that individuals did confront the problem of voting in terms of choice, largely leaving aside factors like membership, identification, and habit. In conclusion, affirming that voting is a choice not dictated by chance makes us take into account those social, economic, and psychological factors that are capable of influencing its outcome. At the same time, recognizing that such a choice is not predetermined leads us to examine what decision-making strategies voters put into action.

Voting as an Individual Choice

Moving beyond explanations based on group membership or partisan identification to consider the voting decision as an individual choice means embracing the task of explaining social phenomena on the basis of their individual motivations and attitudes. The adoption of an individual-based perspective brings into play the interpretative paradigm of methodological individualism, and with it the endless—now almost ritualistic—discussion of which model of actor one should adopt. Here, we will overlook the discussion of whether it is more appropriate to assume a model of *homo economicus* acting in the expectation of future advantages and on the basis of (mostly) selfish motivations or a *homo sociologicus*, consciously (or unconsciously) driven by constraints and resources of the social context in which he is embedded (Elster 1979; Ricolfi 1984; Pizzorno 1989; Goldthorpe 2000; Udéhn 2002).

Instead, we will embrace Jon Elster's pragmatic way of dealing with this issue.

> In understanding behavior, we may begin with all the abstractly possible actions the individual might undertake. The action that we actually observe can be seen as a result of two successive filtering operations. The first filter is made up of all the *constraints*—physical, economic, legal, and others—that the agent faces. The actions consistent with all the constraints constitute the opportunity set. The second filter is a mechanism that determines which action within the opportunity set will be actually carried out. Here I am assuming that the agent chooses the action that will have the best consequences, as assessed by his desires (or preferences). (Elster 2007, 165)

The idea of the two successive filtering processes turns out to be analytically useful. This approach offers a convergence of the stylized images of *homo economicus* and *homo sociologicus*. The reduction of the range of all abstractly possible actions to the set of those that are potentially realizable happens through structural constraints that can be traced back to the social and contextual factors that influence the social actor. The identification of the action to be actually realized from within the set of possible actions is a result of a process of deliberate and intentional choice. The two different modes of explanation are not simply lined up one after the other, however. On the contrary, Elster puts forward a model that is capable of overcoming the major drawbacks of the two previous descriptions of human behavior. His model frees the social actor from sociological determinism by recognizing in him/her a margin of intentional autonomy governed by some kind of decision making. At the same time, Elster remedies the problem of nonexhaustivity of economic theory, especially when it comes to the definition of individuals' preferences and the heterogeneity of their goals. This remedy is found by recognizing how, in the first filtering phase, the reduction of abstractly possible actions to realizable ones can be ascribed to the intervention of structural constraints and therefore to socioeconomic and cultural factors at work in the environment within which individuals define their courses of action.

Compatible with this framework are theories of political action that do not take individual interest and social norms as given, but rather investigate the processes of their emergence and transformation, and find the motivation of political action in the cooccurrence of identity and interest (Gamson 1990; Bearman 1993; Gould 1995; Pizzorno 1983). Without rejecting the idea that actors mobilize to pursue their interests, scholars working in this vein assume that "most individuals act routinely to safeguard and sustain the central sources of meaning and identities in their lives" (McAdam [1982] 1999: xiii). Instrumental behavior occurs within the boundaries of what is admitted and considered possible in the social contexts to which individuals belong (Pizzorno 1983, Calhoun 1991).

Although it has been mostly applied to the study of collective action, this framework is also appropriate for our particular study. The check marked in pencil on the ballot paper can be conceived as the final product of two filtering processes. The voting decision is as much the result of the interest, values, political socialization, context, and socioeconomic conditions of the actors involved as it is of the decision-making strategies adopted by the voter. In this book, our overriding interest is to capture the strategies of choice that guide actors. We will therefore concentrate mainly on "the second filtering phase," i.e., the mechanism—or, as we shall see, the mechanisms—for making a selection among a plurality of possible options. Thus, so far as Elster's framework is concerned, we will exploit in particular the emphasis he places on recognizing the intentionality of the actor, thereby restoring specificity to the individual.

The decision to focus exclusively on the second filtering phase will leave a few readers unsatisfied. In fact, the separation between two distinct phases is merely analytical, and we should be aware of the interdependencies between social constraints and cognitive strategies. Moreover, the interpretative frameworks that people use, the cognitive schemata upon which they base their decision-making process, are shared understandings that emerge from common experiences and patterns of social interaction (DiMaggio 1997; Mohr 1998; Goldberg 2012).[3] While not all these aspects could be taken into consideration in the present research, they should definitely be part of a broader research agenda, in which the important tradition of research on political networks and interpersonal influence (Berelson, Bernard, Lazarsfeld, and McPhee 1954; Katz and Lazarsfeld 1955; Huckfeldt and Sprague 1995; Zuckerman 2005, Mutz 2006; Baldassarri and Bearman 2007) meets recent developments in the field of political cognition.

---

3. The recognition of the intentionality of choice obliges the researcher to trust what individuals say about themselves in the conviction that "we are cultural beings, endowed with the capacity and the will to take a deliberate attitude towards the world and to lend it significance" (Weber 1904, 81). In terms of research practice this will mean distinguishing between individuals exclusively on the basis of their own way of thinking about politics. Accordingly, our typological classification of the electorate will be based on forms of representing politics that emerge from shared modes of structuring information and political beliefs. This will also imply to trust what people say, and to take their stated preferences as reliable, thus following John Levi Martin's invitation to value first-person explanations as opposed to third-person explanations in which actor's own self-understanding is dismissed in favor of a "superior" intellectual authority (Martin 2011).

In Elster's model, the decision-making process occurs in the second stage, and it implies the choice of the action that will have the best consequences for the actor, given his constraints and preferences. Two aspects are relevant here: First, even if one adopts a decision-making process that is based on rational choice principles, thus entailing the maximization of some utility function (Elster 1979), this model of economic choice is used only to explain which action is actually selected from within the spectrum of realizable actions. In other words, the principle of utility maximization is used as a mechanism of choice and not as a general theory of human behavior. Second, and central to our argument, it is not necessary to assume the principle of utility maximization as the only possible mechanism that guides the human decision-making process.

Peter Hedström elaborates on this aspect in his systematization of the DBO theory, a psychologically plausible theory of action according to which "the cause of an action is a constellation of desires, beliefs and opportunities in the light of which the action appears reasonable" (Hedström 2005, 39). In this framework, rational-choice theory, as well as learning theories, can be seen as specific types of action mechanisms, each corresponding to a particular way in which these elements—desires, beliefs, opportunities—combine to determine choices. Neither rational-choice nor learning theory, however, is the only possible, or the most common, form of action mechanism. As will be clear by the end of Chapter 2, in this book we will embrace this philosophy, remaining open to the possibility that the mechanisms of choice might be based on a heterogeneity of cognitive strategies that include different, often alternative combinations of desires, beliefs, and opportunities.

Voting as a Reasoned Choice

The emphasis we have placed on the individuality and intentionality of choice obliges us to spend a few words on the problem of the rationality of the actor.[4] However, anyone who aspires to examine the question of the rationality of human action is almost sure to be daunted by the sheer volume of literature surrounding the debate. In this book, we completely bypass the problem of defining what is a rational course of action and what is not by starting with the assumption that any political choice is characterized by some form of reasoning. Accordingly, our analysis will presuppose that each individual is able to reach a reasoned choice, but will abstain from assessing in any way the "correctness" or the "appropriateness" of the factors involved in the reasoning processes through which these choices are made.

The reason for this pragmatic assumption is easily explained. If we accept the idea of bounded rationality or other similar concepts, which invite us to take into account the cognitive limitations of human decision making and the contextual constraints that characterize any task environment in which the decision-making process takes place, we also accept, as a consequence, that every decision-making procedure has some quality of rationality, limited though it may be. Every choice should therefore be considered a rational (or reasoned) one.

Among social scientists, there has been a widespread tendency to extend and adjust the category of rationality in order to encompass the heteronomous and complex character of human action. This, we argue, has led to the loss of any objective reference point capable of discriminating what is rational from what is not. Herbert Simon, for example, shifts attention from substantive rationality to an idea of procedural rationality, in which

---

4. It is customary to make a general distinction between absolute (economic, Olympic, instrumental) rationality and bounded (limited, situational) rationality so as to organize the numerous definitions that have been proposed of the concept of rationality with a certain degree of coherence. In general, the criteria of differentiation relate to the strength of the conditions for rationality, the consideration of the situational or procedural aspect of rationality, and the general or particular nature of the theory of action one wishes to achieve (Goldthorpe 2000, 20).

existing conditions are considered to be "inside the skin" of actors (Goldthorpe 2000, 131).

> Bounded rationality is simply the idea that the choices that people make are determined not only by some consistent overall goal and the properties of the external world, but also by the knowledge that decision makers do and don't have of the world, their ability or inability to evoke the knowledge when it is relevant, to work out the consequences of their actions, to conjure up possible courses of action, to cope with uncertainty (including uncertainty deriving from the possible responses of other actors), and to adjudicate among their competing wants (Simon 2000, 25).

Human action is subject to internal constraints that are inherent to the individual and therefore inescapable. The rationality of such action cannot be assumed to be absolute. It is necessarily limited and, as a consequence, leads to the selection of courses of action that are not optimal but satisfactory. Humans do not possess an "Olympic" rationality: Limited cognitive capacity and knowledge of the alternative options, as well as information uncertainty, the incommensurability of individual aspirations, and conflict between different goals, are just some of the constraints that prevent the process of choice from conforming to traditional forms of economic rationality.

Admitting the non-optimality of the process of choice leads inevitably to the recognition that an action characterized by bounded rationality may cause outcomes that are unanticipated, even undesirable (Merton 1936). This is a conclusion that is perfectly in line with our everyday experience but that creates a number of difficulties on the theoretical plane. Admitting the possibility that a rational choice may give rise to an outcome that does not conform to the will that animated it means that an action can be considered rational even if it does not lead to the achievement of the desired objective (Pareto 1916). The outcome of a choice no longer constitutes an empirical test of the more or less rational character of that course of action.

Raymond Boudon has dedicated many years to examining the nonintentional, undesired, and perverse effects of action, arguing that very often they stem from erroneous beliefs. He notes that lines of reasoning that are valid in themselves can lead to false beliefs because they are applied in contexts where certain assumptions or implicit propositions are inappropriate. The erroneousness of such beliefs can derive not just from the environment but also from affective dispositions such as desires, fears, or frustrations (Boudon 1995; 1996; 1998). According to Boudon, however, these "incorrect" beliefs originate within the individual through processes analogous to those that give rise to "correct" ones. He concludes that, precisely because they stem from similar processes, scholars should not posit different types of explanation according to whether or not the actions of individuals are based on true or false beliefs. The social and cognitive context furnishes individuals with "good reasons" in accordance with which to define their courses of action (Boudon 2003).

Karl Popper, too, though moving on apparently different ground, proposed an analysis of situational logic, according to which an action should be considered rational if it is "adequate" or "appropriate," given the goals of the actors and given their situation of action, which includes each individual's beliefs (Popper 1957). Along similar lines, Jon Elster identifies actions as rational if they are deliberated in a correct relationship with the subject's desires, beliefs, and available information (Elster 1999). Not only does Elster place desires and beliefs alongside information in the definition of what should be understood as rational but "in order for an action to be rational it *must* have particular relationships with the subject's desires, beliefs and information" (*ibidem*, 154, our italics). The theory of rational choice is thus reformulated according to the maxim that "people draw the maximum possible from what they have—beliefs and preferences included" (*ibidem*, 158).

Both Simon and Boudon, Popper and Elster, argue for a model of rationality in which not only actors' goals but also their beliefs need to be considered as exogenous and for that reason exempt from the application of any criterion of instrumental rationality. Cognitive limits and gaps in information, individual beliefs—whether true of false—the "situation of action," desires and emotions, must all be considered as given and therefore not open to contestation. These phenomena cannot be used to underpin any criterion for distinguishing between rational and nonrational choices. We thus find ourselves facing a dilemma: either we establish a limit to the extension of the concept of rationality or we resign ourselves to not having any criterion of rationality at all, which is tantamount to saying that no action can be considered irrational nor, conversely, is any action rational. In short, given the impossibility of defining its opposite, the category of rationality loses its significance. Neither the optimality of choice, nor the achievement of goals, nor the veracity of beliefs can be used as criteria for establishing the rationality of human behavior.[5]

Having dispensed in this way with the fetish of rationality, other features of decision making assume a central role in our analysis. By no means the least of these are the actual mechanisms that guide the decision-making process, i.e., how information, desires, beliefs, and opportunities come together and contribute to selecting the course of action an individual actually pursues. Once it is established that it is not possible to use the concept of rationality to classify human behavior, the focus of interest shifts from the rationality of choice to the reasoning that leads to it.

Adjusting the concept of rationality to accommodate the cognitive and situational limitations of human action changes how we investigate the decision-making process. Acknowledging the presence

---

5. This entails abandoning any type of nomological aspiration. In fact, the idea of directing attention toward the mechanisms of reasoning by taking account of the internal and situational limitations does not allow one to establish a priori what type of reasoning is to be considered rational and what type is instead "incorrect." This is because individual capacities, information, beliefs, desires, and "good reasons" cannot be subjected to the scrutiny of rationality.

of both internal and external constraints goes hand in hand with recognizing the existence of significant intersubjective differences in the capacities, knowledge, and motivations that manage individuals' decision-making processes. In this light, a single model of decision making is not sustainable. What we need instead is the hypothesis of a heterogeneity of decision-making processes. In other words, once the existence of fully rational behavior is rejected in favor of rationality defined in relation to context and the actual cognitive capacities of the actor, it becomes possible to argue for a range of decision-making strategies, each with their own thought processes.

To sum up, we assume (a) that voting behavior is the fruit of an individual and intentional choice and (b) that this choice is the outcome of some form of reasoning. The methods and elements that produce the decision-making process must be investigated starting from the attitudes and motivations that individuals themselves claim to be at the basis of their choice. The choices in question cannot be evaluated in terms of their correctness because a single criterion of rationality does not exist. It follows, then, (c) that the strategies of choice may be heterogeneous.

Our research on the decision-making strategies of Italian voters will start from the pragmatic assumption that any political choice is the byproduct of reflexive processes, and aim at the identification of these reasoning processes. To do so, we will make use of a certain number of analytical instruments from cognitive and political psychology to understand how individuals represent the world of politics, how they perceive and organize information about it, and what strategies are available to them to orient themselves within it. In the next two chapters, we will examine studies on decision making under conditions of uncertainty. We will pay particular attention, in Chapter 2, to the theme of judgment heuristics and the fast and frugal heuristics research program, while in Chapter 3, we will analyze the contribution of the political cognition approach to the themes of the consistency of opinions, political sophistication, the heterogeneity of cognitive processes, and the use of heuristics in the field of politics.

Human Decision Making and Heuristics of Judgment

The Study of Human Decision Making

It is the destiny of individuals to choose. Formulating judgments and making decisions is a frenetic, everyday exercise. Just as unremitting is the need to evaluate the quality of such choices, the actual consequences they lead to, and their efficacy. The activity of reflecting on our own decisions instinctively unfolds as much on the prescriptive plane—what is the right, rational, best choice?—as on the descriptive and explanatory one—why have I made this choice? How have I proceeded? What errors have I committed? What has conditioned me? What have I overlooked? In fact, these two dimensions often intertwine in people's efforts to respond to the basic need to reason correctly so as to reach the best decision. However, "correct" reasoning is a *naive* aspiration at least with respect to many decision-making tasks, in that it presumes that (a) a best decision (or right choice) does actually exist, (b) that a correct reasoning exists, and (c) that a causal relationship exists between the use of a correct reasoning and the definition of the best choice. These conditions are hardly met in real life. How can one really tell whether she is married to the right person? Or whether she has voted for the optimal candidate? Or even bought the best shoes?

Scholarly approaches to decision making, too, feed off of the same questions and grapple—often implicitly, and by way of more roundabout formulations—with these same assumptions. In this chapter we will examine three of these approaches in detail, starting with the classical *model of the rational actor*, i.e., the normative and prescriptive model that best fits the behavior of *homo economicus*. This approach adopts all of the assumptions listed above: it assumes that each individual has a stable and unvarying order of preferences (hence there exists a best choice); that choice is based on the principle of utility maximization (hence there exists a correct reasoning); and that the optimal choice is defined by a calculation that combines the probability of each possible outcome with the utility that can be derived from its occurrence (the best decision arises out of the correct application of the rules of reasoning).

We will then go on to consider the main findings of two highly fruitful research programs, both interested in the actual nature of the cognitive processes that guide decision making. The *heuristics and biases program*, founded by Daniel Kahneman and Amos Tversky, takes a first step in the direction of denying the existence of a "correct" reasoning. Using a large body of experimental evidence, they demonstrate that individual judgments and decision-making procedures involve systematic shifts and distortions of the normative model rules of inference. They also cast doubt on the existence of a "best decision" by showing, through prospect theory, that individuals' choices are influenced by the manner in which the decision-making problem itself is formulated, invalidating the assumption that rational actors have unvarying preferences.

While the heuristics and biases program has developed as a search for systematic differences between the outcomes prescribed by the normative model and the actual performance of human reasoning, the *fast and frugal heuristics program*, promoted by Gerd Gigerenzer and the ABC Research Group, has shifted attention away from the search for a best choice to a search for a satisficing one, rejecting the existence of correct reasoning procedures in favor of an idea of ecological rationality, according to which reasoning procedures are influenced by the environment and the structure of the information available in it.

As far as our own inquiry into voting choice is concerned, this treatment of the more general topic of decision making should not be viewed as a superfluous ornament. On the contrary, it is an important step toward a full consideration of political choice as a human activity on par with any number of other activities that characterize everyday life. Indeed, if we accept the idea that the formation of political opinion is not something exceptional—almost mystical—but rather an integral part of everyday life, then it is just as necessary to recognize that individuals act, i.e., evaluate and make choices, in the sphere of politics using the same instruments and strategies and in the face of the same constraints that accompany the various other decisions they make in life.

The Rational Choice Approach to Decision Making

The first systematic attempts at studying judgment and decision making were strongly influenced by the theory of rational choice and by the principles of statistical inference (Shafir and LeBoeuf 2002; Gilovich and Griffin 2002). The Bayesian decision theorist Ward Edwards (1954; 1961) was among the first of his generation to recognize the great relevance that the normative and prescriptive models of economic theory had for developing research on decision making in psychology. In particular, he made use of the concept of expected utility to formulate a general normative criterion for decision making in situations of uncertainty. He based his study on the definition of rational behavior as behavior in which the subject chooses the alternative to which he/she attributes the highest degree of expected utility (subjective expected utility, from which derives the acronym SEU) (Von Neumann and Morgenstern 1944; Luce and Raiffa 1957).

Given a set of possible options and a definition of the consequences that could derive from each of these alternatives, the decision-making process can be expressed as a function of (a) the probability that each of the consequences occurs and (b) the value that the decision maker attributes to the eventual realization of these outcomes. In the calculus of the expected utility, each outcome, whether positive or negative, is weighted by the probability of its taking place. The expected utility of a specific option is the sum of the value associated with each outcome multiplied by the probability of its occurrence (Arkes and Hammond 1986).

Let us take an example. Over the last few years, Mr. Rossi has had long periods of unemployment interspersed with a series of temporary jobs and at the present time he is of the opinion that the main task of the government is to address the problem of unemployment. He is able to choose between two parties, Party A and Party B. Party A promises to create new jobs, while Party B proposes to introduce a guaranteed minimum income. Mr. Rossi attributes to the possibility of finding a secure job a utility of 1, while receiving a certain minimum income is worth 0.7. Being unemployed has a utility of 0. At the same time, he believes that the probability that Party A can actually create new employment is 0.3, while the probability that Party B will introduce a guaranteed minimum income, once again according to the estimates of Mr. Rossi, stands at 0.6.

The decision-making tree shown in Figure 2.1 represents Mr. Rossi's situation. The first node on the left is the root decision-making node, from which the two choice options branch out: to vote for Party A or to vote for Party B. Each option can lead to two possible outcomes, each marked for the probability of its taking

Options	Prob.	Outcomes	Values	SEU
Party A	0.3	EMPLOYMENT	1.0	0.3*1.0=0.30
	0.7	UNEMPLOYMENT	0.0	0.7*0.0=0.00
Party B	0.6	MINIMUM INCOME	0.7	0.6*0.7=0.42
	0.4	UNEMPLOYMENT	0.0	0.4*0.0=0.00

FIGURE 2.1 Example of Decision Tree: Calculation of subjective expected utilities (SEUs) for alternative options and outcomes.

place and the subjective value assigned to it. The expected utility for Option A is thus calculated as $(1.0 * 0.3) + (0.0 * 0.7) = 0.30$, while that for Option B is $(0.7 * 0.6) + (0.0 * 0.4) = 0.42$. According to the normative approach, the rational choice for Mr. Rossi is to vote for Party B, because this is the alternative with the highest level of expected utility.

This simple example clearly illustrates the prescriptive nature of this decision-making model. Once the subjective value of each outcome and the probability of it actually occurring are defined, it is always possible to identify the alternative with the greatest expected utility simply by making a few elementary calculations. The image of "Man as an Intuitive Statistician"—the title of a renowned article by Cameron Peterson and Lee Roy Beach (1967)—was the fulcrum for research on decision making throughout the 1960s. Individual inferential capacities were usually studied by asking subjects to estimate averages, proportions, or the correlations between variables, or by examining how they solved problems involving the random extraction of balls from an urn. These tasks were amenable to the use of probability theory and other statistical notions; therefore, the decision-making performance of the subjects could be evaluated by comparing their responses with the "correct" ones, i.e., those that came out of an application of statistical theory (McKenzie 2003a).

This initial emphasis on measuring the relative adequacy of the man on the street's processes of reasoning quickly gave way, however, to discordant positions. While some highlighted the existence of systematic differences between the procedures prescribed by logic and by the rules of probability theory, and the evaluation criteria actually used by individuals (Tversky and Kahneman 1974; Kahneman and Tversky 1979; Kahneman, Slovic and Tversky 1982; Gilovich, Griffin, and Kahneman 2002), others raised doubts about the very significance of such experimental studies and the normative model's utility for researching human rationality at all, underlining how the model of economic rationality was as unrealistic at the theoretical level (Simon 1957; Gigerenzer and Selten

2001) as it was ineffective at the empirical one (Dawes, Faust, and Meehl 1991). According to McKenzie, "errors in the laboratory often appear to be the result of strategies that in fact work well outside the laboratory" (McKenzie 2003b, 403).

Whereas in the former case, the emphasis has been placed on the gap between human reason and the laws of probability, the second type of criticism—and the research project that has grown out of it—brings into question the very concepts of optimization, probability, and utility themselves. But let us proceed in order.

Heuristics and Biases Program

The "dogma" of correct reasoning was progressively abandoned thanks above all to the innovative studies of Kahneman and Tversky, which drew attention to the presence of systematic errors (biases) in the way in which individuals estimate the probability of events and make decisions in conditions of uncertainty and risk (1974; Kahneman, Slovic, and Tversky 1982; Gilovich, Griffin, and Kahneman 2002). "The core idea of the heuristics and biases program is that judgment under uncertainty is often based on a limited number of simplifying heuristics rather than more formal and extensive algorithmic processing" (Gilovic, Griffin, and Kahneman 2002, xv). The actual adequacy of the normative model as a way of explaining human decision making was called into question above all on the basis of empirical observation and experimental investigation. In fact, empirical research has acquired an increasingly central role in the field of cognitive psychology, so much so that, according to Shafir and LeBoeuf, the assumption of rationality can by now be considered "an empirical question" (2002:492).[1]

---

1. "The status of the rationality assumption is ultimately an empirical question (. . .) Consequently, the field of experimental psychology has been at the forefront of the modern rationality debate" (Shafir and LeBoeuf 2002, 492).

From this point of view, the heuristics and biases program is the one that, since the 1970s on, has had the greatest influence on the direction of studies on decision making, giving rise to a line of research that has been as prolific in results as it has been eclectic in the fields to which it has been applied (Fischhoff 2002). Disciplines as far apart as economic theory (McFadden 1999), business studies (Bazerman and Neale 1983; DeBondt and Thaler 2002), law (Saks and Kidd 1980), medicine (Elstein, Shulman, and Sprafka 1978; Gilovich 1991), physics (Henrion and Fischoff 2002) and international relations (Tetlock 2002) have applied the heuristics and biases model in their research.

Heuristics are mental shortcuts that allow individuals to formulate judgments and make decisions in situations and in cognitive and motivational conditions that are less than optimal. The study of these mechanisms of reasoning relies on the assumption that people depend on intuitive strategies and interpretative principles to reduce complex estimation and evaluation tasks to simple and easily accessible operations. In general, heuristics are a useful and effective solution to the problem of decision making, even though at times they lead to distortions and systematic errors, as well as generally violate certain normative principles that characterize the inferential procedures of prescriptive models (Tversky and Kahneman 1974).

Given the impossibility of directly measuring mental mechanisms, the research on heuristics has been oriented toward creating experimental situations in which the use of a cognitive shortcut leads people to commit errors of evaluation. Individuals' statistical intuitions are usually fairly appropriate, even though subject to a certain number of systematic distortions. In a seminal article published in 1974 Tversky and Kahneman introduced three different heuristics capable of explaining the systematicity of the errors they encountered. The *representativeness heuristic* captures the propensity of individuals to estimate the probability that a given object (subject or event) belongs to a particular class by relying on an evaluation of how similar it is to the typical image of the other objects belonging to that class. For example, in estimating the probability that a person is a lawyer, reference is made to the typical image of the members of that professional group, checking to see whether there are any correspondences in terms of clothing, gender, character, attitudes, and so on between the person in question and the professional category. The more analogies there are, the higher the probability will be that the person practices law. In itself, this inferential strategy is appropriate, but it can lead people to overlook other important information; for example, the overall number of lawyers or the likelihood of encountering lawyers in the particular context under observation. In general, then, the more representative a case is, i.e., the more that it appears typical of a certain class of phenomena, the higher the probability is that it will be attributed to that class, irrespective of a series of other possible indicators such as its absolute distribution, the size of the sample, or distortions tied to an erroneous conception of causality or regression toward the mean (Kahneman and Tversky 1972).

The *availability heuristic*, on the other hand, captures the propensity to estimate the probability of an event by referring to the ease with which analogous or correlated events are called to mind (Tversky and Kahneman 1973). However, the readiness with which events come to mind is not exclusively a function of their frequency but also of other factors such as their familiarity and notoriety, their salience and drama, and their visibility and distance in time. Because of these factors, the estimation of the probability of the occurrence of a given event is subject to possible distortions.

Lastly, the *anchoring and adjustment heuristic* points to how the outcome of a process of estimation is influenced by the magnitude of the figure adopted as the numerical value of reference at the outset. In evaluation tasks where individuals make use of processes of progressive adjustment starting out from an initial reference point (anchorage), it is possible to demonstrate that such adjustment procedures are not wholly reliable. In fact, the adoption of different points of initial departure leads to different estimates, distorted vis-à-vis the initial values (Slovic and Lichtenstein 1971).

Researchers have demonstrated that these cognitive shortcuts exist by identifying the systematic errors that they each are prone to produce. In fact, this has been the major objective of the research. The experimental practice of the heuristics and biases research program has led its exponents to concentrate on its "negative" contributions (Strack 2001), i.e., of bringing into question the validity of the rational choice model and revealing the limits of human decision making. Nevertheless, starting from their early work these same proponents have argued for heuristics as effective procedures of judgment, rather than as simply vehicles of "irrationality" (Tversky and Kahneman 1974; Kahneman, Slovic, and Tversky 1982). Moreover, they have always stressed that heuristics based on cognitive processes, though rapid and simplified, are no less sophisticated than those that guide rational choice decision making (Sharif, 1999; Gilovich and Griffin, 2002). Nor have judgment heuristics been considered exceptional procedures, adopted exclusively in highly complex situations; rather, they are seen as intuitive strategies frequently employed to answer specific questions of probability and frequency and, more generally, to evaluate the possibility that given outcomes will occur. More recently, some authors have extended the scope conditions of this approach beyond decision making under uncertainty to include a diverse class of difficult judgments, retrospective evaluations, and so on (Kahneman and Frederick 2002).

The distortions observable in judgment processes cannot be traced back exclusively to the erroneous application of probability theory. In fact, individuals also disregard a number of logical principles when they make choices, as is the case in reversals of preference (Slovic and Lichtenstein 1983) or variations in the propensity to take risks in situations of gain or loss. According to rational choice theory and microeconomic models (Arrow 1951; Downs 1957), the comparative evaluation of preferences should be characterized by the properties of invariance—a subject who is in favor of policy A and opposed to policy B cannot at the same time prefer policy B to policy A—, and transitivity—if policy A is preferred to policy B and policy B is preferred to policy C, then policy A must be preferred to policy C (Druckman and Lupia 2000). According to Tversky and Kahneman these principles imply that "different representations of the same choice problem should yield the same preference" (1987, 69). A large number of experimental results have shown, on the contrary, how the invariance and transitivity of preferences are in fact two assumptions subject to systematic violations (Tversky and Kahneman 1981; 1987).

The major findings in this direction have come from *prospect theory* (Kahneman and Tversky 1979; Tversky and Kahneman 1992; 2000). This descriptive approach aims to understand how subjects actually define their own expectations about the desirability and probability of certain outcomes (Girotto 1996; Shafir 1999; Shafir and Leboeuf 2002). Studies of attitudes toward risk have demonstrated extensively that probability has a nonlinear effect on individuals' decisions. The same estimation of the probability of a given event taking place can lead to different decisions depending on (a) the initial situation in which the decision-making subject finds himself/herself and (b) the way in which the decision-making task is presented. While for an individual who has millions of euros the loss of fifty euros is an almost irrelevant event, the same loss of fifty euros would have extremely negative consequences for a subject who only has a few hundred. This simple situation clearly illustrates how the utility of a gain or the cost of a loss cannot be defined in absolute terms or with intersubjective validity, but must instead be brought back to the subjective value each outcome has for the individual. The attitudes of individuals toward risk, as toward utility, are influenced by the initial level of their affluence. It has been amply demonstrated that in general the evaluation of outcomes and the propensity toward risk are a function of the incremental variation in terms of marginal gains or losses—in the level of affluence of individuals and not, on the contrary, of the absolute value of the gains or losses themselves (Kahneman and Tversky 1979; Prelec 2000).

Moreover, individuals show an aversion to taking risks if the consequences of their choice are presented in terms of gain, whereas, on the contrary, if the same alternatives are proposed in terms of loss, they are more inclined to take risks (Tversky and Kahneman 1981; 1987). In general, the propensity toward risk is subjected to a framing effect. Variation in the formulation of the same alternatives causes the respondent to make different choices, showing the inadequacy of the assumption of decision invariance (Levin, Schneider, and Gaeth 1998).

Finally, *support theory* investigates the distortions involved in subjective perception, examining the distinction between how events unfold in reality and how they are perceived and represented. Backed up by a considerable amount of empirical research, support theory holds that the estimation of the probability that a given hypothesis is true is based on the number of proofs—i.e., on the force of evidence—in support of the hypothesis compared to the weight of the proofs in support of the opposite hypothesis. In other words, according to support theory, probability is not attributed to events themselves, as the traditional normative approach maintains, but rather to the description that is made of them. In fact, different descriptions of the same event can generate different evaluations (Tversky and Koehler 1994; Rottenstreich and Tversky 1997). From this point of view, preferences and judgments are neither predetermined nor immutable; on the contrary, they are constructed in the very process of being elicited, and influenced by the way in which the situation is presented (Shafir 1999).

This conclusion should be added to the numerous research findings that demonstrate how individual preferences are, in general, easily influenced by the way in which questions are put (Druckman and Lupia 2000). Indeed, John Zaller and others have even gone so far as to suggest that citizens do not have "true attitudes" but rather that their preferences are strongly conditioned by what they consider salient at the moment in which a given question is formulated (Zaller 1992, 93).[2]

---

2. It is necessary to keep well in mind the distinction between the more general theme of the formation of opinions and the theory of the response to questionnaires. Availability in the eyes of Kahneman and Tversky and salience in Zaller are certainly similar concepts, but while for the former, availability is conceived in terms of stable cognitive processes, in the latter salience is a property defined by the context in which survey questions are formulated.

Criticisms and Future Prospects of the Heuristics and Biases Program

The amount of criticism a particular approach receives is directly proportional to the level of success it enjoys and the heuristics and biases program is no exception. If we set aside more specific disputes related to the construction of individual experimental situations and their interpretation, the criticism can be summed up by three major objections.

First, a number of scholars have shown fierce hostility toward, if not outright prejudice against, the negative vision of human capacities that this approach implicitly promotes, dismissively associating it with other theoretical proposals centered on the theme of human fallacy and on the image of the individual as a "cognitive miser" (Petty and Cacioppo 1986; Chaiken, Liberman, and Eagly 1989; Fiske and Taylor 1991). In particular, objections have been raised against the fact that the research has focused almost exclusively on identifying errors rather than on demonstrating the utility and efficacy of heuristics (Lopes 1991).

The most recent elaboration of the heuristics and biases approach (Gilovich, Griffin, and Kahneman 2002) gives a partial response to this criticism. This research program has adopted a clear position in favor of the assumption of automaticity and spontaneity in the use of judgment heuristics. This has allowed the study's authors to distance themselves from the postulation of the actor as a "cognitive miser" (Gilovich and Griffin 2002), a characterization that has often been debated.

Heuristics are defined as the natural way through which individuals formulate judgments (Tversky and Kahneman 2002). Their use is automatic and not the product of a deliberate choice (Kahneman and Frederick 2002). This definition of heuristics is incompatible, however, with the assumptions implicit in "dual process" models of cognition, which posit the existence of two alternative mental processes, the one simple and spontaneous, the other more demanding and deliberate.

A classic example of the dual model is Richard Petty and John Cacioppo's (1986) elaboration likelihood model (ELM) of persuasion, according to which individual attitudes can be modified through two alternative and qualitatively different pathways: the central route and the peripheral route. Whether or not individual subjects are persuaded through one or the other pathway depends on their own inclination and ability to elaborate the message. The central route implies intentional and demanding procedures through which individuals elaborate the contents of the persuasive message and base their judgment upon a logical consideration of its arguments. In contrast, the peripheral route does not involve extensive cognitive processing and instead lights upon marginal and superficial characteristics such as the length of the message or the authority and appeal of the source (Petty and Cacioppo 1986, 25–54).

This type of model is not compatible with the assumption of automaticity in cognitive shortcuts. In fact, according to the dual process models, the use of one cognitive process or the other is a function of the individual's degree of commitment, interest, and cognitive ability. This position directly clashes with the hypothesis that the use of cognitive shortcuts is an automatic process. The non-intentionality of the activation of a heuristic excludes the possibility that a variation in the level of commitment or interest can modify the result of the decision-making process. Experimental results, moreover, appear to confirm this position. Increasing incentives, and with them, the commitment of respondents, does not in itself lead to improvements in performance (Camerer and Hogarth 1999). The alternative that Kahneman and his current collaborators propose is a model of reasoning—known as "two systems"—in which two mental processes are at work, operating in parallel. One of these is automatic, rapid, and activated by default, while the other is a deliberate process based on serial mechanisms and special rules of inference (Kahneman and Fredrick 2002; Sloman 2002). Two systems models retain the distinction between a more rapid and intuitive process and a more careful and sophisticated one, but no longer conceived of the two processes as alternatives; rather, if both are active, they work simultaneously.

A second critique, in this case of a philosophical nature, has underlined how the researcher is essentially the one creating the definition of what should be considered correct (normative) in any given experiment. The experimental results may be read, from one point of view, as an expression of the subjects' ignorance of the rules of probability or, from another, as an expression of the researcher's ignorance in defining what the correct normative principles are (Cohen 1981).

However, the criticism that has proved most incisive and productive of new stimuli for research has not focused on the validity of the experimental results in and of themselves but rather on their limited relevance to situations in the real world. In particular, it has been argued that any type of normative model has limited applicability in contexts characterized by a high level of complexity. This is because any normative assessment is based on assumptions that are marked simplifications of reality. It is precisely these simplifications that render ambiguous any attempt to interpret decision-making performance. It is not possible to establish whether any deviation from the normative model is due to the inappropriateness of the human behavior or to the excessive simplification of the normative model itself. The problem becomes even more intractable when it is possible to identify a plurality of alternative normative models for a given situation (Einhorn and Hogarth 1981; McKenzie 2003a).

Opposition to studying human cognition in a vacuum grew over the course of the 1990s, along with a renewed interest in the role of the environment and contextual factors in the study of behavior. In fact, the consideration of the real world leads to different understandings not only of the explanation of individual behavior, but also of what is rational in a given decision-making task (Gigerenzer 2000; McKenzie 2003a). Studies of adaptive behavior, for example, have shown how laboratory errors often prove to be the result of strategies that reveal themselves to be appropriate outside the experimental context (Klayman and Ha 1987; Anderson 1991; McKenzie 2003b). Now, normative models are viewed in research as possible theories of behavior rather than actual standards of action.

Trying to bring the heuristics and biases research program up to date on this issue, scholars have reduced the generality of the prefigured heuristics, reorienting them toward specific domains of application (special-purpose heuristics) in an attempt to close the gap between experimental design and reality (Kahneman and Frederick 2002; Frederick 2002). However, this only partially addresses the abovementioned criticisms concerning the interdependence between cognitive processes and the characteristics of the environment. A radical shift in both theory and methods is in fact needed in order to study real world decision-making processes.

Fast and Frugal Heuristics and Ecological Rationality

Individuals make choices in conditions of uncertainty, with a small amount of information and time at their disposal and with limited computational capacities. Nor does the environment appear to offer them much help, furnishing them with information that is incomplete or redundant, sometimes untrue, and often subject to distortions. In the face of the magnitude and pervasiveness of such cognitive and environmental constraints, it is not possible to limit the research on decision making to comparing performances in experimental settings with those deduced from normative models, be it when the latter are based on complete information and unlimited computational capacities or be it when they are based on a more realistic model of Bayesian decision making (Gigerenzer and Selten 2001). Instead, it is necessary to turn toward a model of rationality capable of reflecting the peculiarities and the limits not just of the human mind but also of the environmental context in which individuals act (Gigerenzer, Todd, and the ABC Research Group 1999; Gigerenzer, Czerlinski, and Martignon 2002).

Herbert Simon's ecological view of human behavior set the basis for a more realistic analysis of decision making under conditions of uncertainty.

"Human rational behavior (. . .) is shaped by a scissors whose two blades are the structure of task environments and the computational capabilities of the actor" (Simon 1990, p.7).

In this perspective, the idea of optimal choice should be abandoned, in favor of that of a satisficing choice. Individuals do not necessarily arrive at the best of the possible alternatives but rather at an alternative that is satisficing, i.e., one that is able to guarantee the achievement of the minimum level aspired to by the decision maker (Selten 2001). According to this model, the decision maker does not engage in a comparative evaluation of all the possible alternatives, nor does he seek the absolutely best choice; rather, he chooses the first option that satisfies his expectations, interrupting at that point the process of sorting and evaluating the available alternatives (Simon 1956, 1990).

There are a number of reasons why this proposal is extremely suitable for researching real-world decision making. In everyday situations, strategies for optimization do not always exist, or it is not always possible to obtain and manage the mass of information relating to the various possible choices and their consequences, and often there is very little time available. Moreover—and most importantly—in many situations actually making a decision is much more opportune than continuing to spend time in a search for the best solution. Finally, there is no guarantee that a strategy aimed at optimization will actually be capable of leading to optimal outcomes. On the contrary, both because of the excessively simplifying nature of the principles of optimization and because of the uncertainty that characterizes the environment, it is often the case that the use of a non-optimal strategy can lead to similar or even better outcomes than those dictated by standard rules of inference.

In the pathway traced by Herbert Simon's theory of bounded rationality (Simon 1957; 1982), Gerd Gigerenzer and his colleagues from the ABC Research Group[3] have proposed a number of *fast and frugal heuristics*, i.e., a set of satisficing strategies that do not require a large amount of information (frugal) and rely on reasoning algorithms that are very simple and rapid (fast) (Gigerenzer et al. 1999; 2002). These heuristics are conceived of as part of an adaptive toolbox that allows individuals to capitalize on their cognitive capacities and the structure of information in various environments. Their efficacy and success cannot be determined per se, but only in relation to the environment in which they are deployed. Breaking with previous models of rational behavior, inferential processes are not evaluated for their logical, but for their ecological rationality.

In general, decision making involves both a search for alternatives and a search for cues by which to evaluate the quality of the alternatives available. Fast and frugal heuristics take for granted the knowledge of the alternatives and concentrate on the procedures of judgment employed in making the choice. Let us consider, for example, the following decision-making task:

Which city has a larger population? (a) Hamburg (b) Cologne (Gigerenzer and Goldstein 1996, 561)

The choice between these alternatives may be based on certain signs or cues like the fact that one or other of the cities is the capital of the province, that it has a football team in the top series, that it has a university, an international airport, and so forth. These cues are capable of differentiating between the profiles of the two cities in

---

3. The acronym ABC derives from *The Center for Adaptive Behavior and Cognition* but it also serves to point to the objective of searching for the ABCs of decision-making heuristics, i.e., the elementary components on which mechanisms of inference are based (Gigerenzer, Todd, and the ABC Research Group 1999).

terms of certain relevant characteristics. The principle guiding fast and frugal heuristics is that once the decision maker identifies a cue with respect to which the alternatives differ—for example, the fact that one city has a university and the other does not—the decision making process is suspended. The inferential process is based on a single, good reason. No form of comparison between options takes place nor is there any compensatory strategy balancing between alternative arguments in support of one or another object of choice. These heuristics are based on a one-reason decision-making model that does not rely on any form of maximization, utility calculation, or probabilistic evaluation (Gigerenzer and Goldstein 1996; Gigerenzer et al. 2002).

Because the process of sorting can be interrupted without all the available information being considered, the order in which the cues are examined takes on great importance. In the case of the *minimalist heuristic* the selection takes place in a random manner. The decision maker is not privy to which information is more important and which less important, so he is not able to distinguish between the cues on the basis of their utility or efficacy in the decision-making task. By contrast, the *take-the-best heuristic* assumes that the subject is aware of which cues are more or less valid and that he consequently takes them into consideration in a sequential manner starting out from the ones he deems most effective. In both cases the decision-making process comes to an end when a discriminating cue is found (Gigerenzer et al. 1999).

Surprising as it may sound, in several instances the predictive accuracy of simple fast and frugal heuristics is comparable to that of the most complex optimization algorithms implemented through the use of multiple regression models, neural networks, and decision trees, despite the latter's use of all the cues (aka predictors) available. In a seminal article, Gigerenzer and Goldstein used the abovementioned task to show that the take-the-best heuristic, which ignores information, is more accurate than other rational inference procedures. They also proved that adding supplemental information might actually lead to less accurate inferences (1996). The robustness of this finding has since been extended to twenty different instances of decision making, including sociological, biological, and economic inference tasks (Czerlinki, Gigerenzer, and Goldstein 1999). This discovery constitutes a serious challenge to a widely accepted dogma in decision-making studies: namely, that the more effort (i.e., information, time, and cognitive capacity) individuals put into the decision-making task, the greater the accuracy of their choice. When compared to the predictive performance of other, more comprehensive decision-making processes, the accuracy of fast and frugal heuristics suggests that the relationship between accuracy and effort should not necessarily be understood as a trade-off: "the mind can have it both ways, achieving more accuracy, with less effort," (Gigerenzer, Hertwig, and Pachur 2011, xxii) as in the motto "less-is-more."

How is this possible? How can take-the-best overcome the accuracy-effort trade-off? The answer lies in the interaction between the characteristics of the inferential process, the structure of the environment, and the number of observations available. This simple heuristic, by ignoring the dependencies between cues, avoids overfitting the observations, and, as a consequence, achieves greater predictive accuracy in an environment where observations are sparse (Gigerenzer and Brighton 2009).[4] In general, fast and frugal heuristics are capable of optimally exploiting the limited amount of information available, while, on the contrary, the absence of complete information represents a serious problem for the optimization algorithm. At

---

4. The authors rely on a predictive error decomposition strategy and on the bias-variance dilemma (Geman, Bienenstock, and Doursat, 1002) to show that ignoring dependencies between cues reduces the "variance" component of the predictive error, thus making the heuristic predictions less sensitive to the content of the particular sample of observations upon which the model is computed. Optimizing models, however, are more sensitive to the sample noise, thus less accurate in making predictions about the broader population. For a more technical account of the environmental structures that favor the take-the-best heuristics, see Martignon and Hoffrage (2002), Katsikopoulos and Martignon (2006), and Diekmann and Rieskamp (2007).

the same time, the take-the-best heuristic is also less subject to distortions created by a redundancy of information, because the choice is made very early and usually not all the information is considered (Martignon, Hoffrage, and Kriegeskorte 1997; Martignon 2001). Thus, the take-the-best heuristic is better suited for the decision-making process in real life, an environment characterized by scarcity and redundancy of information. In these terms, the accuracy of a heuristic cannot be determined according to its intrinsic logic, but depends instead on the structure of the information in the environment. Rationality is ecological, not logical.

"Fast and frugal heuristics can be ecologically rational in the sense that they exploit specific and possibly recurrent characteristics of the environment's structure" (Gigerenzer, Czerlinski, and Martignon 2002, 170).

In general, at the heart of fast and frugal heuristics we find the use of a sequential procedure, which at every step takes into consideration a limited number of informative cues, checks whether they are sufficient for reaching a decision and, only if they are not, proceeds to examine further information, until the conditions for making a satisficing choice are met (Gigerenzer, Czerlinski, and Martignon 2002). The omniscient decision maker capable of calculating probability and expected utility is definitively replaced by decision makers from the real world who use the tools at their disposal to adapt themselves to the environment and to manage its peculiarities to their own advantage. These tools are as varied as the environments in which they are used; while some decision-making contexts are well-suited to the minimalist and take-the-best heuristics described above, others are better suited to the use of the *recognition heuristic,* the simplest of the adaptive instruments, because it exploits the capacities of individuals to make use of their own ignorance (Gigerenzer and Goldstein 1996; Goldstein and Gigerenzer 1999).

For example, in determining which of two teams will win the football championship, which of two politicians is more competent, or which of two cities is the biggest, a subject who is fairly ignorant about the context may make use of a research process based simply on recognition, i.e., indicating a certain alternative as the winning team, competent politician, or biggest city for the simple reason that she has heard the name before. Now, in tasks like that of determining winners or losers, a heuristic in which a subject is a winner if it is recognized may work. For instance, when asked which city is bigger between the two choices of Detroit and Milwaukee, 90 percent of German students got it right, while only 60 percent of American students responded correctly. This is not due to the fact that German students are better at geography: instead, most of them had heard of Detroit, which is the larger city, but not of Milwaukee. They were therefore able to rely on the recognition heuristic and come up with the right answer. In contrast, when the German students were asked to compare Hannover to Bielefeld, their performance was significantly worse. Knowing both cities, they could not rely on the simple but accurate recognition heuristics (Goldstein and Gigerenzer 2002; Gigerenzer et al. 2011). In general, decision making based on ignorance (Todd 2001) is effective in an environment in which ignorance is not distributed randomly. In competitive environments the importance and notoriety of an object is tied to its performance, force, or size and therefore to the possibility that it will prevail over others.

In other contexts the best course of action is the first—and at times the only—one that comes to mind. The *take-the-first heuristic*, based on evaluating possible solutions in the form in which they present themselves to the decision maker, proves itself to be highly effective in tasks that require specific skills, such as piloting an airplane or playing chess, and that involve highly experienced individuals. The effectiveness of the heuristic stems from the fact that, in the case of experts, the process of recognition and categorization brings to mind exactly the elements that are most relevant for the task in question, i.e., precisely the thing that it is actually better to do in that particular situation. On the other hand, the take-the-first heuristic is of limited utility in new contexts, where learning is very difficult, or when the decision-making subject does not possess the necessary experience.

The overall framework of ecological rationality includes social rationality, which encompasses the part of the environment made up of other individuals who enter into relation with the decision maker. Human decision making is without a doubt influenced by the need to act, or appear to act, with transparency, loyalty, and responsibility in order to render choices comprehensible, consistent with expectations and justifiable in the eyes of third parties. Rational strategies that make use of social norms, imitation, and emotions are also, then, a part of the fast and frugal heuristics toolbox (Gigerenzer 2000).

The *imitation heuristic*, for example, is a strategy that relies on the social environment. The search for information takes place through the observation of the behavior of people similar to oneself, and adaptation to the environment follows the simple rule of doing what the majority of the other people do (*imitate the majority heuristic*) or of doing what successful individuals do (*imitate the successful*) (Laland 2001; Boyd and Richerson 2005).

The fast and frugal heuristics research program introduces a few novel guiding principles to the decision-making research agenda. First, it places primary emphasis on the *psychological plausibility* of models, making understanding how human beings actually make decisions the primary objective of research and, in keeping with this, introducing a model of rationality consistent with the cognitive, emotive, social, and behavioral repertory that the human species really has at its disposal.

Second, the realism of the models, and the fact that they do not rely on as-if theories, make it possible to *clearly outline the actual inferential process*, and translate it into a simple computational model that can be studied through computer simulations and tested against real-world scenarios.

Third, it completely abandons any reference to general rules of behavior—like those of the model of subjective expected utility (SEU)—in favor of a set of heuristics that specialize in limited fields and that are characterized by specific dominions of application (domain-specific). Like the various components of a Swiss pocket-knife or the tools in a toolbox, heuristics are nothing other than utensils suited for specific tasks, whose efficacy depends on the environment in which they are put to use.

Mind and environment: ecological rationality concerns the relationship between the cognitive process and the information structure of the environment in which it takes place. Heuristics are *domain-specific* because their operational efficacy depends on how they exploit the information in a given context (Gigerenzer and Selten 2001). The more a heuristic is able to mirror certain features of the environment's information structure, the more likely it is to succeed. Rationality, then, is not found in principles of optimization or consistency but rather in the degree of *adaptation to environmental structures* (Gigerenzer 2001). This approach confers a new, positive meaning to the concept of heuristic. Instead of being considered as suboptimal and inevitably biased cognitive shortcuts, heuristics are now defined as "efficient cognitive processes that ignore information" (Gigerenzer et al. 2011, 2). Information neglect, once considered a limitation, becomes integral part of the inferential process. The rationality of a choice lies as much in ignoring factors that are not relevant as in knowing how to capture those that are: Take the best, ignore the rest.

Looking forward, there are key areas that need to be explored and basic questions that need to be answered, including: (a) which types of decision tasks are most likely to be addressed using which fast and frugal heuristics? And (b) how do individuals select their cognitive strategies in order to match heuristics with environments? With respect to its scope conditions, the fast and frugal heuristics approach has distinguished itself from previous scholarship for a focus on factual inferences (i.e., who will win Wimbledon?) rather than on preferences (i.e., monetary gambles). The reason for this shift was initially pragmatic. Interested in explaining decision making in the real world, the approach needed a benchmark against which to assess the accuracy of its heuristics. Establishing a benchmark for preferences—i.e., the principle of coherence, or the expected utility model—requires making some arbitrary assumptions. External, objective criteria, on the other hand, can establish whether or not an inference is correct. However, in more recent years, the approach has been generalized to preferences and moral judgments. The psychological principles of sequential choice, and one-reason decision making have been shown to be consistent with actual patterns of preferential and moral choice (Brandstätter, Gigerenzer, and Hertwig 2006; Gigerenzer 2010). Indeed, the noncompensatory nature of fast and frugal heuristics makes them a particularly attractive strategy in the domain of moral decisions, because they are a viable solution to avoid trade-offs. Moral behavior, as rational behavior, is therefore considered the byproduct of the mind's interaction with the social environment, from which individuals derive cues about the appropriateness of their conduct. Moral behavior is based not on moral rules or norms but on pragmatic social heuristics, such as imitation (Gigerenzer 2010).

"Adaptive decision making arises from the ability to select a strategy that is appropriate for the current task environment" (Gigerenzer et al. 2011, 243). But how do people select their cognitive strategies? And how can they tell which strategy is the most appropriate for a given task? Although more basic research on this fundamental question is needed, a few interesting hints have been offered already. First, memory and knowledge constrict the set of heuristics available. For instance, if individuals are familiar with only one alternative, like in the case of German students choosing between Detroit and Milwaukee, they would not be able to use the take-the-best heuristic, or any other knowledge-based heuristic and will instead rely on the recognition heuristic. Second, according to Rieskamp and Otto's strategy selection learning theory (2006), individuals learn from experience to select the best adaptive strategy, improving their inferences through reinforcement. Third, there are instances in which individuals' knowledge of the structure of the environment seems to inform strategy selection, even without reinforcement. Finally, scholars have also observed that individuals tend to adopt compensatory strategies in which they consider many cues when facing unknown tasks in nonfamiliar environments, whereas experts are very likely to use take-the-best heuristics (Gigerenzer et al. 2011).

Beyond its specific contribution to the field of cognitive psychology, this approach to the study of decision making should have a substantial impact on many research fields in the social sciences. First, the approach is potentially applicable to a broad range of decision-making situations, namely to those situations in which alternatives are given and the research interest involves the use of information and cues. Second, the centrality of the environment and the structure of information in the real world make it potentially appealing to scholars primarily concerned with explaining human behavior "outside the lab." Moreover, clearly delineating the inferential process and translating it into a simple computational model makes it possible to derive specific expectations and test its implications through a variety of research strategies, both computational and observational. Finally, in the absence of external criteria to assess the accuracy of the inferential process, as in the case of moral judgments, it would still be possible to focus on the process and to provide a descriptive account of how the judgment has been formulated. Indeed, this approach has been already proven to be quite versatile, having been applied to a wide range of real-world instances of decision making, involving both laypeople and experts.[5]

---

5. Professional decision making has been studied in the context of doctors' medical diagnoses, judges' decision to grant bail, and expert burglars' break-in criteria. Laypeople have been used to study geographic profiling, financial investment, targeted marketing, parental investment in their children, and mate-search in the marriage market (Gigerenzer et al., 2011).

Chapter 3

Political Cognition, Sophistication, and Heuristics

The studies represent our effort to make sense of the ordinary citizen's effort to make sense of politics.

—PAUL SNIDERMAN

The Political Cognition Approach

For more than two decades American political scientists have been developing a line of research known as the political cognition approach. This endeavor has had a twofold goal: to investigate how political phenomena are perceived, represented, and evaluated by public opinion, namely to understand "(h)ow people's modest level of political information, plus their similarly modest abilities to process it, conditions how they reason about political choice" (Sniderman, Brody, and Tetlock 1991, 1); and ultimately to "[transform] the discussions about the limits of rationality into more effective explanations of why people do what they do" (Lupia, McCubbins, and Popkin 2000, 1).

The political cognition approach grew out of the cognitivist revolution in psychology, from which it derives its underlying assumption that any explanation of human behavior must take into account how individuals perceive and represent reality. Over time, this field of research has expanded incrementally, drawing on the work of scholars in a wide range of disciplines including political science, economics, psychology, the cognitive sciences, and even philosophy (cf. Lau and Sears 1986; Popkin 1991; Sniderman et al. 1991; Zaller 1992; Lupia et al. 2000; Kuklinski 2001). As a result, the approach is not rigidly structured at a theoretical level and, in fact, has already experienced a number of internal divisions about the definition and empirical ramifications of certain fundamental concepts.

One of the great merits of the political cognition approach is that it has reopened the debate about how politically sophisticated American citizens are, putting forward models of political behavior that take account of the extremely heterogeneous nature of individuals, in terms of their political knowledge and their ability to interpret the political debate.

In this chapter we discuss how the concept of political sophistication has changed over time and demonstrate how the political cognition approach has been able to address the problem of the limited interest and involvement of citizens in the democratic process from a novel perspective. In particular, we focus on how this new approach is more effectively geared toward recognizing the actual evaluation and decision-making procedures that citizens use as opposed to simply asserting that voters have a limited capacity to think in terms of abstract ideological categories.

This new approach to dealing with questions of cognition and political sophistication has been applied with notable success in two areas of research: (a) studies of information processing,[1] which have sought to explain political communication (Zaller 1992), how individuals acquire

---

1. These studies on information processing have contributed a great deal to the description of how individuals acquire, elaborate, and organize political information, giving rise to a number of distinct models. These can be distinguished in terms of the following factors: (a) the assumption that voters acquire all the information available or, alternatively, only a limited part of it (models assuming a high or low level of informational content); (b) the assumption that the quantity of information acquired is the same for each of the possible alternatives in question or, alternatively, is weighted is favor of a subset of candidates (models based on constant or variable information); and (c) the assumption that information is evaluated in a neutral manner and used instrumentally or, alternatively, that it is subject to a process of selection that induces an individual only to expose himself/herself to information destined to confirm and reinforce her preexisting emotional orientations (hot and cold models of information processing) (Campus 2000).

and process information, and the role election campaigns play in determining voting (Bartels 1996); and (b) the development of political decision-making models based on the assumption of heterogeneity in cognitive processes. In what follows we focus on this latter area, exploring in detail the issue of the heterogeneity of decision-making processes and the application of the concept of cognitive heuristics to the field of political research.

The Concept of Political Sophistication

Since their inception, studies of public opinion and electoral behavior have propagated an image of the voter as ill-informed, uninterested in politics, more or less ignorant of the workings of political institutions, bereft of ideological reference points, and largely incapable of abstract thought (Campbell, Converse, Miller, and Stokes 1960; Converse 1964). This picture remained substantially unchanged from the 1950s to the late 1990s (Smith 1980; Luskin 1987; Delli, Carpini, and Keeter 1991), in Europe as in the United States (Popkin and Dimoch 1996; 1999). Nonetheless, in spite of the invariability of the response, the theme of the political sophistication of citizens was continually taken up again, reexamined and reelaborated in the study of political behavior.

This persistent interest is not difficult to explain: the image of a citizen who is ill-informed and incapable of interpreting the dynamics of politics stands in stark contrast to the basic assumptions of democratic theory (Berelson, Lazarsfeld, and McPhee 1954; Carmines and Huckefeldt 1996).[2] Consequently, in the face of the initial, disturbing findings it was not easy to end the

2. "The democratic citizen is expected to be well informed about political affairs. He is supposed to know what the issues are, what their history is, what the relevant facts are, what alternatives are proposed, what the parties stand for, what the likely consequences are. By such standards the voter falls short." (Berelson, Lazarsfeld, and McPhee 1954, 308).

discussion of the putative incapacity of citizens to conceptualize the world of politics; instead, right up to the present, this theme has remained at the center of research and has continually provoked new developments.

These developments have mainly moved in two directions: on the one hand, there has been a progressive redefinition of the concept of political sophistication and a search for measurement instruments better suited to evaluating the modes of cognitive elaboration citizens actually use; on the other hand, there has been an effort to insist that, in spite of their low levels of political cognition, voters are nonetheless able to arrive at satisfactory choices. In what follows we offer a brief account of some of the key phases in the debate.

First, in order to be clear about what is meant by political sophistication and what role this concept has played in political science, let us recall the definition offered by Hamill and Lodge:

> In political science, virtually every descriptive statement about the behavior of citizens and elites must be qualified by their 'level' of sophistication, and almost all attempts to model political behavior introduce one or another measure of sophistication as a control or intervening variable (Hamill and Lodge 1986, 71).

The reason for this is very simple: a person's individual knowledge influences how she perceives, remembers, and interprets reality (*ibidem* 1986).

That said, it is not difficult to see how, precisely as a consequence of its high degree of complexity and abstraction, political sophistication, variously defined as political involvement (Berelson, Lazarsfeld, and McPhee 1954), cognitive complexity (Campbell et al. 1960), political competence (Almond, Verba 1963), expertise (Fiske, Lau, and Smith 1990), or political awareness (Zaller 1991; 1992), has lent itself to a multiplicity of definitions and alternative empirical treatments.

The initial work in the field—the studies of Campbell et al. (1960) and Converse (1964), followed later by, amongst others, those of Nie, Verba, and Petrocik (1976), Carmines and Stimson (1982) and Pierce and Hagner (1982)–concentrated on voters' level of conceptualization, i.e., on "the presence or absence of certain abstractions that have to do with ideology" (Campbell et al. 1960, 221), introducing the idea of a belief system as "a configuration of ideas and attitudes in which the elements are bound together by some form of constraint or functional dependence" (Converse 1964, 207). In both of these works a high level of political sophistication was associated with a high level of education and political involvement.

A second way of defining the concept of political sophistication, especially prevalent in the field of political psychology, has involved what are referred to as cognitive schemata[3] (Lodge, McGrawn, Conover, Feldman, and Miller 1991). According to this approach, there are a range of possible schemata that can be applied to politics and which one a given individual adopts is influenced by his level of political involvement and expertise (Fiske and Kinder 1981). This approach maintains similarities with Converse's (Lawrence 2003) to the extent that it is based on the idea of knowledge organized in cognitive structures (analogous to the concept of belief system) but it diverges by rejecting the idea that the political belief system only manifests itself in a single form, recognizing instead that different people organize their vision of the political world in different ways (Conover and Feldman 1984) and that even less-sophisticated voters possess some form of schemata (Fiske and Kinder 1981; Hamill, Lodge, and Blake 1985).

Even though a great deal of vigorous criticism has been directed at the concept of schemata, especially its definition and operationalization

---

3. A schemata is defined as "a cognitive structure of organized prior knowledge, abstracted from experience with specific instances that guide the processing of new information and the retrieval of stored information" (Fiske and Linville 1980, 96).

(Kuklinski, Luskin, and Bolland 1991; Luskin 2002), this line of research can take credit for introducing the concept of political expertise, which has been widely used by subsequent scholars as a synonym for political sophistication (Luskin 1987), into the debate. Political expertise is a very general and abstract concept capable of encompassing the particular capacities, attitudes, and behaviors that distinguish the way in which individuals relate to politics.

For Krosnick, for example:

> political experts are presumed to be keenly interested in political affairs, to expose themselves to lots of political information (. . .), to pay close attention to the political information they encounter, and to reflect on the meaning and implications of that information (Krosnick 1990a, 4).

According to Krosnick (1990b), interest in and exposure to politics (the quantity and quality of information available) are distinct factors each capable of exerting its own particular effect, even though they are both a part of the concept of political expertise (Lawrence 2003). Sophistication has also been defined by the means which individuals have at their disposal: their general cognitive capacities; their motivations, such as incentives for acquiring and making use of information; and the opportunities available to them, such as access to information (Gordon and Segura 1997, 129). Luskin, on the other hand, conceives of political sophistication as the organization of cognitions in each individual's particular belief system. Individual political belief systems vary in terms of the number of cognitions (size), the coverage of the political universe (range), and the organization of the system itself (constraints); these three elements, when combined, indicate the level of political sophistication (Luskin 1987, 859–860).

A crucial problem in most of this discussion has been to explain how citizens with limited political cognition nonetheless manage to arrive at satisfactory choices (McKelvey and Ordeshook 1985;

Sniderman et al. 1991).[4] As we will see in the following sections, one of the most promising solutions to this problem has emerged from adopting the concept of heuristics and, in particular, the assumption that in reaching decisions, individuals use a range of cognitive and affective shortcuts, according to their level of political sophistication.

The question of how to measure political sophistication has given rise to as many debates and alternate proposals as the question of its definition has (Luskin 1987). Given the highly abstract nature of the concept, it is not surprising that it has been expressed as a product of several different factors. To measure political sophistication, scholars have used ideological abstraction and the capacity to conceptualize (Campbell et al. 1960; Converse 1964; Nie, Verba, and Petrocik, 1976; Carmines and Stimson 1982; Pierce and Hagner 1982), the degree of association between political knowledge and political beliefs (Conover and Feldman 1984; Hamill, Lodge, and Blake 1985), the level of political information (Luskin 1987, Bartels 1996), actual knowledge about politics (Zaller 1992; Delli Carpini and Keeter 1993; Popkin and Dimoch 1999), interest in politics (Fiske, Kinder, and Larter 1983; Lodge and Hamill 1986) and level of education (Sniderman et al. 1991).

The Heterogeneity of Cognitive Processes

As the concept of political sophistication has evolved, the initial emphasis on individuals' capacity to abstract and conceptualize has gradually given way to a more attentive consideration of the cognitive and affective factors that influence the construction of the political belief system. This development can be seen in the content and tenor of criticism directed toward the original works by subsequent scholars.

---

4. From a rational choice approach, voters' limited involvement in politics is a perfectly understandable phenomenon: ill-informed voters act rationally given that the advantage deriving from acquiring new information rarely exceeds the cost of obtaining it (Downs 1957).

In *The Nature of Belief Systems in Mass Publics* (1964) Converse describes a political belief system in terms of the constraint, the consistency, and the level of conceptualization of citizen opinions. Constraint is defined as the degree of coherence between a given individual's various opinions. Consistency is a measure, instead, of the stability of opinions over the course of time. Finally, conceptualization is gauged by the reasoning that individuals offer to justify their judgments on candidates.

Converse's conclusions, extensively confirmed by numerous subsequent studies, paint a picture of the typical voter as an individual with minimal levels of constraint, consistency, and conceptualization. In other words, whether in terms of positions on the issues or their stability over time, the majority of voters have no ideological coherence—to such an extent that the widely shared view that the American electorate is "innocent of ideology" seems plausibly justifiable (Kinder and Sears 1985; Sniderman 1993). Even Luskin finds himself obliged to recognize that

> the American public is extremely unsophisticated about politics and has not became appreciably more so over the past two-and-a-half decades. Other publics, abroad, are similarly unsophisticated. It is time to close the book on these questions and turn to others (Luskin 1987, 889).

Nevertheless, though more or less accepted in its general outline, this far-from-comforting description of the mass public has been widely criticized with respect both to its methodology for measuring and estimating the inconsistency and instability of voters (Luskin 1987, 865–873), and its actual contents. In particular, the following criticisms have been made of this type of research: that it overestimated the volume of information necessary for individuals to be considered politically competent (Conover and Feldman 1981; Kinder and Sears 1985; Sniderman et al. 1991); that it systematically underestimated the cognitive capacities and political competencies of citizens (Nie and Andersen 1974); and that it described the belief system exclusively in terms of opinions, without taking into consideration values and expectations (Sniderman et al. 1991).

But the thing that made many scholars reject this way of analyzing public opinion was its assumption that the relationship between ideological identification and specific opinions could be conceived of in only one way—an assumption that had been implicit in the decision to investigate the structure of belief systems by calculating the correlations between distinct and predefined pairs of idea-elements (i.e., political attitudes, partisanship, ideology) (Converse 1964, 207).

In fact it is possible that different types of people would connect such idea-elements in different ways, as a function of the nature of the problems considered and of the characteristics of the individuals in question (Sniderman et al. 1991). Affirming that principles and political preferences can relate to each other in a multiplicity of ways precludes the existence of a single coherent belief system and instead prompts the researcher to investigate the processes of judgment through which individuals form their own particular opinions and structure their own particular beliefs. This shift in focus from the coherence of opinions to the study of cognitive structures has led scholars of public opinion and information processing to embrace the hypothesis of a heterogeneity of citizens or, in other words, to accept the idea that "people make up their minds in different ways" (Sniderman et al. 1991, 8).

This heterogeneity is the outcome of a judgment process that combines two contrasting subprocesses: integration and differentiation. Integration, the act of connecting idea-elements, reduces the complexity of the belief system by limiting the number of separate units of information that are considered. Differentiation, understood as the number of different evaluative dimensions necessary to formulate a judgment, increases the complexity, as a rise in the number of evaluative dimensions necessarily leads to an expansion in the number of considerations that need to be made (*ibidem*, 5–7).

Individuals differ in terms of the degree of integration and differentiation within their belief systems and, as a result, they take into account considerations that vary according to the various evaluative dimensions at their disposal. For example, a voter capable of acquiring, checking, and understanding a substantial amount of the available political information might structure her judgments of the political parties in a contest around evaluative dimensions like the ideological content and salience of the political platforms, the credibility of the leaders, and the stability and unity of the party alliances. In a case like this, the voter will have a very large volume of information and considerations to manage.

At the same time, though, the complexity produced by this high level of differentiation is reduced by integrating information using certain political categories: i.e., the concepts of economic liberalism, moral conservatism, reformism, and left and right. A relatively unsophisticated voter, however—and one who, in addition, is neither able nor motivated to manage a high volume of information—will not be equipped with many of the concepts necessary for integrating information. By the same token, however, her need to reduce complexity is more limited, because the number of evaluative dimensions that she requires is more limited.

The processes of judgment and choice are not limited by any type of normative consideration: there does not exist *ex ante* any strategy of choice that is "right" or even "better" than others. The only assumptions for this analysis are that: (a) "choice is the product of reason, where reason is the human process of seeking, processing, and drawing inferences from information" (Lupia et al. 2001, 1); and (b) the objective is to identify the "elements of reasoning": the systematic steps in the process through which different individuals gather and make use of information (*ibidem*, 2).

It should be noted that the assumption of heterogeneity does not have anything to do with the simple—and banal—observation that each individual organizes his political opinions in his own way. On the contrary, an interest in heterogeneity spurs us to identify and explicate the criteria involved in decision making and to search for systematicity and uniformity in the processes of reasoning within groups that are homogenous in terms of political sophistication (*ibidem*, 20).

Voting Heuristics

It has long been evident that citizens have a limited knowledge of the practice of government and that they pay only sporadic attention to what happens in politics; nonetheless, it is no less evident that they have opinions, formulate judgments, and are often capable of indicating possible solutions for their communities' problems. How is it possible for individuals with a limited capacity to acquire and process information (Simon 1957; 1958), to make choices that are approximately rational (Sniderman et al. 1991)?

Normally the hypothesis that citizens are able to participate competently in the process of public decision making, despite limitations, is supported in two quite distinct ways: on the one hand, by arguing that they make use of shortcuts in judgment, or heuristics, to reduce the number of separate units of information necessary for decisions (Sniderman et al. 1991, Popkin 1991); and on the other, by claiming that they participate to a collective rationality (Converse 1990; Page and Shapiro 1992; Bartels 1996; Kuklinski and Quirk 2000).

This latter claim is based on an extension of Condorcet's theorem (Miller 1986; Johnson 1998), according to which a group of individuals is able to reach better decisions than a single person because the process of aggregating opinions tends to cancel out the effects of individual errors of judgment. Consequently, the *collective opinion* that emerges from an electoral process fully represents the real will of the citizens involved (Page and Shapiro 1992). What makes it possible for individual errors to fall away in the process of aggregation is that such errors are attributable exclusively to chance;

i.e., they are not systematic. This randomness, according to the proponents of the theory, is guaranteed by the essential inconsistency and instability of public opinion, which, as we have seen, has been an assumption taken for granted since Converse. Paradoxically, then, the very fact that citizens do not demonstrate stable attitudes in relation to politics becomes a guarantee that the outcome of public choice is an actual expression of the people's will.

The main criticism of this theory of "rationality as collective outcome" casts doubt precisely on the assumption that the errors made by individual citizens in formulating political judgments are fortuitous. Cognitive psychology has amply demonstrated how human cognitive processes give rise to systematic distortions and errors. And since individual voters find themselves in the face of the same cognitive tasks and have at their disposal bodies of information of the same nature, it is logical to suppose that they also make the same types of errors (Kuklinski and Quirk 2000).

By contrast, the first argument in support of citizens' political competence does not make any appeal to the collective outcome but rather emphasizes the *effectiveness* of the judgmental processes, and is based on the assumption that:

> Citizens frequently can compensate for their limited information about politics by taking advantage of judgmental heuristics (Sniderman et al. 1991, 18).

A heuristic, understood here as a judgment shortcut capable of organizing and simplifying political choices, represents an "effective" solution to the problem: it requires a limited quantity of information and is capable of providing definite responses, even to complex problems (*ibidem*, 19; Kuklinski, Quirk, Jerit, and Rich 2001). This, at any rate, is its supporters' optimistic view. However, even amongst the proponents of the political cognition approach, there are many who have assumed more cautious positions, especially with regard to the systematicity of heuristics' use and the appropriateness of the political decisions that emerge out of them (Kuklinski and Quirk 2000).

The concept of heuristics was first applied, in the study of political attitudes and opinions, to those cognitive processes in which the procedures of inference reduce or eliminate the need to acquire specific information. There are a number of clear examples of such inferences: attributing particular issue positions to a candidate based on his demographic characteristics or those of his constituents and supporters; inferring a candidate's political temperament from the cues of his personal character (Popkin 1991); relying on retrospective evaluations to judge a government's economic performance, assuming that its leader has control over the economy (Fiorina 1981); formulating judgments about candidates and policies by relying on the opinions expressed by political representatives, or interest groups connected to them (Lupia 1994); and relying on partisan stereotypes to judge political candidates (Rahn 1993).

Other types of heuristics are based instead on the idea that limited information can be compensated for by affective judgments. The process of choice is not confined exclusively to its cognitive features or to logical processes of opinion formation; rather, it is also influenced by feelings of attachment to and repulsion toward social groups, issues, parties, or political leaders. This is particularly true in the case of affective dispositions that are lasting, strongly felt, and focused, as opposed to states of mind that are fleeting, changeable, and vague (Sniderman et al. 1991, 7–8).

Starting from the hypothesis that people make use of various heuristics to compensate for a lack of information, depending on the specific level of information on hand, Sniderman, Brody, and Tetlock have developed the idea of an "interactive sophistication." They argue that political sophistication influences not only the decision-making process but also the way in which other factors, namely affective ones, influence reasoning (Sniderman et al. 1991, 20–22).

The introduction of affective and emotional factors is certainly not a novelty in the political behavior field of research (Markus 2000; Rahn 2000). The originality here lies in claiming that such predispositions influence political reasoning differently depending on the individual's level of the political sophistication. In fact, given that affective inferential processes are facilitated by how relatively accessible the sphere of the emotions are to most people, while cognitive processes necessarily require competencies and information not always at the disposal of the mass public, it is plausible to hypothesize that relatively unsophisticated citizens make greater use of affective reasoning than their more sophisticated counterparts do. However, this does not mean that individuals endowed with high levels of sophistication base their reasoning exclusively on logical processes (*ibidem*, 23).

The "likeability" heuristic (Brady and Sniderman 1991) is based on the idea that individuals use their own affinity toward certain social categories or political groupings to define the political position that such groups assume on particular issues. Individuals attribute positions to liberals and conservatives by combining their own feelings toward those political groupings with their own positions on the issues in question. In this way, through recourse to their own affective disposition—their own "likes and dislikes" (ibidem, 93)–individuals, even without concepts like liberalism and conservatism, nonetheless manage to estimate quite effectively what the positions of liberals and conservatives are.

There is a component of affectivity in ideological reasoning as well. Although commonly viewed as a form of judgment guided by cognitive processes, ideological reasoning is, in fact, rooted as much in what individuals feel as in what they know. The idea that ideological reasoning is centered on abstract categories and deductive inferences is brought into question by the significant role party attachment plays in giving an ideological position substance: the force of ideological reasoning is sustained more by support of an affective nature than by logical arguments (Chubb, Hagen, and Sniderman 1991).

In sum, there is no way of empirically establishing the relative influences cognition and affectivity have on the decision-making processes; nor is that the objective of this analysis. Investigating the heterogeneity of processes of judgment does not mean seeking to distinguish between who structures her own mind "well" and who does so in the "wrong" way (Sniderman, Glaser, and Griffin 1991, 178). On the contrary, the powerful idea behind this research proposal is that it is by structuring their mental schemes in distinct ways that ill-informed voters arrive at roughly rational or at any rate reasoned choices (*ibidem*, 165; Popkin 1991; Lupia 1994). This is also, obviously, the theory's most controversial feature.[5]

Experimental Studies of Political Cognition

While most research in the field of political cognition has been carried out using survey data, in recent years scholars have also used laboratory and field experiments to address basic questions concerning political persuasion, especially with respect to the effects of diverse types of messages, sources, and media (Cobb and Kuklinski 1997; Lupia and McCubbins 1998; Green and Gerber 2008); preference formation and framing (Druckman 2004; Druckman, Hennessy, Charles, and Webber 2010); party cues and policy information (Bullock 2011; Rahn 1993); interest group endorsements (Arceneaux and Kolodny 2009); candidate positioning (Tomz and Van Houweling 2008), and so on.

A relevant experimental advancement in the study of information processing and cognitive heuristics was Richard Lau and David Redlawsk's *How Voters Decide* (2007), in which they deploy an innovative research method called "dynamic process tracing" to study

---

5. For a critical overview of the main problems relating to the concept of heuristics such as (a) the suitability of their deployment, i.e., whether citizens systematically make use of certain heuristics in the case of particular situations and if this occurs with regularity and (b) the optimality of their use, i.e., whether such heuristics are capable of leading to reasonable decisions, see Kuklinski and Quirk (2000).

how voters acquire and use information. Their work was a basic step toward a better comprehension of how individuals decide how to vote, and greatly contributed to our understanding of the process of information acquisition. With the support of computer technology they simulated, in a laboratory setting, primary and presidential campaigns that reproduced many crucial aspects of actual US campaigns. They adapted the information board methodology, which makes it possible to record every action taken by the decision maker, to model the dynamic flow of information during the electoral campaign, recording the amount and type of information that people gather, as well as its sequencing and symmetry.

Reviewing the political science and psychology literature, Lau and Redlawsk identified four models of individual decision making: (a) the rational choice model, in which a dispassionate voter performs a rational calculus based on as much information as possible; (b) the early socialization model, in which individuals develop a strong party identification in the formative years of their lives, gather information occasionally, and process it selectively to maintain their cognitive consistency; (c) the fast and frugal heuristics model; and (d) the bounded rationality decision-making model, both of which are based on an attempt to minimize the amount of information processed via the use of heuristics. While the former two models are directly derived from classic political science theories (the Downsian model of economic voter and the Michigan model of party voter, respectively), the latter two are inspired by more general developments in psychology. Each of these four models defines an ideal strategy of information search. Voters are classified in one of the four different categories based on the depth and sequence of search and whether they deploy a compensatory (the same information is searched for every alternative) or noncompensatory strategy.

Lau and Redlawsk's findings confirm a basic expectation about political sophistication: political experts perform a more thorough search of available information and are more likely to adopt compensatory strategies than other voters. More interestingly, though, they show that certain features of campaigns affect the type of information processing strategies that people adopt. For instance, the proportion of people using compensatory strategies is much lower when there are four candidates than when voters have to choose between only two. Similarly, when the ideological differences between the candidates are minimal, voters are more likely to rely on intuitive strategies. More generally, the harder the decision task, the more likely people are to rely on heuristic strategies that minimize the amount of information necessary for the choice.

In addition, a voter's method and amount of information processing can be a relevant predictor of voting decisions. For instance, people who consider a larger amount of information for both candidates are more likely to cross party lines. Finally, most people seem to rely on political heuristics such as group endorsement, partisan and ideological schemata, person stereotypes, and candidate viability. However, those who seem to benefit from their use are the political experts, thus casting some doubts, according to Lau and Redlawsk, on the argument that cognitive heuristics "are the saving grace of the apathetic American voter" (252).

The Art of Making It Simple: Heuristics
in the Social Sciences

As we have seen, the concept of heuristic, as originally conceived in the field of psychology, means a cognitive process that was rapid and effective but distinct from perfect reasoning: it is not the best choice; indeed, used in contexts that are inappropriate, it may lead to wrong judgments. It is a shortcut, and as such is inevitably imperfect (Aronson et al. 1999, 86–87).

It is curious to observe, then, how this concept has been taken up in the analysis of public opinion and political attitudes. The term heuristic has been introduced as a synonym for an efficient choice or rational strategy that compensates for ignorance, a far cry from its use in psychology, where it has been an abiding object of study precisely because of the systematic errors that characterize it (Kuklinski and Quirk 2000, 166). The political cognition approach shares this semantic gap with other disciplines.

In studies of artificial intelligence, for example, which analyze human problem solving and reasoning mechanisms in order to create software capable of simulating them, the concept of heuristic has been used as an alternative to algorithmic reasoning characterized exclusively by logical consequentiality. Newell, Shaw, and Simon (1962) argue that the principle characteristics of heuristics can be inferred by observing human behavior as individuals solve complex problems.

> The success of a problem solver who is confronted with a complex task rests primarily on his ability to select—correctly—a very small part of the total problem-solving maze for exploration. The processes that carry out these selections we call heuristics. (*ibidem* 1962, 96).

A heuristic is a "process of creative thought" in which imagination (i.e., a change in perspective, or backward-looking learning), not conventionality, is necessary for resolving problems (*ibidem*, 97–114).[6] This is also true in the case of artificial intelligence. In these studies, heuristics have not been viewed as a simplification of perfect thought, because in the face of complex problems so-called perfect thought would require considering a huge quantity of information and evaluating a vast array of possible solutions.[7] They have

6. It could be objected that, while this type of approach lends itself well to the study of scientific thought, it is much less suitable for capturing the inferential processes of the common man. But in actual fact there may be little difference between a scientist's way of thinking and that of the common man—for instance, Albert Einstein's political opinions were founded on arguments analogous to those of any other moderately well-informed citizen (Pais 1982).

7. A further example of this approach is Johnson-Laird's theory of mental models (TMM). According to this theory, individuals, starting out from an innate condition of incompleteness of information, make use of simplified models of reality to draw inferences and reach creative solutions (Anolli and Legrenzi 2001, 147–178).

been viewed, instead, as essentially and necessarily creative processes. In chess the number of moves that are permissible at every turn and the number of countermoves that these moves can prompt in turn are in the order of thousands; in order for a game to be brought to an end, players must come up with creative solutions.

But what about political choices? Political issues are intrinsically complex. It is not in the interests of politicians to provide voters with really pertinent information about themselves; nor do the structures of modern democracies encourage voters to pay particular attention to politics; nor, finally, can citizens evaluate with confidence the actions of the government (Kuklinski and Quirk 2000). In contrast to many economic choices, for example, it is very unlikely that a political choice is reached starting out from a set of individual preferences that is complete, transitive, continuous, and coherent.

The problem of defining an "order of political preferences" stems from two factors: (a) the plurality of goals in any given political undertaking and the related difficulty of making tradeoffs and establishing hierarchical relations between different interests—be they economic, ethical, or value-based—especially when these interests are in conflict (as they often are); and (b) our extremely limited capacity to foresee the future and the practical impossibility of making comparative costs-benefits analyses.

We might, perhaps somewhat colorfully, suggest that *in politics what's missing is the price*. There is no synthetic, intersubjectively shared measure that allows actors to communicate through a code—the price—and to evaluate the advantages and disadvantages that might result from an exchange. This fact renders politics much more complex, unpredictable—and intriguing—than other forms of interaction between human beings. Nonetheless, this absence does not, in itself, necessarily preclude the possibility that individuals behave in politics just as they do in other areas of social life.

The concept of heuristic is of considerable use in accounting for how voters manage the complexity of the political system.

Nevertheless, cognitive shortcuts should not be invested with virtues that they do not possess: in particular, it is not possible to make any claims about either the quality of their outcomes or the systematicity of their use. It would appear appropriate, then, to circumscribe our assumptions about the use of heuristics to a single incontrovertible fact—that individuals use heuristics to reach decisions in complex situations—thereby excluding any consideration about the quality of the decisions they produce or the degree of awareness involved in their use. Heuristics are applied immediately every time the opportunity for using them arises. This alone constitutes a huge advantage, as amply demonstrated by George Polya. The computational velocity guaranteed by heuristics allows individuals to spontaneously deal with an enormous number of everyday situations (Polya 1945), including the choice of for whom to vote.

PART TWO

The Cognitive Shortcuts of Italian Voters

Chapter 4

The Heuristics of Italian Voters

The motto "Take the best, ignore the rest" is a good starting point to understand voters' decision-making strategies. This motto, in fact, encapsulates the general principle—take note only of the important cues and leave the remaining information aside—that enables citizens to get their bearings in the political environment, find a shortcut, and arrive at a decision. Similarly, in our investigation of voter's cognitive shortcuts, our goal will be to capture organizing principles of voting decision making that are systematic, widely shared, and consistent over time, and disregard individual idiosyncrasies and contingencies that do not belong to the ecology of the political environment.

In our search and analysis of the decision-making mechanisms that guide Italian voters we will combine (a) the more general perspective of the adaptive approach to the study of human decision making—in particular, following the guiding principles of fast and frugal heuristics, and (b) specific contributions from the field of political cognition concerning the political sophistication and heterogeneity of the electorate. These two fields of research are united by the idea that individuals make use of cognitive shortcuts in order to reduce the complexity of decision-making tasks.

Theoretical Framework and Research Hypotheses

How can the conceptual tools of the adaptive approach to decision making be employed in the study of voting behavior? As researchers, the large amount of uncertainty and complexity that distinguishes the decision-making process in the political context makes it very problematic to define what constitutes the "best or right choice" for a certain voter or what is the "correct reasoning" strategy that citizens should adopt.[1] As a consequence, both the use of a normative model and the search for systematic errors in the processes of judgment and choice turn out to be fairly sterile exercises when applied to voting behavior and the study of public opinion. As an indirect confirmation of this, one should consider the scarce capacity of spatial models of voting behavior, which are based on the standard model of rational decision making, to account for actual voting choices (Budge et al. 2001; DeSio 2011; Page and Shapiro 1992; Pizzorno 1983).

However, this does not necessarily mean that voting must be considered a choice *sui generis* and void of any rationale, nor can it justify an investigation of the decision-making process based on categories and reasoning strategies different to those used in other decision-making contexts. The fast and frugal heuristics approach, with its shift from the search for the "best choice" to the study of the principles of ecological rationality (Chapter 2), allows us to take into account both the specificities of the political context and at the same time bring them into relation with the more general framework of

---

1. See, however, the interesting attempt by Lau and Redlawsk at identifying "substantive criteria for judging if voters can and do vote their informed interests" (2007, 16). Namely, they "define a correct vote decision as one that is the same as the choice that would have been made under conditions of full information" (2007, 75) and measure it in two different ways. First, they ask the participants in the mock election experiment to review, after they have completed their decision-making task, *all* the information available, and to decide whether under a condition of full information, they would have voted for the same candidate. Second, they compute a normative measure of naïve vote preferences based on a voter's own values and an objective evaluation of the information gathered by the voter (and what the voter should have looked at) and compare it to the actual choice. They find that an average of 70 percent of participants do indeed vote for the "right" party.

The validity of this method depends on two basic assumptions: (1) that full information would inevitably lead to the "right" choice, and (2) that the information environment does indeed contains all the information that is necessary for "making the right choice." While these assumptions might sound plausible in the American political system, neither assumption is fully defendable in more complex political systems, like the Italian one.

decision making in conditions of uncertainty. The study of political judgment in the light of the guiding principles of the fast and frugal heuristics approach makes it possible to heed the specificity of political choice without succumbing to the temptation of thinking that everything that pertains to political action is invariably and necessarily different from the rest of human behavior.

Fast and frugal heuristics are domain-specific: in the context of political judgment, they rely on cues that are encrypted in the ecology of the political system. In fact, according to the principle of ecological rationality, it is the environment that furnishes the elements on which the judgment process is based and heuristics are all the more effective the more they succeed in reproducing the information structure of the context in which they are applied and in exploiting its peculiar conformation. In other words, it is not possible to define in an absolute way the applicability and efficacy of a heuristic, because the performance of any model of reasoning depends on the type of information that the environment offers and the way in which it is configured.

According to Simon, human decision making is shaped by a scissor whose two blades are the capacity of the human mind and the structure of the environment. Of these two elements, scholars have mostly investigated the constraints of the human mind, ignoring the decision-making context, or deliberately trying to strip it away in laboratory experiments. The study of political cognition is no exception. As one can easily infer from the content of Chapter 3, political psychologists have mostly invested in the study of cognition and political sophistication, devoting only scant attention to the structure of the political environment.

In this book, we instead start from a careful consideration of the political environment and show how the cognitive shortcuts of Italian citizens are forged by the combination of the specific configuration of the political context and voters' cognitive and affective dispositions. This shift in focus justifies the choice of relying on observational data relative to real political campaigns—i.e., survey interviews—rather than experimental results that simulate only some features of the electoral campaign.

Structured interviews administered to nationally representative samples are the most common tool to study public opinion and political behavior, whereas most research in decision making is carried out through laboratory experiments. The advantage of the latter is the possibility of tracing the decision-making process in real time, and control the type and amount of information that subjects gather. The disadvantage is that the campaign context is simulated, and therefore it is representative of reality only for those elements that are already known by the researcher and that he decides to reproduce in the mock election. Observational data, in contrast, do not allow for a careful mapping of information processing, but have the advantage of capturing a snapshot of respondents' view of a real political campaign, which reproduces, although indirectly, the way in which information is encrypted in the political context of the campaign. For a study that posits as its major goal the identification of the ecological as well as the cognitive constraints that guide the decision making of Italian voters, therefore, it seems reasonable to rely on the method that better reproduces these ecological features (i.e., how political information is "bundled" in the political context under investigation).

A second distinctive feature of the adaptive approach—alongside the principle of ecological rationality—is the attention it gives to the psychological plausibility of the models. This concern entails that the decision-making process described by a model has to conform to the actual cognitive capacities of the subjects involved and to the social reality in which the decision making is taking shape. So far as research practice is concerned, this means that it should be reflected in how citizens perceive and interpret the public debate.

In our analysis, we make use only of forms of representation of the political system that the mass public itself makes use of. Moreover, any consideration relating to the level of sophistication or political competence of single individuals is argued for on the basis of the actual use of such forms of representation. Thus, for example, we will say that a particular subject has the concepts of left and right at his disposal only in the case that he is able to position parties on the ideological continuum in accordance with an inter-subjectively shared order. In general, the availability of specific cognitive competencies will have to be "certified" at the level of the individual by the fact that he is able to make use of such analytic categories.

The criterion of psychological plausibility, then, does not just mean the rejection of the image of an omniscient voter capable of controlling and processing an immense quantity of knowledge. As well as the general limitations on the cognitive capacities of human beings, it is also necessary to take account of the limits relating to the interaction between individuals and their environment, in particular with respect to the degree of familiarity that individual subjects have with the conceptual categories inhering to public debate and the different capacities they have to interpret and understand the information that arises out of it. In short, the acceptance of the principle of psychological plausibility translates empirically into a requirement to check whether individuals really do have at their disposal the cognitive capacities necessary for the strategies of reasoning attributed to them. In this chapter, we classify individuals according to clearly outlined inferential processes.

The principle of ecological rationality and psychological plausibility can be coherently integrated with the basic assumption, quite popular among scholars of political cognition, of voters' heterogeneity. Taken together, they contribute to the specification of our research hypotheses. Assuming that voting is an individual choice, that it is the fruit of (some form of) reasoning and that a heterogeneity of decision-making strategies are possible, we classify Italian citizens according to the following principles:

Assumption I—in their political judgments individuals make use of heuristics that enable them to reduce the complexity of decision-making tasks;

Assumption II—political judgments rely on cues that are encrypted in the ecology of the political system. It follows that these political schemata are based on the objects that populate the political environment (i.e., parties, leaders, and issues) and on inter-subjectively shared forms of representation (i.e., forms that are common to a substantial number of voters);

We will then use the typology of Italian voters that emerges from this classificatory exercise to test the following four general hypotheses:

Hypothesis I—*Political sophistication*—voters use different cognitive shortcuts in accordance with their level of political sophistication.

Hypothesis II—*Sistematicity*—voters use cognitive shortcuts systematically: they apply the same heuristics any time they face specific decision-making tasks.

Hypothesis III—*Effectiveness*—the cognitive shortcuts should lead to effective decision making: the decision-making performance of voters using certain heuristics should be equal or even better than that of people with the highest levels of political sophistication.

Hypothesis IV—*Heterogeneity of the effects*—political objects do not have the same importance for all voters: The use of a particular heuristic leads a voter to take into consideration some political objects and to overlook others.

The assumption of a heterogeneity of voters—in order for it not to remain a mere suggestion—requires us first of all to divide voters into different types and to then examine the decision-making dynamics of each type. The remaining part of Chapter 4 is dedicated to construct a typology of voting heuristics; Chapter 5 provides a description of the sociodemographic profile of each type, as well as a test of Hypothesis I. The following empirical chapters then test the validity of the typology. Chapter 6 tests the systematicity of use and effectiveness of the alternative decision-making strategies here identified (Hypotheses II and III). Chapter 7 investigates the heterogeneity of the decision-making strategies and shows the relative importance of diverse political objects in voting choice (Hypothesis IV).

The "Ecology" of the Italian Political System

In Western democracies, the landscape of politics is populated by a fairly well delineated set of objects, such as parties, leaders, and political issues. However, the relative importance of each of them, as well as the way in which these objects combine, varies across countries and over time. The left-right dimension (or the liberal-conservative dimension in the United States) represents the major ideological divide in most societies, although the specific issue positions that are associated with the left and right categories vary from country to country. Moreover, in some societies the political conflict is not confined to the ideological dimension exclusively, but involves also ethnic or other types of cleavages. Countries also vary widely with respect to the number and role of political parties, and their electoral rules (Sartori 1976, Lijphart 1968, Fabbrini 1998). Countries with numerous parties tend to have proportional systems of representation, in which party coalitions are as important as the parties themselves. Instead, majoritarian systems are often characterized by competitions in which two major (presidential) candidates attract most of the attention, and their personalities might become, at times, as important as the party agenda.

These considerations, and many others along similar lines, are meant to support the idea that the overall ecology of the political system is likely to affect how bits of information are bundled together during a campaign. People conceptualize politics relying on the cues that are available in the political context, as well as on their own personal evaluation of the single political objects. The electoral system, the number of parties, the dimensionality of the spatial competition (i.e., left-right ideology vs. multiple cleavages), the strategic alliances among parties, the importance of leaders, and the accountability of the political establishment are all factors that contribute to the architecture of the political landscape, and will therefore guide citizens' perception of it (Denzau and North 2000; Sniderman 2000; Kuklinski et al. 2001).

The Italian political landscape of the Second Republic is un-equivocally complicated, but constitutes a great opportunity for the study of political decision making, for reasons that will be easy to comprehend after a short summary of Italy's recent political history. For more than fifty years after Italy became a Republic in 1946, the same party coalition led by the Democratic Christian party held both cabinet control and a consistent congressional majority. During the period of the so-called First Republic (1946–1993) election outcomes were fairly stable and highly predictable. Although electoral campaigns were held in a very confrontational climate, they were never perceived as real competitions. Consequently, electoral volatility was minimal (Mannheimer and Sani 1987). Partisan affiliations were very strong, and rooted territorially (Galli et al. 1968). Through the 1970s and 1980s corruption grew rampant and affected virtually the entire political class. At the beginning of the 1990s, widespread judicial investigations of political corruption, which were started in Milan by the Mani Pulite (Clean Hands) investigation pool in February 1992 and rapidly spread through the country, led to the arrest of many politicians and the collapse of the entire party system. Changes were dramatic and invested many aspects of the political and economic life of the country (Gilbert 1995).

It is customary to date the beginning of the Second Republic in 1993, with the adoption of a new electoral law. The electoral system during the First Republic was a nearly pure proportional representation system, which led to a proliferation of small parties, the fragmentation of the political system, government instability, and more importantly, favored parties' insulation from the electorate (parties had full control over the nomination of the candidates, leaving little actual choice to the voters). Citizens promoted via two abrogative referenda an electoral reform aimed at establishing a majoritarian representation system that was expected to terminate vote-exchange practices ("voto di scambio") and start a new era of political accountability. The law that was eventually passed by Congress was a mixed electoral system, with three-quarters of seats allocated using a first-past-the-post electoral system, and one-fourth using a proportional method.

The new electoral law was first implemented in the national general election of 1994, and Silvio Berlusconi, a media tycoon turned politician to salvage his own business (and himself) from corruption investigations (Stille 2006), won large consensus and became prime minister. Rising from the ashes of the First Republic, the political scene in 1994 was characterized by great uncertainty. Almost all parties were brand-new or rebranded, and none of them could really estimate their relative value. In this climate they formed a few pre-electoral alliances: The left-wing parties, among which the Partito Democratico della Sinistra (PDS), the Partito della Rifondazione Comunista (PRC) and Partito dei Verdi and other smaller parties, such as, for instance, what was left of the Partito Socialista Italiano (PSI), formed a progressive alliance. Similarly, there was a coalition of parties, heirs of the Democrazia Cristiana (DC), the Democratic Christian party that ruled the country for the previous fifty years, which occupied the center of the political spectrum. Finally, Mr. Berlusconi's newly founded party, Forza Italia (FI), was in alliance in the northern districts with Lega Nord (LN), a Northern federalist and racist party that had capitalized in the previous few years on citizens' disappointment with the national political establishment, while in the central and southern districts it formed an alliance with Alleanza Nazionale (AN), a newly established, conservative party home to many members of the former fascist party (Movimento Sociale Italiano). Berlusconi's astute strategy of a "variable" alliance made it possible for him to win the general election, but failed to provide consistent support in Congress, and he was forced to resign eight months later. Overall, although the new electoral rule did not bring about the bipolar party system and reduction in the number of parties that scholars had anticipated (and citizens hoped for), it surely started an era in which elections became real competitions determining winners and losers, political campaigns acquired real meaning, and electoral volatility increased.

This book analyzes the subsequent two general elections of 1996 and 2001. In 1996, although the party system was still in turmoil, parties could rely on some previous experience, which led them to the formation of two major political alliances. The center-left coalition, the Ulivo, was lead by Romano Prodi, an economist and statesman coming from the reformist wing of the DC. The Ulivo comprised most left-of-center parties and one important party from the center of the political spectrum, the Partito Popolare Italiano (PPI), the direct heir of the DC. Particularly telling of the growing bipolar nature of the emergent political landscape is the fact that several PPI members who came from the right-wing tradition of the DC and opposed the alliance with the center-left parties, abandoned the PPI to form the Centro Cristiano Democratico and Cristiani Democratici Uniti (CCD-CDU) and then converged in the right-wing coalition. In fact, on 1996, CCD-CDU, FI, and AN formed Berlusconi's center-right alliance, the Polo delle Libertà, while the Lega Nord, which had caused the crises of Berlusconi's Cabinet in 1994, ran alone. Romano Prodi and his center-left coalition won the elections by a slim margin. Prodi had to quit in 1998 after the PRC withdrew its support to his Cabinet, but the center-left coalition managed to form new Cabinets and governed the country until the end of their mandate.

The 2001 general national election was similarly characterized by a center-left coalition, the Ulivo, and a center-right coalition, the Casa delle Libertà, although their composition differed slightly from the previous election. The Ulivo did not comprise PRC, which had been responsible for bringing down Prodi's government and included instead a group of parties from the center running under the label of Democrazia é Libertà—Margherita (Dem), which had been founded by Romano Prodi himself, while the Lega Nord re-entered the Casa delle Libertà alliance. There were also a few parties running alone in the center of the political spectrum.

Overall, the major novelty of the Second Republic was the formation of preelectoral political alliances, and the personalization of the political campaign. However, parties did not lose their importance—indeed they remained central actors in the political landscape. Moreover, issues did not manage to attract a lot of attention. Historically, policy issues have always had scarce importance in the national debate, and the 1996 and 2001 elections were no exception. For instance, Legnante and Sani (2002) report that more than 70 percent of political information provided by the media in the days before the 2001 election were concerned with personal information about the leaders and campaign and personal issues, and less than 20 percent covered policy or political issues.

Finally, the Second Republic did not stop the growing sense of inefficacy and disaffection that has characterized the history of Italian democracy since World War II. On the contrary, voter turnout declined by almost 10 percent in the 1990s, and the disconnect between the political class and "the people" increased. The scarce legitimacy of its institutions has always been a problem of Italian democracy. The level of trust in parties, politicians, and the Parliament has been in constant decline for decades. In 2004 only one-fourth of Italians had some trust in parties, and around one-third said that Parliament, public administration, or the press could be trusted. Similarly, citizens' sense of political efficacy is among the lowest in Western democracies. In 1975 three-quarters of Italians thought that they had no influence on what the government did. In 2004 almost 90 percent was of that opinion (Segatti and Vezzoni 2007).

However, during the First Republic, strong partisan identifications would alleviate the scarce legitimization of the political system. The Catholic and communist political subcultures had strong territorial roots and were capable of permeating the economic and social life of many Italians, thus favoring their integration in the national polity (Lipset and Rokkan 1967; Almond and Verba 1963). Although the credibility of these institutions had been significantly compromised by widespread patronage and corruption practices, their sudden disappearance left many citizens orphans of their political identities, fostering disillusion and cynic realism. Disaffection, mistrust, and a disgusted rejection of all-things-political are diffused sentiments among Italian citizens. One example well captures this spirit. During the electoral campaign in 2001, a reporter for RAI 3 news show interviewed passersby in a central street in Naples asking who they hoped would win the upcoming election. A polite man in his sixties graciously replied: "To me, doesn't matter who wins. Those people (politicians) won't ever be able to rule us!" Although we should not make too much of a single line, it is interesting to notice here how the disappointment with the political establishment did not simply translate into skepticism and apathy—the indifference toward which party will win—but went as far as to elicit a sense of resistance.

There are three main reasons why it is particularly attractive to study political judgment in the first decade of the Italian Second Republic. First of all, the sudden collapse of the entire party system and the emergence of a new one, in a context in which not only parties and leaders but also the dynamic of electoral competition had changed dramatically, is a perfect setting in which one can study political judgment "*en plein air*." One can even think of it as a quasi-experimental setting. New or "refurbished" parties had to cope with novel rules, form preelectoral alliances, and run political campaigns in a climate of great uncertainty. In this context, *voters had to make up their minds.* They could not rely on their preexisting political identities, nor they could rely on the experience of the previous decades, or information collected in the past. They had to evaluate and decide in a new political environment. Of course, they could rely on old heuristics, as well as come up with new ones. As we will see, they did both.

Second, the Italian political landscape, in which the multiparty and coalitional competition intertwine in unexpected ways, presents a high level of complexity, especially when compared to the "minimalist" American two-party system. If it is true, as research on cognitive shortcuts suggests, that *mater artium necessitas* (necessity is the mother of invention), we can expect that people who have to deal with such complexity will be more likely to rely on cognitive shortcuts.

Finally, this research extends extant work—which is mainly based on and about the American voter—to other electoral contexts. Indeed, the study of the Italian case represents a good opportunity to extend the scope conditions of the theory of political decision making by testing its validity in a different institutional and social context. The research shows that some core findings extend beyond the United States to a country whose political tradition is quite different. At the same time, the comparison allows for the identification of institutional factors (like, for instance, electoral laws, party systems, and coalitions) that might vary across countries.

Toward a Classification of Italian Voters

The idea that voters do not constitute a homogeneous mass but, on the contrary, need to be investigated in terms of their heterogeneity is certainly not new. So far as the case of Italy is concerned, academics have for a considerable time been oriented toward an interpretation of political behavior of a classificatory kind, making frequent recourse to voter typologies (Legnante 1998). Some of these are not much more than snapshots of a particular moment in political history and as such do not have any more than a passing impact. Others instead devote greater attention to the Weberian insistence on "the need to elaborate an ad hoc conceptual form that expresses the purity of the phenomenon to which it refers" (Barlucchi 1998, 67) and, in fact, succeed in identifying characteristics that constitute elements of differentiation that tend to be stable and lasting.

These latter typologies vary in terms of the classificatory principles that inform the division of subjects into different groups. The most well-known—frequently evoked and often misunderstood—is the voting typology[2] proposed by Arturo Parisi and Gianfranco Pasquino, based on the "formal characteristics of the relationship that ties "voter" and "voted"" (Parisi and Pasquino 1977b, 220). These authors distinguish between a vote "of opinion," a vote "of membership" and a vote "of exchange"[3] (ibidem, 219–228).

Other typologies that have been proposed for the voting behavior of the Italian electorate are based on different criteria (Marradi 1992). For example, Giacomo Sani and Giovanni Sartori divided voters along two dimensions: their dominion of identification and space of competition (Sani and Sartori 1978; 1983). Core to their classification is the distinction between voters who can be placed in an electoral space (or space of competition), i.e., voters who could potentially change their voting preference, and voters who, on the contrary, do not experience voting as a choice—this latter set constituting a category analogous to that of "membership" voters in the Parisi and Pasquino typology. Renato Mannheimer and Sani, on the other hand, propose a typology of voting motivations, dividing voters into the categories of voters "for ideals," "for interest," "for habit," and "for

2. This typology, put forward at the end of the 1970s to account for certain changes in voting orientation (Parisi and Pasquino 1977a), has maintained its validity long after and by now has for some time constituted a point of reference for the study of voting behavior in Italy. However, it is only in recent years that attempts have been made to test empirically its resilience (Cartocci 1990; Legnante 1998; Parisi 1995).

3. The "opinion" voter makes a choice by evaluating the policy proposals of the parties in terms of the pursuit of his personal interest. The subjective benefit is conceived as deriving out of the outcome of future governmental action undertaken within the more general pursuit of some collective objective. As a consequence, in the vote of opinion the pursuit of interest has a "mediated nature" (*ibidem*, 221–223). By contrast, in the vote of exchange the relationship between vote and pursuit of interest is "immediate and individual" (*ibidem*, 226), i.e., here the vote reproduces the logic of exchange in the market, in which in exchange for one service (a vote) there takes place a counter-exchange that is immediate and directed *ad personam*. The third type of vote, on the other hand, "much more than an expression of choice is a testimony to a membership." The voter experiences the vote as "the affirmation of a subjective identification with a political force that he believes has a relationship of organic identification as opposed to mere institutional representation" with his social group (*ibidem*, 223–225).

exchange" according to the reasons that voters themselves declare for their voting choice (Mannheimer and Sani 1987, 51–59). The typological approach has also been used to investigate voting mobility (Biorcio and Natale 1989), the nature of individual political identity (Biorcio and Diamanti 1987), types of *cives*, understood in terms of the composition of citizens' political knowledge and feelings (Sani 1994), and the ways in which people are exposed to political communication (Baldini, Bucchi, and Fava 2001).

In general, many scholars of Italian public opinion have come to recognize that to "speak of the "voter" as if there existed some sort of ideal "average" is to say the least, rather imprecise" (Mannheimer and Sani 1994, 11). However, up to the present, very little if any attention has been given to the fact that, even before they are considered in terms of individual motivations and identifications, citizens need to be differentiated in terms of the way in which they interpret and represent political phenomena. Our division of voters, then, in contrast to previous ones, will pay close attention to how individuals organize their preferences and define courses of action in the domain of politics.

The heterogeneity of voters stems from the different ways they have of understanding politics. Our classification, then, comes about starting out from the availability and use of different ideological representations of public debate, where, by "ideological representation," we mean the particular structure of the system of political beliefs that makes it possible for the individual to control and organize her knowledge, opinions, attitudes, and behavior (van Dijk 1998, 48; see also Converse 1962). In fact, in order to be able to argue that voting choice is based on certain conceptual categories, it is necessary first of all to check that such categories do actually exist at an acceptable level of inter-subjectivity. In operational terms, this means that a survey respondent is attributed an ideological representation by virtue of the fact that she organizes specific information, opinions, and/or attitudes according to a framework that is defined and shared by a significant number of other individuals.

We identify three different ways of interpreting political debate. In addition to the traditional representation of the competition through the categories of left and right (Baldassarri 2004), widespread throughout the majority of Western democracies (Mavrogordatos 1987), a second way of organizing political reality is the interpretation of the competition as a conflict between coalitions and, in particular, in the dualism unleashed by candidates' competition for the premiership (Baldassarri and Schadee 2004).

From the point of view of ecological rationality, not just the availability but also the refusal or incapacity to make use of the interpretative categories suitable for a particular environment are factors that influence the dynamics of decision making. As a consequence, we consider as a third possible form of representation, the absence of the traditional ideological categories—a condition that opens up the possibility of using alternative interpretative criteria (Baldassarri and Schadee 2005).

The principle players in our analysis, then, will be (a) the voter *utilius*, who understands the political competition using the left-right yardstick and defines her own voting preference following a principle of spatial proximity; (b) the voter *amicus*, who conceives of politics as a dichotomy, i.e., reduces the political competition to a contraposition between the two major coalitions and their leaders; and (c) the voter *aliens*, who is unable or unwilling to govern political debate through traditional ideological categories. This voter, as we shall see, is animated by a rejection of politics and seeks in every possible way to keep her distance from it. Nevertheless, even though she cultivates a general feeling of distrust, she still makes a choice, choosing parties both to the right and to the left. Lastly, there is the voter *medians*, a residual category, which includes all the cases that do not fit into the previous three types. In a large number of our analyses *medians* voters represent a middle way between *utilius* and *amicus* voters, on the one hand, and *aliens* voters, on the other, and they will serve as a category of comparison vis-à-vis the other three.

The analysis is based on two surveys on the political opinion and electoral behavior of Italians carried out by the research group Itanes (Italian National Election Studies). The 1996 Itanes survey was conducted via telephone interview on a sample of 2,502 individuals in the month following the 1996 national Italian elections. The respondents were drawn from a larger random sample of individuals who have been interviewed already in the course of the election campaign. This double selection led to a distortion in the sample because "the mechanisms of self-selection normally present (...) weighed on the sample two times" (Corbetta and Parisi 1997, 364). In particular, there is a systematic overrepresentation of respondents who are very interested in politics and are politically active. There are also some biases with respect to the political identification of the interviewees. However, since the focus of this work is on the relationship between the variables, the above-mentioned problems in relation to the sample do not impact on the contents of the analysis; nevertheless, they should still be taken into consideration in any comparison of the two surveys.

The 2001 Itanes survey consisted of 3,209 face-to-face interviews, conducted in the period immediately following the 2001 national elections, and was based on a three-stage probabilistic sample (Itanes 2001). There are no particular distortions with this sample.

Utilius: The Spatial Voter

The concepts of "left" and "right" entered the political vocabulary during the French Revolution of 1789, following an intense debate among members of the National Assembly: members who were loyal to religion and the king sat to the right of the president, while those members who supported the revolution clustered in the left side. From then on, a large part of the political debate in Western societies has developed according to this dichotomy (Inglehart and Klingemann 1976; Bobbio 1999). The content of these categories has changed over time and varies between countries, to the point that there is a certain ambiguity among scholars as to whether these labels have any meaning in themselves—e.g., equality *versus* freedom—or serve instead as empty boxes that are filled with meaning by the actual issues that are associated with them in any given historical period (Bobbio 1999, Sartori 1982; Schadee 1995). Either way, the left-right ideological continuum has been the most salient political cleavage in Western democracies for at least a century, and does not seem to be losing its power as an organizing principle of the democratic debate (Lipset and Rokkan, 1967; Bartolini and Mair, 1990; Caramani 2004). Finally, the left-right, or liberal-conservative, ideological continuum is at the basis of spatial theories of voting, insofar as they stem from the intuition that the political competition can be conceptualized as the movement of parties and voters along a single, or a few, dimensions of ideological differentiation.

Citizens who are familiar with the left and right categories can use them as a powerful guidance to political judgment. In this perspective, the left-right ideology functions as a cognitive shortcut in the sense that it represents a particular configuration of the political information that voters can make use of to simplify their decision-making process. In fact, the labels of left and right make it possible to condense a multiplicity of attitudes on specific issues (such as, for example, health care, education, welfare, etc.) into a single synthetic position along a one-dimensional continuum. So, for voters who dispose of these conceptual coordinates, the voting choice may simply be based on an evaluation of the position that the parties assume on the left-right axis. Obviously, the more public debate is structured around these categories, the more effective will this strategy of choice be.

The first type of voter, *utilius*, makes use of the left-right dimension as an ideological representation of the political space. He reproduces the framework of behavior of the rational voter described by Downs (1957). This framework assumes that (a) the position the voter takes up within political space constitutes a synthesis of his preferences in relation to particular issues; that (b) the parties engaged in the electoral competition are placed in the same space; and that (c) the distance that separates voter and party decreases in proportion to the increase in the benefit that the voter would enjoy as a consequence of the victory of the party.

The conditions necessary for the identification of the *utilius* voter are (a) that the voter agrees to place himself on the left-right dimension, (b) that he demonstrates the ability to place the parties according to a commonly agreed left-right order, and (c) that he has voted for the party closest[4] to his own position. Only if all three conditions are true can we assume that a voter uses this strategy for simplifying political judgment.

These selection criteria are useful in that they distinguish (a) the cognitive element, in the form of a capacity to use the left-right dimension to organize the party system, from (b) the actual satisfaction of the criterion of spatial proximity, a distinctive trait in the strategy of choice of the *utilius* voter. This makes it possible, on the one hand, to make the selection of *utilius* voters hinge on the availability of a sufficiently detailed map of the distribution of the parties in political space and, on the other, to separate out those voters who, though being able to order the parties according to ideological categories, nonetheless do not appear to adopt this decision-making strategy.

The construction of a measure of the capacity of an individual to place parties requires a rather elaborate procedure (for further

4. Note that the utility in the model proposed here is exclusively a function of spatial distance. No account is taken of other factors that could plausibly contribute to influencing the choice, such as the size of parties, their visibility, or the probability of victory accredited to them. The literature on spatial models has explored all these aspects and many others, as a great deal of effort went into developing mathematical models aimed both at reproducing Downs's spatial model with greater formal rigor and at integrating into it less restrictive assumptions about the level of information and the cognitive capacities at the disposal of actors (Hinich and Pollard 1981; Enelow and Hinich 1984; 1990; Fiorina 1990; McKelvey and Ordeshook 1990; Hinich and Munger 1994). However, the goal here is to use the left-right ideology as a fast and frugal single cue that simplifies the decision-making task.

discussion see Baldassarri 2003). In the first place, it is necessary to identify an order of reference that is shared by the electorate and in relation to which it is possible to compare the sequence of parties advanced by each individual.

It is possible to define the position of the parties along the left-right axis in at least three different ways: by making use of the opinion of privileged witnesses (Laver and Hunt 1992), by evaluating the declarations and the policies of the parties and leaders (Budge, Robertson and Hearl 1987; Kleinnijenhuis and Pennings 2001; Pennings and Keman 2002), and by referring to the opinions expressed by citizens in specific surveys (Bartolini and Mair 1990; Schadee 1995; Venturino 2000). This last method is the most appropriate for investigating the presence of ideological representation within voters, and so it is to the responses of the voters themselves that we refer to define the order of the parties in political space in Italy.

Figure 4.1 shows the relative positions of the parties according to the average value assigned to them by our interviewees in relation respectively to the 1996 and 2001 national elections. The variable indexing party placement in the 1996 Itanes survey is constructed by way of the combination of two questions: in the first, the respondent is asked to associate each party with one of the following categories: left, center-left, center, center-right, and right. The response to this is then refined by way of a further question[5] that makes it possible to represent the definitive response in terms of a 7-scale variable indexing placement along the left-right continuum.[6]

---

5. In particular, a respondent who replies "Left" to the first question is asked "Do you really mean left or more towards the center-left?," a respondent who replies "Center-left" is asked "More towards the left or more towards the center" and a respondent who replies "Center" is asked "More towards the center-left or more towards the center-right?" Obviously, questions analogous to these are asked of respondents who reply "Center-right" or "Right" (Itanes Survey Questionnaire 1996, 242–244).

6. The choice of this method of data collection is tied to the fact that the 1996 Itanes survey was conducted by way of telephone interview. In this situation, where it is not possible to have respondents view visual supports, it is in fact inadvisable to pose questions with a large

In the 2001 survey, on the other hand, the acquisition of the data on party placement on the left-right ideological dimension takes place by means of a more traditional visual support card representing a continuum numbered from 1 to 10.[7] The similarities and differences in relation to the placement of the parties in the two years under consideration have been discussed elsewhere and a possible explanation of the phenomenon has been proposed (Baldassarri and Schadee 2004). In the present study the placement of the parties along the left-right axis will simply be used as a standard order of reference in relation to which to compare the order of each individual voter.

In general, the analysis of the data in aggregate form allows us to maintain that there is a roughly consistent, collective view of the placement of the parties and that the categories of left and right still represent an effective map for orienting oneself in political and electoral space (Ricolfi 1999; Segatti and Schadee 2003; Baldassarri 2003). But this does not in itself guarantee that each individual voter possesses an order that is perfectly consistent with the one represented in Figure 4.1. And it would be just as unrealistic to expect that every voter was able to reproduce the continuum in a detailed manner. The capacity to divide the parties into a left area as opposed to a right or center area is perhaps fairly widespread but it is a much more complicated exercise to define the precise position of each party.

---

number of possible responses. This multiphase type of data collection process, however, leads to "results that are not unlike those obtained by way of a single question containing all the graded alternatives" (Corbetta 1999, 245) and so it was decided to make use of the series of two questions. The 7-scale variable was constructed by attributing one-unit intervals between one category and the next, except in the space in the center, where the interval between center-left (3) and center (3.5) and between center and center-right (4) is half a unit (cf. Appendix, Baldassarri 2002).

7. The question is asked as follows: "A lot of people, when they talk about politics, use the terms "left" and "right." Here they are on this card: a continuum of boxes that go from left to right (. . .) where would you place the following parties? If you do not know the party or do not know what response to give, just say "I don't know,"" followed by a list of the major Italian political parties (Itanes 2001).

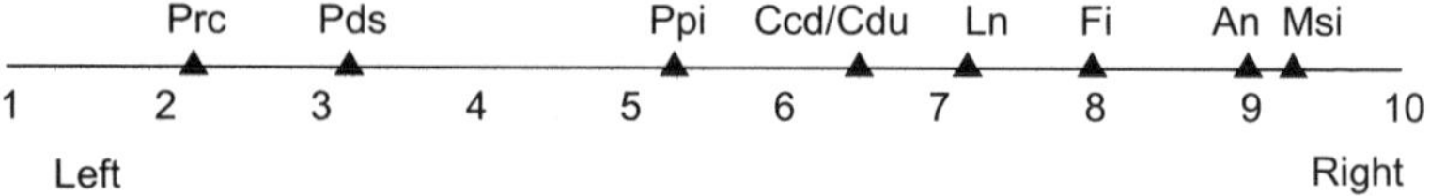

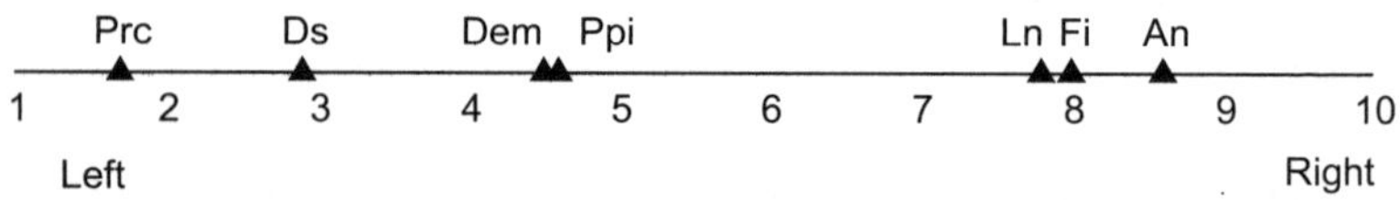

FIGURE 4.1 Placement of the parties on the left-right ideological continuum. Average values. To facilitate comparison across years, both left-right continua have been reported on a 1–10 interval scale.

Source: Itanes 1996 and 2001.

In keeping with the assumption of voters' heterogeneity, we expect that some respondents are able to correctly reproduce the order, that others make some errors, and that for still others, the left-right axis is in fact something rather unclear or indeed unknown. To capture these differences within the electorate it is necessary to study the sequence of the parties at the level of single individuals and to compare these results with that of the general order of reference. Given the information that we have available, i.e., the position assigned to each party, such a comparison can be made in two ways: either (a) by measuring the distance between the average position of each party and the position assigned to it by the individual respondent, or (b) by considering the order of the parties, i.e., whether party A is to the left, to the right, or in a same position as party B. The use of a cardinal measurement, as in this case, the calculation of distance, is based on the assumption that all respondents assign the same semantic content to the categories used. This assumption is not very realistic. As far as the substantive meaning of the categories "center-left," "right," "center more towards the right," and so on is concerned and as far as the meaning attributed to the positions in the numbered continuum is concerned (Marradi 1993, 95),[8] it is difficult to argue that all the voters make use of the same standard of measurement and criteria of meaning. The only way to overcome the problem of inter-individual comparison is to construct a measure of the capacity to place the parties that is based exclusively on infra-subjective comparisons. This means renouncing the use of information in relation to distance and taking into consideration only the ordinal properties of the sequence.

Operationally, this involves considering only the relative sequence of the parties, ignoring their position in absolute terms (Schadee 1995, 88). In particular, for every respondent, account is taken of the reciprocal position assigned to each pair of parties. Every comparison between party A and party B can result in any of three outcomes: (1) A is to the left of B; (2) A is to the right of B; and (3) A and B are in the same position. A comparison with the standard order of the parties makes it possible to establish which of the outcomes (1) and (2) is to be considered correct and which instead constitutes an inversion. Outcome 3, on the other hand, is defined as a coincidence. The capacity to place the parties is measured in terms of the number of correct or incorrect positionings that the individual respondent generates.

Three general criteria were formulated to count the errors committed by each respondent. Given the order of reference for each year obtained by starting out from the average position of the major parties (Figure 4.1), (a) it is possible to place in a position of coincidence only contiguous parties, and, on the contrary, the case in which two non-contiguous parties are positioned at the same point is counted as an error. This means, for example, that given the order RC DS PPI, placing

---

8. In self-anchoring scales only the two extreme categories are invested with meaning, while the intermediate categories are evaluated in terms of their distance from the extremes. In particular, it is held that the subject is inclined to move along the continuum according to a criterion of equidistance between the categories (Corbetta 1999, 242–243).

RC and DS, or DS and PPI, in the same position is not considered an error. Instead, in the case in which RC, DS, and PPI are all in the same position an error is counted, because it is not possible for RC to have the same position as PPI; (b) no type of inversion in the position of the parties is permitted. For example, the placement of RC to the right of DS would be counted as one error, while two errors would be counted in the case that RC were positioned to the right of PPI.

Finally, starting out from the principle that every reciprocal position between two parties is to be considered acceptable if it is chosen by a substantial number of individuals, it is established that (c) any outcome chosen by more than one-sixth of voters (i.e., 16.7 percent) is not in any case to be considered as an error. This last criterion renders the measurement of the capacity of the individual to place parties more sensitive to the peculiar characteristics of specific elections. In particular, it induces the researcher not to consider as errors a certain number of inversions attributable to a limited degree of real differentiation between the parties, as opposed to a limited cognitive capacity on the part of voters.[9]

In summary, both the coincidence of noncontiguous parties and any type of inversion are counted as errors, with the exception of those cases in which such positionings are shared by at least one out of six voters. Up to this point, the criteria have been deliberately expressed in a general form in order to render them potentially applicable to a range of years and to different countries (Baldassarri and Schadee 2003). Let us examine now how these criteria take concrete form in relation to the specific case of the Italian national elections under examination.

In the case of the 1996 elections, the order of reference is made up of seven parties: Partito della Rifondazione Comunista (RC),

---

9. In 1996 the only borderline case is the 15.3 percent of respondents who place the CCD/CDU to the left of the PPI—an outcome counted as an error. In 2001, on the other hand, the inversion of the Democratici and the PPI (17.7 percent), the inversion of the Lega Nord and FI (36.9 percent), and the coincidence of the Lega Nord and AN (24.4 percent) are not considered as errors, whereas the inversion of FI and AN, effected by 14.6 percent of respondents, is counted as an error.

Partito Democratico della Sinistra (PDS), Partito Popolare Italiano (PPI), Centro Cristiano Democratico/Cristiano-Democratici Uniti (CCD/CDU), Forza Italia (FI), Alleanza Nazionale (AN), and Movimento Sociale Italiano (MSI). The previously described criterion for counting errors leads us to consider as an error any coincidence between noncontiguous parties and any inversion. In 1996 about 85 percent of respondents agreed to place all the parties and about half of these (45.8 percent) managed to do so without making any errors (Table 4.1). In short, as many as two out of five voters show absolutely no difficulty in reading the competition between the parties in terms of the categories of left and right.

In the case of the 2001 elections the order of reference is PRC, Democratici di Sinistra (DS, formerly PDS), Democratici (DEM), PPI, LN, FI, and AN. However, as it is clear from Figure 4.1, there is a considerable amount of disagreement about how to define the relative positions of the Lega Nord, Forza Italia, and Alleanza Nazionale. The order of these three parties is far from clear: 37.5 percent of respondents place the LN to the left of FI, while 36.9 percent place it to the right. Similarly, according to 34.4 percent of respondents, the Democratici are to the left of the PPI, whereas for another third the Democratici are to the right. Thus, in keeping with the principle that no party placement can be considered incorrect if it is chosen by at least one-sixth of respondents, we consider legitimate both the inversion of the LN and FI and of the Democratici and the PPI and the coincidence of the LN and AN.

In 2001 too, of the respondents who agree to place all the parties, as many as 44.1 percent do so in a way that is consistent with the order of reference. However, because about half of the respondents refuse to place at least one of the parties, the figure, vis-à-vis the entire sample, for those who do not make any errors in reproducing the order is 22 percent, lower than the 38 percent registered in the 1996 sample (Table 4.1).

Generally speaking, a fairly large number of individuals are able to define the position of the parties in terms of the ideological dimension of left and right and this confirms how these categories are

TABLE 4.1 Distribution of respondents according to the number of errors in the placement of the parties.

Number of errors		0	1	2	3	4	5	6	7	8 or more	Total
1996	N	963	387	159	163	106	49	59	25	192	2103
	%	45.8	18.4	7.6	7.8	5.0	2.3	2.8	1.2	9.1	100%
2001	N	718	388	187	125	68	43	31	23	44	1627
	%	44.1	23.8	11.5	7.7	4.2	2.6	1.9	1.4	2.8	100%

Source: Itanes 1996 and 2001.

in general to be considered a pertinent form of representation of political competition.

As a prerequisite for the ideological proximity heuristic, then, we establish that a necessary condition to belong to the *utilius* category is to not commit any errors in defining the placement of the parties. As a consequence, the *utilius* voters, made up of those who (a) agree to place themselves (nine out of ten voters in 1996 and more than four out of five in 2001), who (b) are able to reproduce the order of the parties along the left-right axis, and, finally, (c) who choose the party that is closest to themselves, constitute 17 percent of the sample in 1996 and 9 percent in 2001 (Table 4.2). The third condition is satisfied in the case in which the distance between the self-placement of the voter and the position of the party voted for is the smallest distance that separates the voter from any party.

In conclusion, the number of voters that can be ascribed to the *utilius* category varies between one-tenth and one-sixth of the electorate depending on the year considered. The difference between the two years is due to the sampling bias that lead to an overrepresentation of highly interested voters in the 1996 dataset. In fact, the

TABLE 4.2 Classification of the *Utilius* voters. Percentage of the sample.

	Self-placement	Placement of all the parties	Correct party order	Classified as *Utilius*
1996	91.1%	84.1%	38.5%	17.3%
2001	82.7%	50.7%	22.4%	9.1%

proportion of those who choose the closest party vis-à-vis those who are able to place the parties, remains the same in both years.

> "All men are enemies. All animals are comrades."
> George Orwell, *Animal Farm*

Amicus: **The Sympathetic Voter**

According to Carl Schmitt, "The specific political distinction to which political actions and motives can be reduced is that between friend (*Freund*) and enemy (*Feind*)" (1927 (2007), 26). Although one may or may not agree with Schmitt's controversial political philosophy, it is undeniable that conflict is an intrinsic aspect of political life. As such, it can also serve as an organizing and simplifying principle, especially in contexts where the political competition presents itself as a battle between two opposite camps. Two-party systems with majoritarian representation are, in this respect, the ideal setting for this type of heuristic, while a multiparty system and proportional electoral rules are more likely to generate a less divisive environment, reflecting the consensual (or consociative) nature of their politics (Lijphart 1968).[10]

---

10. Indeed, it is for this reason that in countries where there was a high potential for political conflict, constituent assemblies quite often have opted for proportional systems of representation.

After the introduction of a majoritarian component in the electoral law—75 percent of the seats in both Chambers are assigned through a single member first-past-the-post method—the Italian general election campaigns have increasingly concentrated on the composition, leadership, and political agenda of the two major partisan alliances. Although the campaigns are still populated by a plurality of parties, there is evidence of the fact that Italian citizens are inclined to consider party coalitions as an important actor in the political competition (Baldassarri and Schadee, 2004). Accordingly, here we identify a type of voter, the *amicus* voter, as distinguished by the fact that he represents politics as a dichotomy, and tends to think, reason, and choose by reducing the political debate to the conflict between coalitions and their leaders. The *amicus* voter will, therefore, organize his preferences in terms of his affinity with one or other of the political line-ups.

As we will discuss in more detail in the conclusions, the *amicus* type resembles certain traits of the "likeability heuristic" introduced by Brady and Sniderman (1985), in which people manifest a bipolar organization of preferences and tend to magnify the differences between themselves and the exponents of the opposite side. In this perspective, the reinterpretation of the political debate in bipolar terms constitutes a cognitive strategy that benefits from both affective and cognitive elements. Assuming a more radical perspective, one can also argue that the antithesis inheres to reality, i.e., to the way in which the political space is structured. For instance, Melvin Hinich and Michael Munger (1994) propose a concept of ideology according to which contraposition inheres to the very terms of political debate themselves and expresses itself in a tension between orthodox and heterodox ideology. In particular, the tension between groups of contrasting ideas can be translated into a political space characterized by a limited dimensionality. This is because the set of positions, in relation to a group of issues, is not defined on the basis of an internal coherence within the positions of each ideology but rather on the basis of the contraposition that distinguishes the two ideologies from each other (Hinich, Munger 1994, 16–18).[11] In this way, then, it is possible that the simplification of the political space is inherent to reality: the range of positions that parties can occupy is drastically reduced by the logic of the competition. The orthodox ideology maintains a position and ineluctably the heterodox ideology contrasts it. In this perspective, the dichotomy is encrypted in the structure of the political competition: it is the terms of the debate themselves that are contradictory.

Whether the simplification takes place at the cognitive level, or instead is encrypted in the structure of the information, the dichotomous nature of this form of ideological representation translates, in the process of choice of the amicus voter, into a comparison between just two objects: the party coalitions. The principle choice takes place between the Polo/Casa delle Libertà and the Ulivo, whereas the parties receive only secondary consideration. This process makes it possible to simplify the decision-making task in that the major effort of evaluation is focused on only two objects. This also reduces the complexity of the subsequent choice of party, both because the subjective perception of the importance of the decision is lower and because the range of the parties available to consider is limited to those making up the chosen coalition. As a consequence, this reduces the amount of information necessary for party choice. In fact, in contrast to a choice that right from the outset requires a consideration of all the parties, such as for instance in the case of the *utilius* voter, the *amicus* voter will consider only the parties that make up his favorite coalition and ignore all the rest.

On the other hand, the *amicus* voter has to deal with the need to confer homogeneity on the party alliances, to think of each of them as a single body, even though in actual fact they manifest themselves through a variety of parties and leaders. Indeed, parties do try to

---

11. In other words, given a number x of issues held to be important, these can be represented in a political space with a number of dimensions inferior to x. This is because the position in respect of each issue is defined starting out from positions assumed by the orthodox ideology.

differentiate themselves not only from the opposite alliance, but also from the parties that belong to their own coalition, thus sending somehow contradictory signals to voters who focus primarily on the coalitions. In sum, *amicus* voters have to make an effort to organize and integrate the relevant information, so as to confer coherence to the party line-ups.

This propensity to interpret public debate according to a pattern of contraposition between two party alliances is especially evident in the way in which a large number of voters structure their judgments in relation to the major political leaders. In fact, such voters tend to systematically evaluate in a favorable manner the leaders of the parties that belong to their own coalition. Conversely, they tend to represent in a negative manner those of the opposing coalition. This means that their evaluation of a particular leader is not based on the leader's personal characteristics alone. Nor can it simply be traced back to the party that the leader represents. Rather, it has to do with the system of alliances within which parties and their leaders operate (Baldassarri and Schadee 2004).

We measure the propensity to use an *amicus/hostis* evaluation strategy by comparing the judgments voters give on each leader of the Ulivo with the evaluations they make of each leader of the Polo/ Casa delle Libertà. For each respondent, we consider all the possible pairwise comparisons between leaders of opposite coalitions, and count the number of comparisons systematically favorable toward the leaders of the same coalition.

With respect to 1996, we consider the judgment expressed in relation to eight party leaders, of whom four belong to the Ulivo alliance: Romano Prodi, Massimo D'Alema, Oscar Luigi Scalfaro, and Lamberto Dini, and four to the Polo delle Libertà alliance: Silvio Berlusconi, Gianfranco Fini, Pierferdinando Casini, and Marco Pannella. This process produces sixteen possible comparisons. Of those who agree to give a mark to each one of the eight leaders (i.e., 87.4 percent of the sample), 21 percent systematically give a more positive judgment to the politicians of the Ulivo than they give to the representatives of the Polo delle Libertà, whereas 8 percent judge the leaders of the Polo superior in absolute terms to those of the Ulivo (Table 4.3). In general, then, in 1996 one out of four voters systematically structures his judgment according to the *amicus/hostis* logic and this figure reaches 40 percent if we take into consideration those that make at least fourteen out of sixteen comparisons in favor of one or other of the two sets of leaders.

With respect to 2001, the data at our disposal make it possible to compare the judgments expressed in relation to six leaders, three from the Casa delle Libertà: Silvio Berlusconi, Gianfranco Fini and Umberto Bossi, and three from the Ulivo: Francesco Rutelli, Massimo D'Alema, and Giuliano Amato, giving rise to a total of nine comparisons.

About four-fifths of the sample agrees to evaluate all nine political players. Of these, 20 percent show a systematic preference for the leaders of the Ulivo, while 9.3 percent express a clear preference for those of the Casa delle Libertà (Table 4.4). In this case, too, about one-fourth of the voters follow the *amicus/hostis* logic, even though it is necessary to take account of the fact that the number of comparisons considered is less than in 1996. The relationship between the coalitions also remains more or less the same. In both 2001 and 1996, the systematic structuration of the preferences seems to guide twice as much voters in the case of the Ulivo as it does with respect of the Polo/Casa delle Libertà.

The count of the comparisons in favor of the Casa delle Libertà, however, is influenced by the very negative judgment of Umberto Bossi, the controversial leader of Lega Nord. In fact, more than half the voters attribute to him marks of 1 or 2 and only one out of seven voters attribute to him at least a pass mark (i.e., 6). For this reason, we will also count as comparisons favorable to the Casa delle Libertà the comparisons in which Bossi receives a mark equal to that of the leaders of the Ulivo. In this way, the percentage of voters who make their evaluations according to a dichotomous framework and who have a preference for the center-right coalition increases by almost 6 percent, going from 9 percent to 15 percent.

TABLE 4.3 Distribution of respondents according to the number of leader comparisons in favor of a coalition (N = 2,187).

Number of comparisons	Victories for leaders of the Polo delle Libertà		Victories for leaders of the Ulivo	
	N	%	N	%
0	701	32.1	326	14.9
1	108	4.9	95	4.3
2	132	6.0	111	5.1
3	113	5.2	88	4.0
4	134	6.1	121	5.5
5	65	3.0	53	2.4
6	89	4.1	74	3.4
7	54	2.5	70	3.2
8	89	4.1	97	4.4
9	71	3.2	88	4.0
10	76	3.5	95	4.3
11	59	2.7	76	3.5
12	118	5.4	131	6.0
13	60	2.7	98	4.5
14	80	3.7	122	5.5
15	63	2.9	93	4.3
16	175	8.0	449	20.5
	2187	100.0	2187	100.0
14–16		14.6		30.3

Source: Itanes 1996.

Amicus voters are classified according to the following two criteria: (a) they make a systematic use of the *amicus/hostis* criterion of evaluation, and (b) they vote for their preferred coalition.

In 1996 a quarter of our sample shows a structure of judgment completely organized in these terms. To these we add other cases that generate a very small number of inconsistencies, thereby showing that, in essence, they too make use of the *amicus/ hostis*

TABLE 4.4 Distribution of respondents according to the number of leader comparisons in favor of a coalition (N = 2,582).

Number of comparisons	Victories for leaders of the Casa delle Libertà		Victories for leaders of the Casa delle Libertà (compensatory criterion for Bossi)		Victories for leaders of the Ulivo	
	N	*%*	*N*	*%*	*N*	*%*
0	794	30.8	702	27.2	494	19.1
1	135	5.2	144	5.6	202	7.8
2	167	6.5	166	6.4	255	9.9
3	206	8.0	201	7.8	428	16.6
4	189	7.3	175	6.8	155	6.0
5	155	6.0	151	5.8	123	4.8
6	439	17.0	302	11.7	180	7.0
7	143	5.5	204	7.9	139	5.4
8	113	4.4	157	6.1	90	3.5
9	241	9.3	380	14.7	516	20.0
	2582	100.0	2582	100.0	2582	100.0

Source: Itanes 2001.

evaluation criterion. In particular, we consider as potential amicus voters all those who make at least fourteen out of sixteen comparisons in favor of the leaders of a particular coalition, i.e., almost two-fifths of the sample. Of these, 83 percent cast a vote consistent with their judgment on the leaders. The *amicus* voters amount to one-third of the sample (Table 4.5): 22 percent are Ulivo voters and 11 percent are Polo delle Libertà voters.

In 2001, on the other hand, we consider as potential amicus voters all those who generate all nine preferences in favor of a particular coalition (taking account of the less restrictive criterion in respect of the judgment on Bossi). These amount to little more than one-fourth and in this case too the majority of them (84 percent) vote for their preferred coalition. In 2001 the amicus voters made up

TABLE 4.5 Classification of the *Amicus* voters. Percentage of the sample.

Year	Judges all the Leaders	Dichotomous Judgment	Amicus
1996	87.4%	39.2%	32.5%
2001	80.5%	27.9%	23.4%

23.4 percent of the sample: 10 percent line up with the Casa delle Libertà and 13.4 percent with the Ulivo (Table 4.5).

Aliens: The Voter "Innocent of Ideology"

Both *utilius* and *amicus* rely on cognitive shortcuts that derive from the institutional features of the political environment: the party and coalitional competition. However, a large component of the Italian voters mistrust and reject politics. They have a negative view of everything that has to do with politics and its protagonists. In our classification of voters, we identify the *aliens* voter as someone who is extraneous to the traditional forms of ideological representation. He is either not able to make use of the categories of left and right or actively refuses to make use of them. Because of this he falls under a negative form of classification, which points to the absence of particular criteria for organizing the political world as opposed to the presence of possible alternative cognitive frameworks. In this respect, we would not outline *ex ante* a specific cognitive shortcut that the voter is supposed to follow, but we will investigate a few possibilities in a more inductive fashion through the analysis.

The absence of an ideological representation does not constitute a limit in itself. On the contrary, it can be seen as an opportunity if one recognizes the existence of systems of belief that are not ideological but rather pragmatic (Sartori 1995, 114–15). The "innocence of ideology," in other words, can be a precondition for a form of choice that is an alternative to the ones discussed above—one that is free from the constraints of an ideological belief system. Or at least it is potentially free. In fact, according to Sartori, the function of ideology is not to orient the acquisition of knowledge but rather to persuade. What distinguishes ideological thought is the fact that ideas lose their characteristics of logicality and verifiability and transform into "social levers"[12] (Sartori 1995, 113). In contrast to this, Sartori points to pragmatic forms of thought and he identifies in "cognitive authorities" or, more particularly, the way in which each individual relates with the authorities that say what is true and what is not true the distinguishing element between the two forms of thought. The ideological mentality is characterized by a closed, rigid, impermeable, and dogmatic mind that entrusts itself to an absolute authority. A pragmatic mentality, by contrast, takes the form of an open, permeable cognitive structure (*ibidem*, 114–20).

This emphasis on the persuasive component of ideology—not considered up to now—is particularly useful for capturing the potential inhering to an investigation of the *aliens* type. In particular, is it possible that the lack of or rejection of traditional ideological representations is an index of a substantial independence of judgment and autonomy in decision making? Or is it, on the contrary, simply a measure of marginality, lack of interest, and mistrust? This is a basic question that we will address in the following chapters, although it should be recognized that survey data will hardly give us definitive answers concerning the functioning of "pragmatic thought" or the specific cognitive heuristics that might inform the cognitive strategies of detached voters. To anticipate our results, the following pages will depict an image of the *aliens* voter as a citizen who is extraneous—alien—to politics and characterized by a profile of social marginality. This image cannot be easily reconciled with the idea of

12. In Sartori (1995, 113), cited in D. Bell, *The End of Ideology*, Collier Books, New York, 1962, p. 440.

a "free spirit" capable of evaluating politics without allowing himself to be swayed, but more of a distracted and annoyed voter that relies on fast and frugal one-reason decision-making heuristics based on easily accessible cues.

We classify as *aliens* voters (a) those respondents who refuse to place themselves along the left-right continuum or (b) those respondents who do not have any capacity to make use of the coordinates of ideological space. In particular, with respect to the second criterion, we consider as devoid of ideological understanding those respondents who refuse to place even one of the four major parties, PDS/DS, RC, FI, or AN, or who place PDS-DS or RC to the right and FI or AN to the left of the political spectrum.

In 1996 9 percent of respondents do not assume a position along the continuum and 15 percent are bereft of ideological coordinates. Overall, *aliens* voters make up 20 percent of the sample. In 2001 the figure for voters that do not place themselves is 17 percent, while those that are not capable of placing DS, RC, FI, and AN even in a general way amount to 19 percent (Table 4.6). In 2001 the *aliens* voters make up 30 percent of the total number of respondents. It also needs to be underlined that in both years, half of those that do not place themselves are also incapable of locating the parties.

There are two possible criticisms that can be made of the *aliens* type we have constructed and both are tied to the degree of the heterogeneity of its components. First, there is a substantial difference between a "deliberate" refusal to place oneself within the left-right space and the incapacity to use such conceptual categories. Second, the very recognition of a high level of heterogeneity implies that multiple heuristics may be at work in this group of voters.

With respect to the first problem, we should keep in mind that the *aliens* category can contain both individuals who deliberately conceive of their own political position as detached from the traditional labels of left and right (this can occur, for example, with voters of the Lega Nord) and, on the contrary, subjects that are conditioned by a real cognitive deficit that severely compromises their

TABLE 4.6 Classification of the *Aliens* voters. Percentage of the sample.

Year	Does not Place Himself	Refuses or is not Capable of Placing the Major Parties	Aliens
1996	8.9%	15.4%	19.8%
2001	17.3%	18.8%	29.5%

capacity to understand the political system through the classical ideological categories. However, as we will see in Chapter 5, after examining the level of political sophistication of the *aliens* voter, we would conclude that most of these voters do not make use of the ideological dimension more because they do not possess its coordinates, i.e., they have no idea what it is, than because of a voluntary choice to define themselves according to alternative conceptualizations. But this does not mean that there is nothing at all political about their mode of reasoning and choosing.

The second problem with the heterogeneity of the *aliens* voter concerns the possibility that diverse decision-making processes are informing their choice. Indeed, our decision not to formulate a "behavioral framework" for this type of voter *ex ante* has been due more to the fact that a few frameworks are possible than to any lack of a hypothesis in this regard. Unfortunately, not all the possible hypotheses can be tested.

For instance, since we have excluded ideology and party identification, the most common long-term factors used to explain voting decisions, we can hypothesize *aliens* voters to be the ones who have the greatest propensity to make choices based on short-term factors such as certain specific issues or the image of a leader. Alessandro Pizzorno, for example, argues that a new form of politics is emerging— one that he defines in terms of ethicality—and that this is substituting the politics of ideology, ideology-based mass parties, and churches. He sees a "shift of attention away from the contents of programs aiming at material well-being towards symbolic contents" and argues that as a result of this there is a corresponding shift away from a judgment based on criteria relating to ideology, the issues and governmental capacity toward judgments on "the virtue of the candidates" (Pizzorno 2001, 232). But changing the object of judgment brings with it a modification in the decision-making strategies. Fast and frugal heuristics, like the minimalist, or take-the-best strategies, can serve these voters who rely mostly on short-term factors quite well.

A similar argument can be made for heuristics based on the popularity and availability of the political objects. Generally speaking, the space that the mass media dedicate to political leaders is directly proportional to their importance, and leaders' exposure is related to their visibility among the mass public. In particular, it is unlikely that a voter who pays little attention to political events will remember minor leaders and she is even less likely to have an opinion about them. As a consequence, her range of alternatives is reduced to the one or two most well known leaders. But it is precisely this selection of information that may render more practicable her decision-making task, because the reduction in the alternative is not random. The environment selects the most central leaders, i.e., those who are the real players in the game. In other words, it is precisely her ignorance about the existence of the other leaders that makes it possible for the uninterested voter to reduce the choice options to the most important political figures.

Finally, a decision-making strategy of an altogether different nature—and, above all, one that is difficult to test empirically—is that of imitation/delegation. Starting out from a principle of the division of labor, it is perfectly reasonable to hypothesize the existence of voters who systematically refer to or depend on the opinion of others for their own voting choice. Be they relatives, friends, or work colleagues, what counts are everyday experiences, regular contact, and esteem. In other words, the sharing of values and lifestyles and the recognition of oneself in common patterns of interaction constitute indirect ways to evaluate politics through the political choices of others. Politics, then, is not known and lived directly, but rather seen through the lenses of others. Namely, individuals look to others they like and respect for cues about politics. What is involved is not just a simple imitation or assimilation of the political orientation of others, but rather the evaluation of a political orientation taking departure from the judgment one makes of a person from one's own milieu. Unfortunately, the data at our disposal, as most research in public opinion, do not place us in a position to capture this type of decision making.

The Typology of Political Heuristics

Our division of the respondents into the *utilius*, *amicus*, and *aliens* types does not cover all the respondents. We assign the remaining cases to a residual category, the *medians* voter, which turns out to have the empirical peculiarity—by no means to be taken for granted—of reproducing the characteristics of the sample as a whole. In fact, it clearly emerges that for both the years under consideration, the sociodemographic profile of the *medians* voter is very similar to that of the average respondent. Because of this peculiarity this category constitutes a useful point of comparison for the other three groups. Since there is no positive selection criterion in operation in our construction of the type, it is reasonable to presume that *medians* voters are characterized by a high level of internal heterogeneity. They constitute 40 percent of the sample in 1996 and 45 percent in 2001.

The fact that we classify two-fifths of respondents in a residual category is something that could provoke some concern. There are, however, two quite distinct arguments that render this solution preferable to other possible solutions. First, the major goal of this research is to identify and study different heuristics of judgment. This has made it preferable to deploy restrictive criteria of classification. It would have been possible, in other words, to include a larger number of respondents in the first three categories, but we have preferred to strengthen the analytical capacity of the groups as much as possible, instead of pursuing the goal of classifying as many people as possible.

Second, it is important to acknowledge that the problem of limiting the major focus of the research on someone limited part of the sample is shared by virtually every study on voting behavior that makes use of survey data. In fact, even if in theory the traditional explanatory models of voting are applied to entire samples, in actual research practice a very large number of respondents are excluded on account of missing responses with the result that the heart of the analysis and the interpretation of the results end up being based on the responses of as little as a half or a third of the total number of respondents (Pisati 1997; Clarke, Sanders, Stewart, and Whiteley 2003a).

Obviously, this reduction of the sample does constitute a problem in that the respondents who do not provide responses have characteristics different from those who do. So what takes place, in other words, is a kind of "natural" selection of respondents, which tends to exclude precisely the category of subjects less involved in public debate and more extraneous to political competition—exactly those that in our analysis are captured by the *aliens* type. In conclusion, even if our analysis cannot escape from the criticism of having lent too little attention to part of the respondents, it is nonetheless certain that the selection criteria we have adopted have had a less distorting effect on the composition of the sample than takes place customarily.

In order to have an accurate estimate of the distribution of the various groups in the population it is preferable to refer to the 2001 survey, given that the sampling procedure in the 1996 survey was subject to a particular type of distortion that presumably overestimated the weight of the *utilius* and *amicus* types. In this respect too, moreover, it should be underlined that the choice of less restrictive criteria could increase the number of respondents that can be classified in the first two categories.

As Figures 4.2 and 4.3 illustrate, the criteria for dividing voters according to the ideal types do not guarantee the mutual exclusivity of the categories. On the contrary, there are a number of cases of substantial overlap both between *amicus* and *utilius* and between *amicus* and *aliens*.

The existence of voters that can be classified as both *utilius* and *amicus* is perfectly understandable. The two strategies of choice are not mutually exclusive, in that spatial representation in terms of the left-right continuum does not in any way preclude the possibility of perceiving contraposition in dichotomous terms. The overlap between *amicus* and *aliens*, on the other hand—which is relatively limited—involves for the most part voters who structure their judgments in a dichotomous manner without consenting to place themselves or the parties. In the analyses that we undertake in the following chapters,

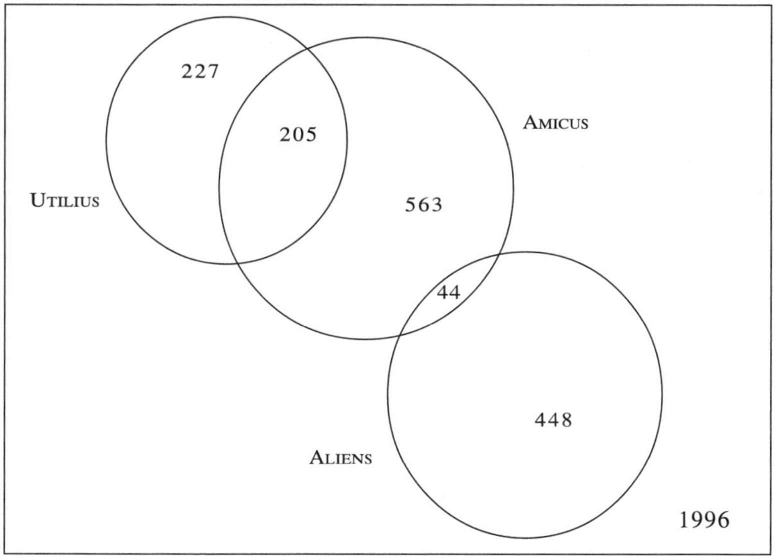

FIGURE 4.2 Number of respondents per type and overlap between types.

Source: Itanes 1996.

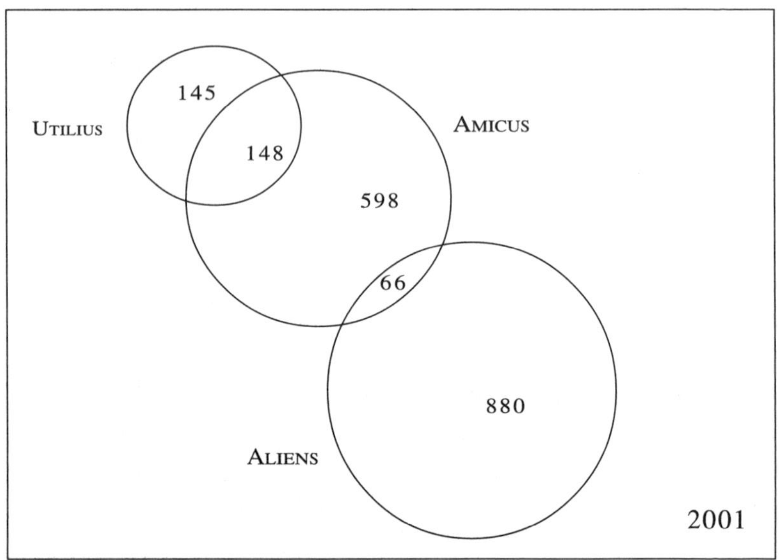

FIGURE 4.3 Number of respondents per type and overlap between types.

Source: Itanes 2001.

the cases of multiple membership are handled in the following manner: respondents who satisfy the characteristics of both the *utilius* voter and the *amicus* voter are assigned exclusively to the *utilius* category, whereas those who correspond to both *amicus* and *aliens* are placed in the *amicus* type.

The nonexclusivity and nonuniqueness of the selection criteria together with the large number of respondents classified in a residual category expose our typology of voting heuristics to possible criticisms in respect of its construction. However, as will become clear in the chapters to come, this "lack of elegance" in the definition of the typology's selection criteria is amply counterbalanced by its extreme simplicity and classificatory capacity. In fact, the efficacy of a typology should be judged not in terms of criteria internal to its construction, but rather in terms of whether or not the partition that it identifies is also capable of distinguishing between voters in terms of other important factors independent of its construction. As we will begin to demonstrate in the next chapter, by making use of just a few items of data—self-placement on the left-right continuum, the placement of parties and judgments on leaders—we have constructed an identikit of *utilius*, *amicus*, *aliens*, and *medians* that really is able to delineate the profile of voters in terms of a number of other important characteristics inhering to them.

Chapter 5

Who are *Utilius, Amicus, Aliens,* and *Medians?*

The typology of political heuristics that we have constructed has the virtue of being frugal. Respondents are categorized based on just a few batteries of responses—the voters' self placement and parties' placement along the left-right axis and judgments on political leaders. Up to this point, however, this typology has been just one of many possible ways to classify individual voters. To substantiate this division into groups, it is necessary to demonstrate that other important differences are also structured along the same dividing lines. In other words, in order to maintain that *utilius, amicus,* and *aliens* really do constitute different types, we should find that the classification captures differences between respondents with respect to variables that were not used in constructing the types.

In line with Hypothesis I, stating that voters use different cognitive shortcuts according to their level of political sophistication, in this chapter we show that our typology does indeed distinguish between voters along several measures of sophistication, such as level of education, interest in politics, and political knowledge. We also provide a detailed description of the sociodemographic profiles of our four types of voters. After having assessed the discriminatory capacity of our classification, we use predictive models (multinomial logistic regressions) to estimate the relative weight of cognitive and sociodemographic factors in driving our classifications.

All the analyses reported in this chapter have been conducted for both the 1996 and the 2001 general national elections. The results are for the most part analogous and, unless otherwise specified, the conclusions should be considered valid for both years. We have adopted this manner of exposition precisely because of the extensive correspondences we encountered. This fact gives us strong confirmation of the validity of the typology, and, in particular, of its capacity to capture cognitive structures that are stable and consistent over time. For greater detail and/or areas of special interest we encourage the reader to refer to the tables.

Heuristics and Political Sophistication: a Cognitive Profile

Measurement and Hypotheses

Before formulating any predictions about each type's cognitive profile, it is necessary to discuss how best to empirically measure the concept of political sophistication. In fact, as we have already observed in Chapter 3, the problem of measuring the concept of political sophistication is still far from being resolved. The concept's high degree of abstraction and polysemic nature make it extremely problematic to identify a single indicator or even a composite index sufficiently comprehensive to encapsulate it. To what extent can education, political interest, or level of information account for the dimensionality and organization of a political belief system? (Luskin 1987) And how do they influence the processes of integration and differentiation? (Sniderman et al. 1991)

The problem does not simply stem from how general the concept is, but also from its ambiguity. It combines—and at times confuses—the idea of sophistication, i.e., the "style of manipulating information," with political cognition, understood as a measure of political information and competence. The integration of these two concepts is certainly very intriguing, but it leads to a number of arbitrary reductions at the empirical level. However, this problem is not particularly relevant in our analysis, since we do not need to select a single measure, or to combine different dimensions into a single index. Indeed, we will consider all the major dimensions of political sophistication. This is possible because, in the present analysis, we introduce measures of political sophistication simply to test the validity of our classification; they do not play any role in the construction of the typology. This stands in contrast to most studies of political cognition and voter heterogeneity, where some operativization of political sophistication is used as a criterion for dividing subjects into different groups.

As we conceive of it, political sophistication has three dimensions: (a) the means, or, more precisely, the cognitive capacities, (b) the motivations, i.e., the incentives that induce individuals to acquire and make use of political information, and (c) the opportunities, understood as the characteristics of the environment that influence the quantity and quality of the information individuals obtain (Luskin 1990; Gordon and Segura 1997; Campus 2000). These three dimensions are measured respectively using: (a) *education*, particularly the level of formal education,[1] as an indicator of cognitive capacities and cultural formation; (b) *interest*, measured using an index that combines interest in politics and interest in the election campaign,[2] to gauge the degree of motivation; and c) *information*, assessed by differentiating the quantitative aspect—frequency of exposure to the media[3]—from the qualitative aspect—type of

---

1. With respect to education, we distinguish between possession of a middle or elementary school certificate; possession of a high school certificate (mainstream or technical); and possession of a university degree.

2. The measure of political interest is constructed as a combination of the questions "How interested are you in politics: a lot, a little, or not at all?" and "How much interest did you take in the recent election campaign: a lot, a reasonable amount, little, or none?" (Itanes 1997). Comparable questions were available in the 2001 Itanes election survey. In both years, the respondents who declared that they were very or reasonably interested in both politics and the campaign are classified as "interested"; all others are considered "not interested."

3. The index of exposure to the media captures the frequency with which people make use of mass media and divides respondents into those who are exposed to mass communication every day and those who make less frequent use of mass media.

media (e.g., TV, radio, and newspapers).[4] While acquiring information is a considerable cost in some decision-making contexts, it seems reasonable to assume that this is not the case in a national election campaign, in which political information is available at the negligible cost of spending a few hours listening or reading about it. Thus, political information should be seen as an opportunity citizens exploit in a variegated manner, not as a "scarce resource."

After having defined our measures of political sophistication, let us now formulate a few hypotheses about the link between cognitive characteristics and decision-making strategies.

The decision-making strategy of the *utilius* voter requires highly specific cognitive capacities—he has to have at his disposal a detailed map of the political space—so we hypothesize that he is highly educated, interested in politics, and very receptive to available political information.

The *amicus* voter, too, shows interest in politics. She relies on a moderately demanding strategy of choice; the systematic organization of judgments on political leaders requires some general knowledge of how the two coalitions are composed. At the same time, however, her judgment criterion could be more affect-driven (Brady and Sniderman 1991), i.e., influenced by evaluations based on personal sympathies. The influence of cognitive factors could be reduced by affective elements. Compared to the *utilius* type, then, level of education may be less important for the *amicus* voter. A similar comparison holds true for the acquisition of information. Ideological representation in dichotomous terms does not require special cognitive insights into the contents of policy proposals, so the volume and the diversity of information involved could also be more limited. However, as we have already observed, a structured evaluation in terms of an *amicus/hostis* logic requires that the party alliances be

---

4. A distinction is made between respondents who declare that they only watch TV and respondents who also make use of other sources of information such as the radio and newspapers (Corbetta and Mazzoleni 1995).

represented as homogenous—as a unit in contraposition to an external body. The effort of conferring this homogeneity increases the need to obtain information that will allow for its satisfactory integration in the belief system. In sum, the *amicus* voter may be a bit less sophisticated than the *utilius* voter, but still possesses a quite good understanding of the political competition.

The *aliens* voter understands the political competition without using traditional ideological categories. As we have already pointed out, this disposition can be seen as a sign, theoretically, as much of a deliberate rejection of classical ideological interpretations of the political world, as of a real incapacity to manage its complexity (and therefore of a more general condition of social marginality). This interpretative ambiguity will be resolved at least in part by our analysis. If *aliens* voters were characterized by a level of political sophistication analogous to that of the other types, it would be possible to assume that they were relying on decision-making strategies equivalent to those that guide *utilius* and *amicus* voters, albeit based on representations of a different kind. On the other hand, if *aliens* voters' level of political cognition and sophistication proved to be significantly lower, their decision-making process would have to be one that was intelligible to and used the forms of reasoning and political representation actually at their disposal. Arguing in favor of one or the other alternative will also help guide our subsequent investigation of voting heuristics, allowing us to calibrate our hypotheses about the factors of choice based on the cognitive and motivational preparedness of the subjects in question.

A Cognitive Profile

We expect our typology to be able to differentiate voters based on their levels of political cognition and sophistication. Examining the figures clearly shows that all of our political sophistication indicators successfully differentiate among the types.

Tables 5.1 and 5.2 illustrate the profile of each type in terms of education, interest in politics, and information, for each of the two years under consideration. Running down the tables row by row, it is easy to compare the types in terms of percentage distribution of our variables of interest. Figure 5.1 shows the same information for year 2001 in graphic form. Looking at education, for instance, we discover that 57 percent of *utilius* and 42 percent of *amicus* voters hold a high school or college degree, while, in contrast, almost three-quarters of *aliens* voters did not reach high school. With respect to political interest, we observe that almost half of the *utilius* and 38 percent of the *amicus* voters are interested in politics and the campaign, compared to a mere 6 percent of *aliens* voters. Finally, most people listen to the news every day: more than 90 percent of *utilius* and *amicus* voters, and 76 percent of *aliens* voters. However, among the latter, 44 percent rely exclusively on TV news, while 89 percent of *utilius* and 82 percent of the *amicus* voters also listen to the radio and/or read the newspapers.

In general, we find that the *utilius* voter has a high level of education, a keen interest in politics, and a strong propensity to differentiate between mass media. The *amicus* voter also has a high education level, is very interested in politics, and frequently relies on a diversified range of information sources, albeit to a lesser degree than the *utilius* where education and differentiation between the media are concerned. Among *aliens* voters, by contrast, there are a large number of individuals who do not have educational credentials beyond a middle school certificate, are not very interested in politics, and have little inclination to make use of sources of information other than TV news programs.

In sum, *utilius* and *amicus* voters have a higher level of political sophistication than both *aliens* and *medians* voters. At the same time, the level of sophistication of *aliens* voters is considerably lower than that of *medians* voters. Finally, it should be noted that the profile of *medians* is very similar to that of the entire population.

Consistent with our expectations, then, the types are characterized by substantially dissimilar levels of political cognition and sophistication. This first test confirms the "predictive" capacity of the

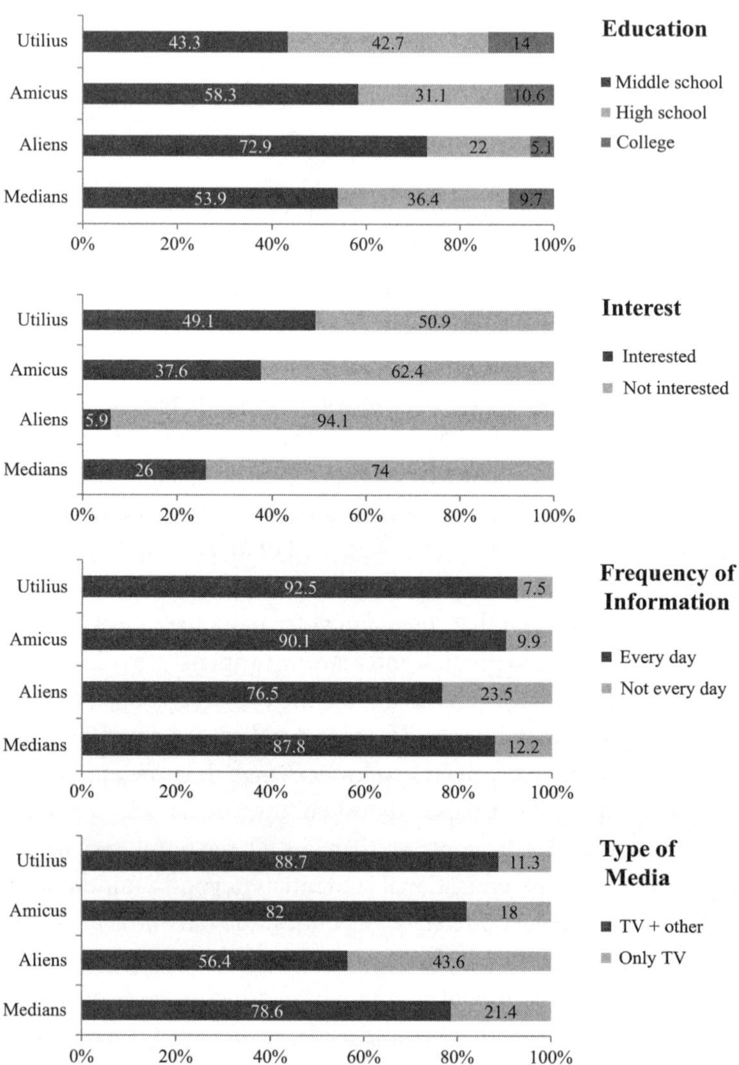

FIGURE 5.1 Barplots of the level of political sophistication for each type of voter. Percentage values.

Source: Itanes 2001.

TABLE 5.1 Level of political sophistication by type of voter. Percentage values.

		Utilius	Amicus	Aliens	Medians	All
Education	Middle school	20.9	33.9	59.1	37.8	38.3
	High school	54.5	49.3	34.4	49.2	47.5
	College	24.6	16.8	6.6	13.0	14.2
		100%	100%	100%	100%	100%
Interest	Interested	59.4	58.2	15.4	43.4	42.9
	Not interested	40.6	41.8	84.6	56.6	57.1
		100%	100%	100%	100%	100%
Frequency of media exposure	Every day	82.6	90.1	71.7	82.7	82.5
	Not every day	17.4	9.9	28.3	17.3	17.5
		100%	100%	100%	100%	100%
Type of media	TV + other	89.0	81.2	47.6	75.0	74.2
	Only TV	11.0	18.8	52.4	25.0	25.8
		100%	100%	100%	100%	100%

Source: Itanes 1996.

typology. It should be noted, moreover, that the distinctive traits of each voter type's profile turn out to be stable over the two successive election years (Table 5.1 and 5.2). This lends substantial support to our claim that the organizing principles of voter decision making, upon which we based classification, are systematic and consistent over time.

Let us now focus on the specific characteristics of the *aliens* type. The *aliens* voter's low level of political sophistication precludes the possibility that his or her political beliefs are organized in forms analogous to those of the *utilius* or *amicus* voter's. The limited amount of attention that *aliens* voters dedicate to political events makes it highly implausible that they have at their disposal very highly structured forms of reasoning. Thus, in seeking to identify factors capable of influencing and motivating the way *aliens* vote we must look at factors that are less sophisticated than

TABLE 5.2 Level of political sophistication by type of voter. Percentage values.

		Utilius	Amicus	Aliens	Medians	All
Education	Middle school	43.3	58.3	72.9	53.9	59.0
	High school	42.7	31.1	22.0	36.4	32.0
	College	14.0	10.6	5.1	9.7	9.0
		100%	100%	100%	100%	100%
Interest	Interested	49.1	37.6	5.9	26.0	24.8
	Not interested	50.9	62.4	94.1	74.0	75.2
		100%	100%	100%	100%	100%
Frequency	Every day	92.5	90.1	76.5	87.8	85.4
of media	Not every day	7.5	9.9	23.5	12.2	14.5
exposure		100%	100%	100%	100%	100%
Type of	TV + other	88.7	82.0	56.4	78.6	74.4
Media	Only TV	11.3	18.0	43.6	21.4	25.6
		100%	100%	100%	100%	100%

Source: Itanes 2001.

ideological representation and accessible even to a public that is not very interested in the political debate and is substantially incapable of managing and interpreting it through ideological categories.

Our initial hypotheses about *utilius* and *amicus* voters' relatively high level of political sophistication have been confirmed. However, keeping in mind that the variables indexing sophistication and political cognition are not independent of each other, the differences between the two types need to be further investigated.

Having established the heterogeneity of the profiles, let us now consider the relative importance of the various dimensions of political sophistication in determining how respondents are classified into types. Our measures of political sophistication are in fact related to each other. More educated people, for instance, are more likely, on average, to be interested in politics. Similarly, people who are not interested in politics are also less likely to listen to political information every day, or to make use of the radio and newspapers to gather it. We used multinomial logistic regression models to account for the interdependence of sophistication variables. Model 0 in Tables 5.7 and 5.8 (at the end of the chapter) reports, for each year, the probability of being *utilius* as opposed to *amicus* or *aliens* as a function of four independent variables: education, interest, frequency of exposure to the media, and type of media. This descriptive exercise allows us to determine which political sophistication variable is likely to have the most direct influence in dividing subjects into types, thus providing a better understanding of the characteristic traits that distinguish the types from one another. We are nonetheless aware that these results should not be overinterpreted, and cannot be used to support any causal claim.

Overall, in both years, the estimated coefficients are significant, suggesting that all three dimensions of political sophistication exert some autonomous leverage in determining the type of cognitive decision making that people adopt. We interpret this as an additional confirmation of the fact that these variables represent various dimensions of the same concept. They are correlated amongst themselves, but each one exerts an independent role in determining membership in the *utilius*, *amicus*, or *aliens* types.

Although results overall are comparable for the two election years, there are a certain number of peculiarities that provide an opportunity to describe the models in greater detail. In 1996 education played an important role in each of the comparisons between types. High levels of education increased the probability of belonging to the categories *utilius* and *amicus* as opposed to *aliens*, as well as the probability of being *utilius* as opposed to *amicus* (Table 5.7, Model 0). Interest distinguished the members of the *amicus* and *utilius* categories— obviously characterized by a higher degree of interest—from those of the *aliens* category, who revealed a substantial lack of interest in politics. On the other hand, no differences emerged between *utilius* and *amicus* in terms of political interest. So far as the information variables were concerned, the use of media other than TV was much more widespread among *utilius* members than among *amicus* and *aliens* members, even though *amicus* members distinguish themselves from *aliens* members in this regard.[5]

In 2001 (Table 5.7, Model 0) education distinguished *utilius* from *aliens* and *amicus* voters, with the former being more likely to possess a high school certificate, while there was no difference between *amicus* voters and *aliens* voters in terms of educational certificates. Interest distinguished *utilius* and *amicus* voters from *aliens* voters in a very marked way. Additionally, *utilius* voters appeared slightly more interested than *amicus* voters. The two variables relating to information further distinguished *utilius* and *amicus* voters on the one hand from *aliens* voters on the other, but *utilius* voters and *amicus* voters were alike in terms of frequency of use and differentiation between the media.

In general, considering the regression outcomes for both 1996 and 2001, it is possible to conclude that:

1. *Utilius* voters differ from *aliens* voters in terms of education, interest, and type of media.
2. *Amicus* voters differ from *aliens* voters in terms of interest and frequency and type of media, while level of education is significant only in 1996.
3. *Utilius* voters differ from *amicus* voters essentially in terms of a higher level of education, while the role of interest and information varies depending on the year considered.

---

5. To sum up, in 1996 *utilius* voters and *amicus* voters differed from *aliens* voters in terms of a higher level of education, a greater interest in politics and the election campaign, and a strong propensity to make use of sources of information other than TV. In addition, *amicus* voters were distinguished from *aliens* voters in terms of a more frequent exposure to information. *Utilius* voters in their turn were different from *amicus* voters both in terms of a higher level of education and a stronger propensity to make use of different sources of information. On the other hand, *utilius* voters and *amicus* voters did not differ in their level of interest in politics.

Let us take as established, then, the substance of the division achieved by starting out from the different forms of ideological representation. *Utilius, amicus,* and *aliens* have levels of political sophistication that differ in terms of all four measures we used. This is a first indisputable point in favor of the typology that we are proposing.

Heuristics and Social-Contextual Factors: A Sociodemographic Profile

Who lies behind the labels *utilius, amicus, aliens,* and *medians*? Here we provide descriptive profiles in terms of a range of demographic, social, and economic characteristics.

Hypotheses

Our typology is based on characteristics relating to cognitive processes. We have made no reference, up to now, to any relationship between voter types and their sociodemographic characteristics. According to our hypothesis, the strategies of choice have their origins in different forms of ideological representation and are a function of the individual's level of political sophistication. There is no reason to expect that contextual or sociodemographic factors would directly determine the use of particular decision-making strategies. In other words, aspects such as area of residence or social class are probably not in themselves factors that are capable of influencing the type of decision-making process voters use. Nevertheless, there are links between, for example, area of residence and social status, or between occupation and level of formal education (Cobalti and Schizzerotto 1994; Müller and Shavit 1998).

These considerations about the relevance of an individual's socioeconomic profile in determining his level of political sophistication and therefore, indirectly, his decision-making strategy, lead us to formulate the following general expectation: demographic, economic, and social characteristics do not directly influence the nature of the decision-making process but rather determine its preconditions, in particular by defining the level of the individual's political sophistication. This allows us to derive two specific hypotheses. First, we expect that *utilius, amicus,* and *aliens* will differ with respect to their sociodemographic profiles and, second, that sociodemographic and contextual factors will not directly influence an individual's odds of using a particular decision-making strategy; rather, their action will be mediated instead by their level of political sophistication.

This hypothesis is in line with the description of human behavior—discussed in Chapter 1—as an outcome of a dual filtering process composed of (a) a phase governed by a "set of structural constraints," i.e., social and environmental factors, in which abstractly possible actions are reduced to those that are realizable, and (b) a phase guided by "deliberate and intentional choice" that leads to selecting the action that will actually be realized (Elster 1983, 190–91).

A Sociodemographic Profile

In general, we hypothesize that the classical distinction of social centrality *versus* marginality (Bardi and Pasquino 1995; Caramani 1997) will apply to our typology, where *utilius* and *amicus* are expected to have socially central profiles, while *aliens* should resemble socially marginal citizens. In the Italian context, social centrality is heavily determined by gender, age, occupational status, and area of residence. With respect to the latter, we consider not only the level of urbanization[6] but also the geopolitical area. As discussed in Chapter 1, the First Republic has been characterized by the country's marked division into macro-political areas, in which

---

6. We distinguish between towns of up to 10,000 inhabitants, mid-size cities (10,000 to 100,000 inhabitants), and large cities of more than 100,000 inhabitants.

the North East (also called, in the political lingo, the "White" area) was heavily dominated by the Christian Democratic Party while in the Center-North (the "Red" area) there was a similarly strong communist subculture. These are also the most industrialized and modern areas of the country. We therefore expect that, for political and economic reasons, people living in the North and Center-North will be more likely to use ideologically driven decision-making strategies. In Tables 5.3 and 5.4, we describe the profile of each voter type for each election year in terms of geopolitical area of residence, urbanization, gender, age, and occupation. A quick glance at the tables, and at the barplots of Figure 5.2 for the year 2001, confirms our expectations.

Aliens voters are underrepresented among the inhabitants of the North and Center-North, while they are overrepresented in Southern Italy. In addition, this group is almost two thirds women, with a large number of housewives and unemployed. Indeed, among *aliens* there are proportionally three times as many housewives and almost twice as many unemployed individuals as there are among *utilius*. By contrast, *utilius* voters are disproportionally men and people who hold a stable job. They are overrepresented among the inhabitants of the Northwest and among those who live in highly urbanized area (more that 100,000 inhabitants). *Amicus* voters have a profile fairly similar to that of *utilius* voters, albeit less marked. They too are characterized, in contrast to *aliens* voters, by the presence of a substantial number of men, but the distribution in terms of gender within this category does not differ greatly from that of the sample as a whole. On the other hand, the number of *amicus* voters living in the Center-North—aka the Red area—is above the average (Figure 5.2 and Tables 5.3 and 5.4).

A word of warning: although it is useful to trace the profile of our voter types, we should keep in mind that the *aliens* voter is not necessarily a housewife who lives in the South, nor is the *utilius* voter necessarily a man from a large city in the Northwest. In fact, about two-fifths of *aliens* voters are men and about a third of *utilius* voters

TABLE 5.3 Sociodemographic profile by type of voter. Percentage values.

		Utilius	Amicus	Aliens	Medians	All
Geopolitical area	North-West	29.2	24.5	23.7	31.0	27.8
	North-East	10.2	11.7	12.7	10.9	11.3
	Center-North	22.7	22.6	14.5	17.4	19.1
	Center	15.0	12.5	11.6	13.4	13.1
	South	22.9	28.7	37.5	27.2	28.7
		100%	100%	100%	100%	100%
Urbanization	Town	29.2	32.0	35.0	33.4	32.6
	City	41.9	37.1	45.5	41.7	41.3
	Large city	28.9	31.0	19.4	24.9	26.1
		100%	100%	100%	100%	100%
Gender	Male	64.4	50.9	34.6	55.4	52.1
	Female	35.6	49.1	65.4	45.6	47.9
		100%	100%	100%	100%	100%
Age	18–24 years	14.4	11.9	12.9	13.6	13.2
	25–34 years	25.5	18.6	28.1	23.7	23.6
	35–44 years	28.2	28.0	23.4	26.3	26.5
	45–54 years	18.8	21.7	15.0	19.3	19.0
	55–64 years	7.2	9.9	14.1	10.2	10.3
	65–74 years	4.6	6.3	5.4	4.5	5.1
	More than 75 years	1.4	3.6	1.1	2.4	2.3
		100%	100%	100%	100%	100%
Occupation	Unemployed	7.2	7.6	11.4	8.1	8.4
	Student	11.3	9.9	5.8	10.6	9.7
	Housewife	6.3	11.7	23.2	8.9	11.7
	Retired	9.0	17.0	12.3	13.1	13.2
	Public Employee	25.9	20.1	9.4	20.1	19.2
	Private Employee	22.7	20.6	27.0	23.9	23.5
	Professional	17.6	13.2	10.9	15.3	14.4
		100%	100%	100%	100%	100%

Source: Itanes 1996.

TABLE 5.4 Socio-demographic profile by type of voter. Percentage values.

		Utilius	Amicus	Aliens	Medians	All
Geopolitical area	North-West	31.1	29.1	22.2	26.0	26.0
	North-East	9.2	11.4	10.2	13.1	11.7
	Center-North	18.1	22.4	12.4	18.4	17.5
	Center	17.4	12.4	14.5	16.6	15.3
	South	24.2	24.7	40.7	26.0	29.6
		100%	100%	100%	100%	100%
Urbanization	Town	34.1	30.0	36.4	31.8	32.9
	City	34.5	43.0	42.7	43.3	42.3
	Large city	31.4	27.0	20.9	24.9	24.8
		100%	100%	100%	100%	100%
Gender	Male	67.6	52.8	36.9	53.9	50.3
	Female	32.4	47.2	63.1	46.1	49.7
		100%	100%	100%	100%	100%
Age	18–24 years	7.8	7.5	11.1	9.9	9.6
	25–34 years	19.5	20.4	19.1	22.6	20.9
	35–44 years	18.8	15.2	18.8	19.7	18.5
	45–54 years	22.2	21.4	13.0	16.3	16.9
	55–64 years	15.7	18.4	14.0	15.4	15.6
	65–74 years	11.9	12.6	15.6	10.7	12.5
	More than 75 years	4.1	4.6	8.5	5.4	6.0
		100%	100%	100%	100%	100%
Occupation	Unemployed	4.5	3.5	8.4	5.3	5.8
	Student	7.2	5.8	4.4	7.4	6.3
	Housewife	7.5	13.5	20.2	13.6	14.9
	Retired	21.2	27.4	27.1	23.4	25.0
	Public Employee	19.2	11.7	9.9	13.1	12.5
	Private Employee	25.7	24.0	20.1	21.4	21.9
	Professional	14.7	14.0	9.8	15.7	13.7
		100%	100%	100%	100%	100%

Source: Itanes 2001.

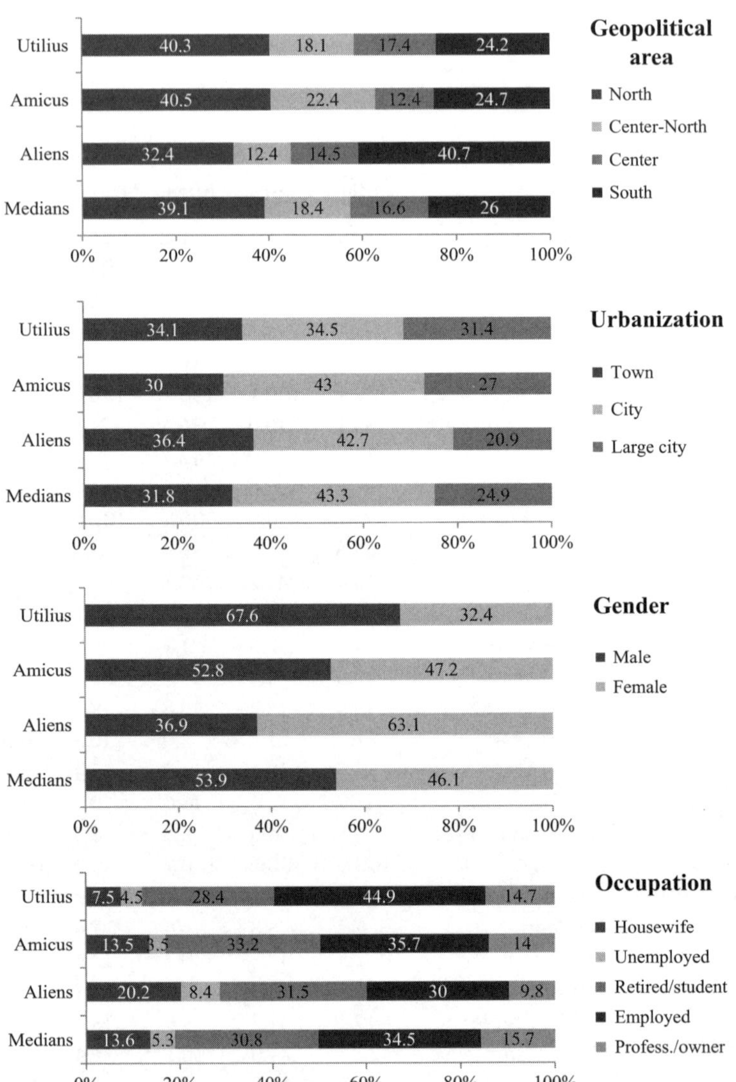

FIGURE 5.2 Barplots of the sociodemographic profile for each type of voter. Percentage values.

Source: Itanes 2001.

live in a small town. Our typology is not constructed on the basis of these categories and each type is distinguished by a marked heterogeneity in terms of the sociodemographic profile of its members. In general, describing social profiles is useful for understanding some of the peculiarities of the members of a type, but the reader should not under any circumstances feel encouraged to construct a "social" image of the types. This warning also applies to what has been said about the level of political sophistication. In this case too, *utilius* voters should not all be labeled interested and educated, because about half of them do not take an interest in politics and only a fifth on average have a degree.

Political Participation

Having voiced this *caveat*—which is valid through the entire book— let us now consider the distribution by type of a series of other variables relating to political participation and embeddedness in associational life. We will focus in particular on the frequency of political discussion,[7] political activism,[8] consistency in voting behavior,[9]

7. The index of political discussion relies on name-generator questions and is built combining the number of people with whom respondents talk about politics and how often they engage in political discussions. In the 1996 Itanes survey, we consider a respondent prone to talk about politics if he speaks with at least two people about politics and does so with one of the two "often" and at least "occasionally" with the other or, at a minimum, "fairly often" with both. In the 2001 Itanes survey, we consider a respondent prone to talk about politics if he talks at least "sometimes" with two people or more.

8. The index of political activism classifies as "politically active" those individuals who declare that they have performed at least two out of three possible political actions such as, for 1996, following the political debates, seeking out information on their local candidate, and participating in the nomination of a candidate or the presentation of a list of candidates. For 2001, the action of seeking out information on the local candidate is replaced by reading political flyers.

9. We consider "consistent" voters those who have voted for the same party (or, in case of a party disappearance, its legitimate heir) in two successive elections. In 1996 consistency is measured with respect to both the immediately preceding elections (1994–1996) and the long-term period (extending back to 1992–94).

the timing of the voting decision,[10] religiosity,[11] and associational participation.[12] As expected, our typology captures systematic and quite substantial differences among voters along these indicators (Tables 5.5 and 5.6, Figure 5.3). For instance, only 17 percent of *aliens* voters discuss politics on a regular basis with family or friends, compared with half of *utilius* and *amicus* voters. Similarly, only 5 percent of *aliens* voters are politically active, while around a third of *utilius* and *amicus* are. *Aliens* are also much more likely to change party from one election to the next (88 percent), and to make up their mind about which party to vote for only a short time before elections (55 percent). They are on average more likely to go to church, but they avoid political associations, while there are no differences between *aliens* and the other types of voters with respect to their membership in nonpolitical associations.

Overall, to grasp the intensity of the difference between the types along these dimensions of political participation, one should consider the fact that the number of *utilius* voters who have a propensity to discuss politics with others, are engaged in associations, are politically active, are nonreligious, and are consistent in their voting pattern is invariably at least twice that of *aliens* voters.

Although *utilius* and *amicus* have a fairly similar profile when contrasted with both *aliens* voters and the sample as a whole, there are differences between *utilius* and *amicus* too: with respect to the

10. A distinction is made between those who had definitively decided whom to vote for "a long time before" and the rest, i.e., those who decided "a few weeks before," "in the last week" or "in the polling booth at the moment of voting."

11. We define as "practicing believers" those who go to church more than two or three times a month, "nonpracticing believers" those who participate in religious ceremonies only two or three times a year, and "nonbelievers" those who declare themselves to be such (Itanes 2001, 53).

12. "Members of associations" are considered in general to be those who participate at least occasionally in the activities of an association; we distinguish between membership in "political associations" such as parties, unions, or professional associations, and "nonpolitical associations."

TABLE 5.5 Political participation by type of voter. Percentage values.

		Utilius	Amicus	Aliens	Medians	All
Political	Does not talk	27.5	37.2	73.2	47.4	46.1
discussion	Talks politics	72.5	62.8	26.8	52.6	53.9
		100%	100%	100%	100%	100%
Religiosity	Practicing	39.3	40.5	47.3	45.2	43.4
	Non-practicing	40.7	39.7	41.6	38.1	39.5
	Non-believer	20.1	19.8	11.1	16.7	17.1
		100%	100%	100%	100%	100%
Associational	Non-member	49.3	54.1	71.3	58.5	58.1
membership	non-political assoc	36.7	32.9	23.5	32.1	31.6
	political association	14.0	13.0	5.1	9.5	10.3
		100%	100%	100%	100%	100%
Poltical	Non-active	65.7	62.1	85.0	74.3	71.8
activism	Active	34.3	37.9	15.0	25.7	28.2
		100%	100%	100%	100%	100%
Continuity	Non-consistent	47.0	50.1	82.1	65.2	61.4
in voting	Consistent	53.0	49.9	17.9	34.8	38.6
'92–'94		100%	100%	100%	100%	100%
Continuity	Non-consistent	25.9	41.5	66.9	55.5	48.7
in voting	Consistent	74.1	58.5	33.1	44.5	51.3
'94–'96		100%	100%	100%	100%	100%
Timing of	A long time before	71.5	74.0	34.1	49.9	56.9
decision	A short time before	28.5	26.0	65.9	50.1	43.1
		100%	100%	100%	100%	100%

Source: Itanes 1996.

proportion of people who engage in political discussions (56 percent vs. 48 percent) and activism (32 percent vs. 21 percent), continuity in voting (69 percent vs. 54 percent) and membership in political associations (35 percent vs. 29 percent). The only exceptions to this trend are the moment of voting choice and religiosity, which are distributed in a similar way among *utilius* and *amicus* voters, and predisposition toward political activism, which in 1996 was more common among *amicus* voters.

TABLE 5.6 Political participation by type of voter. Percentage values.

		Utilius	Amicus	Aliens	Medians	All
Political	Does not talk	44.4	51.5	83.4	55.9	61.5
discussion	Talks politics	55.6	48.5	16.6	44.1	38.5
		100%	100%	100%	100%	100%
Religiosity	Practicing	29.7	32.8	42.5	37.6	37.3
	Non-practicing	41.0	38.6	37.7	40.3	39.3
	Non-believer	29.4	28.6	19.8	22.1	23.4
		100%	100%	100%	100%	100%
Associational	Non-member	45.1	54.0	66.0	53.3	56.2
membership	non-political assoc	19.8	17.4	18.2	21.0	19.4
	political association	35.2	28.6	15.8	25.7	24.4
		100%	100%	100%	100%	100%
Poltical	Non-active	67.9	77.8	94.5	82.5	83.6
activism	Active	32.1	22.2	5.5	17.5	16.4
		100%	100%	100%	100%	100%
Continuity	Non-consistent	30.7	45.7	87.7	65.0	64.4
in voting	Consistent	69.3	54.3	12.3	35.0	35.6
'96–'01		100%	100%	100%	100%	100%
Timing of	A long time before	78.5	78.1	45.1	59.8	61.6
decision	A short time before	21.5	21.9	54.9	40.2	38.4
		100%	100%	100%	100%	100%

Source: Itanes 2001.

Voting Heuristics Rooted in Cognition and Political Culture

Having established that *utilius, amicus,* and *aliens* have different sociodemographic profiles, we now consider the second part of our hypothesis: that these structural constraints will not directly influence the probability that an individual will use either decision-making strategy, but that their effect will instead be mediated by individual levels of political sophistication and related measures of political participation.

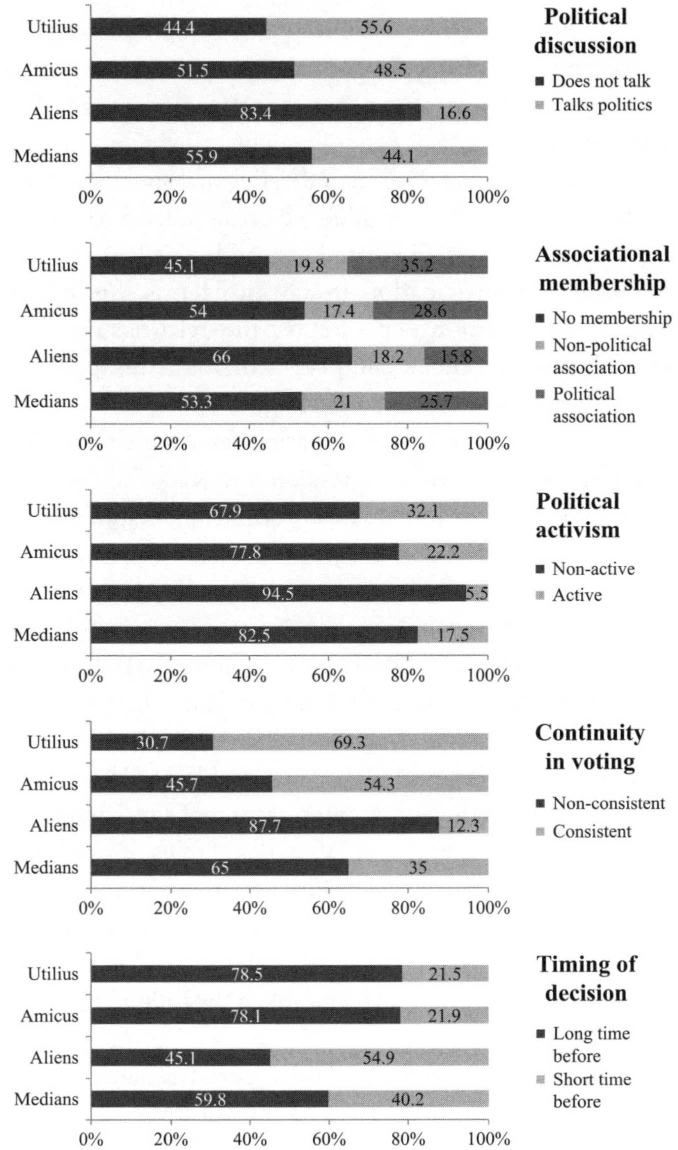

FIGURE 5.3 Barplots of the political participation for each type of voter. Percentage values.

Source: Itanes 2001.

Just as we did in our analysis of political sophistication, let us now move from describing the particular composition of each type to estimating the relative importance of each sociodemographic, behavioral, and cognitive factor in influencing in which type an individual might be classified. Our hypothesis is that sociodemographic variables do not have a direct influence on an individual's decision-making strategy, which is mediated instead by his level of political sophistication and participation. In statistical terms, this hypothesis can be tested by looking at whether the relationship between sociodemographic predictors and types of voters disappears once we control for political sophistication.

We test this hypothesis by comparing the results from two different multinomial logistic regression models: the first model (Model 1, Tables 5.7 and 5.8) includes both all the sociodemographic predictors we described above (geopolitical area of residence, urbanization, gender, age, and occupation), as well as measures of political participation and behavior, such as frequency of political discussion, associational participation, political activism, consistency in voting patterns, and the timing of the voting decision. In the second model (Model 2, Tables 5.7 and 5.8), we introduce in addition to the variables in Model 1, the variables indicative of political sophistication: education, interest in politics, frequency of exposure to the media, and type of media. Tables 5.7 and 5.8 also report the model in which we consider only political sophistication variables as predictors (Model 0), as discussed previously in this chapter.

We can reduce the possible scenarios to the following three:

1. The sociodemographic variables could remain significant while those indexing political sophistication and participations do not. This would mean that political sophistication is an expression of sociodemographic characteristics and that it is not an autonomous factor in influencing the nature of decision-making mechanisms.

TABLE 5.7 Multinomial Logistic Regressions (reference categories in parenthesis).

Utilius/Aliens 1996		*Model 0*	*Model 1*		*Model 2*	
Geopolitical area	North-West		1.16*	(.25)	1.16*	(.27)
(South)	North-East		.79*	(.31)	1.01*	(.34)
	Center-North		1.30*	(.28)	1.29*	(.30)
	Center		.57	(.30)	.52	(.33)
Urbanization	Town (< 10.000 inh.)		-.50*	(.24)	-.12	(.26)
(Large city: > 100.000 inh.)	City (10.000–100.000 inh.)		-.47*	(.23)	-.16	(.25)
Gender (Female)	Male		.95*	(.20)	.85*	(.22)
Age	18–24 years		.10	(.82)	.44	(.91)
(More than 75 years)	25–34 years		-.19	(.78)	-.13	(.87)
	35–44 years		-.13	(.77)	-.01	(.86)
	45–54 years		-.06	(.77)	.31	(.86)
	55–64 years		-.75	(.76)	-.21	(.84)
	65–74 years		-.36	(.80)	-.27	(.87)
Occupation	Unemployed		.08	(.39)	.19	(.42)
(Professional/Employer)	Student		.78	(.45)	.47	(.48)
	Housewife		-.74	(.38)	-.24	(.42)
	Retired		-.66	(.42)	-.61	(.47)
	Public Employee		.61	(.33)	-.04	(.36)
	Private Employee		-.66*	(.29)	-.57	(.32)

(continued)

TABLE 5.7 (*continued*)

Utilius/Aliens 1996		Model 0		Model 1		Model 2	
Political discussion	Talks about politics			1.53*	(1.53)	.95*	(.21)
Religiosity	Practicing			-.24	(-.24)	-.20	(.31)
(Non-believer)	Non-practicing			-.38	(-.38)	-.18	(.31)
Associational membership	Non-member			-.37	(.34)	.34	(.37)
(Political association)	Non-political association			-.07	(.35)	.20	(.38)
Political activism	Active			.34	(.21)	-.14	(.24)
Continuity in voting pre'92–'94	Consistent			.89*	(.21)	.97*	(.23)
Continuity in voting '94–'96	Consistent			1.15*	(.19)	1.19*	(.21)
Timing of decision	A long time before			1.03*	(.19)	1.02*	(.20)
Education	High school	1.26*	(.17)			1.31*	(.22)
(Middle school)	College	2.37*	(.31)			2.16*	(.36)
Interest (Not interested)	Interested	1.51*	(.18)			.92*	(.23)
Frequency of media exposure	Every day	-.06	(.20)			1.08*	(.24)
Type of media	TV + other	1.48*	(.20)			-.22	(.26)
	Costant	-2.43*	(.24)	1.67	(.95)	-1.24	(1.10)
χ^2		454.844		600.006		710.909	
df		10		56		66	
N		1445		1337		1337	

Amicus /Aliens 1996		*Model 0*	*Model 1*		*Model 2*	
Geopolitical area	North-West		.69*	(.23)	.58*	(.24)
(South)	North-East		.60*	(.27)	.76*	(.29)
	Center-North		.93*	(.25)	.83*	(.27)
	Center		.17	(.27)	.08	(.30)
Urbanization	Town (< 10.000 inh.)		-.43	(.22)	-.12	(.23)
(Large city: > 100.000 inh.)	City (10.000–100.000 inh.)		-.65*	(.21)	-.44	(.22)
Gender	Male		.31*	(.18)	.20	(.20)
Age	18–24 years		-.66	(.72)	-.48	(.77)
(More than 75 years)	25–34 years		-.83	(.67)	-.79	(.72)
	35–44 years		-.51	(.67)	-.46	(.72)
	45–54 years		-.40	(.66)	-.18	(.71)
	55–64 years		-1.17	(.64)	-.83	(.68)
	65–74 years		-.94	(.68)	-1.07	(.72)
Occupation	Unemployed		.05	(.36)	.16	(.38)
(Professional/Employer)	Student		.89*	(.42)	.60	(.45)
	Housewife		-.36	(.32)	-.08	(.35)
	Retired		.12	(.37)	.09	(.41)
	Public Employee		.42	(.32)	-.14	(.34)
	Private Employee		-.45	(.28)	-.40	(.30)

(continued)

TABLE 5.7 (*continued*)

Amicus /Aliens 1996		Model 0		Model 1		Model 2	
Political discussion	Talks about politics			1.13*	(.17)	.66*	(.18)
Religiosity	Practicing			-.42	(.27)	-.35	(.29)
(Non-believer)	Non-practicing			-.52	(.26)	-.36	(.29)
Associational membership	Non-member			-.28	(.32)	-.25	(.34)
(Political association)	Non-political association			-.01	(.33)	-.14	(.35)
Political activism	Active			.61*	(.19)	.08	(.22)
Continuity pre'92–'94	Consistent			1.00*	(.19)	1.06*	(.21)
Continuity '94–'96	Consistent			.41*	(.17)	.38*	(.18)
Timing of decision	A long time before			1.21*	(.17)	1.16*	(.18)
Education	High school	.71*	(.15)			.14	(.18)
(Middle school)	College	1.59*	(.30)			-.26	(.29)
Interest	Interested	1.58*	(.17)			1.20*	(.21)
Frequency of media exposure	Every day	.67*	(.20)			.17	(.22)
Type of media	TV + other	.87*	(.16)			.68*	(.17)
	Costant	-1.79*	(.21)	2.84	(.84)	.43	(.95)

Standard errors in parentheses. *p < 0.05

Source: Itanes 1996.

TABLE 5.8 Multinomial Logistic Regressions (reference categories in parenthesis).

Utilius /Aliens 2001		Model 0		Model 1		Model 2
Geopolitical area	North-West		1.00*	(.24)	.79*	(.25)
(South)	North-East		.72*	(.31)	.45	(.32)
	Center-North		.62*	(.27)	.45	(.28)
	Center		.48	(.27)	.19	(.28)
Urbanization	Town (< 10.000 inh.)		-.44	(.22)	-.16	(.24)
(Large city: > 100.000 inh.)	City (10.000–100.000 inh.)		-.86*	(.22)	-.66*	(.23)
Gender (Female)	Male		1.15*	(.20)	1.00*	(.21)
Age	18–24 years		-.19	(.59)	-.36	(.61)
(More than 75 years)	25–34 years		-.15	(.51)	-.37	(.53)
	35–44 years		-.34	(.50)	-.44	(.52)
	45–54 years		.04	(.49)	-.11	(.51)
	55–64 years		-.06	(.45)	-.24	(.47)
	65–74 years		.20	(.45)	.16	(.47)
Occupation	Unemployed		.12	(.46)	.33	(.47)
(Professional/Employer)	Student		1.43	(.48)	1.13	(.49)
	Housewife		.17	(.39)	.37	(.41)
	Retired		-.22	(.36)	-.05	(.38)
	Public Employee		.65	(.33)	.48	(.37)
	Private Employee		.13	(.29)	.20	(.30)

(continued)

TABLE 5.8 (*continued*)

Utilius /Aliens 2001		Model 0		Model 1		Model 2	
Political discussion	Talks about politics			1.19*	(.19)	.79*	(.20)
Religiosity	Practicing			-.14	(.23)	-.24	(.24)
(Non-believer)	Non-practicing			.01	(.22)	-.01	(.23)
Associational membership	Non-member			-.28	(.22)	-.19	(.23)
(Political association)	Non-political association			.03	(.20)	.02	(.28)
Political activism	Active			1.32*	(.24)	.91*	(.26)
Continuity in voting '96–'01	Consistent			2.52*	(.19)	2.52*	(.20)
Timing of decision	A long time before			.81*	(.19)	.63*	(.20)
Education	High school	.63*	(.17)			.70*	(.22)
(Middle school)	College	.31	(.27)			.21	(.34)
Interest (Not interested)	Interested	2.26*	(.20)			1.21*	(.24)
Frequency of media							
exposure	Every day	.66*	(.26)			.81*	(.25)
Type of	TV + other	1.13*	(.21)			.45	(.30)
media	Costant	-3.20*	(.26)	-3.64*	(.63)	-4.65*	(.71)
χ^2		430.741		805.772		864.582	
df		10		54		64	
N		1705					

Amicus / Aliens 2001		Model 0	Model 1		Model 2	
Geopolitical area	North-West		.76*	(.18)	.53*	(.19)
(South)	North-East		.70*	(.23)	.49*	(.24)
	Center-North		.71*	(.21)	.54*	(.22)
	Center		.14	(.22)	-.09	.23
Urbanization	Town (< 10.000 inh.)		-.41*	(.18)	-.21	(.20)
(Large city: > 100.000 inh.)	City (10.000–100.000 inh.)		-.45*	(.17)	-.25	(.18)
Gender	Male		.54*	(.15)	.33*	(.16)
Age	18–24 years		.21	.44	.22	.46
(More than 75 years)	25–34 years		.44	.38	.44	.40
	35–44 years		-.06	.37	.01	.40
	45–54 years		.57	.37	.56	.39
	55–64 years		.23	.33	.20	.35
	65–74 years		.15	.33	.12	.35
Occupation	Unemployed		-.27	.36	-.23	.38
(Professional/Employer)	Student		.88*	.39	.71	.40
	Housewife		.40	.28	.41	.30
	Retired		.29	.29	.45	.30
	Public Employee		.06	.28	-.01	.30
	Private Employee		-.01	.24	.02	.25

(continued)

TABLE 5.8 (*continued*)

Amicus /Aliens 2001		Model 0		Model 1		Model 2	
Political discussion	Talks about politics			1.11*	(.15)	.81*	(.16)
Religiosity	Practicing			-.28	.19	-.31	.19
(Non-believer)	Non-practicing			-.16	.18	-.15	.19
Associational membership	Non-member			-.18	.18	-.07	.19
(Political association)	Non-political association			-.11	.22	-.03	.23
Political activism	Active			.96*	(.22)	.59*	(.24)
Continuity in voting '96–'01	Consistent			1.74*	(.15)	1.76*	(.16)
Timing of decision	A long time before			.98*	(.14)	.84*	(.15)
Education	High school	.13	(.14)			.14	(.18)
(Middle school)	College	-.10	(.24)			-.26	(.29)
Interest	Interested	1.98*	(.18)			1.20*	(.21)
Frequency of media exposure	Every day	.46*	(.18)			.17	(.22)
Type of media	TV + other	.85*	(.14)			.68*	(.17)
	Costant	-1.70*	(.19)	-2.35	(.48)	-2.99	(.53)

Standard errors in parentheses. *p < 0.05

Source: Itanes 2001.

2. It is possible, instead, that the sociodemographic variables will become nonsignificant in Model 2, thus supporting our hypothesis that political sophistication mediates the effect of social and contextual variables.
3. Finally, both political sophistication and the sociodemographic and participatory factors could remain significant.

Focusing on the results of Model 2, we find, in accordance with our hypothesis about the role of political sophistication in determining decision-making strategies, that education, interest, and information continue to be significant even in the presence of the sociodemographic and participatory variables. Our theory is confirmed for both years and most of our political sophistication indicators. Education, interest, and information—with the exception, in a few cases, of frequency of media exposure—each have a substantial role in predicting which type an individual is likely to belong to, even in the presence of numerous other control variables. The strength of the estimated coefficients is substantial, albeit smaller than the values reported in Model 0. Similarly, a few measures of political participation remain significant even when controlling for the sociodemographic profile of the respondent: namely, political discussion and activism, timing of the choice, and consistency in voting patterns. This clearly rules out the first of the three scenarios above, and suggests that the type of decision making that individuals adopt is a function of individual cognitive capacities, motivations, and opportunities, and not just a "consequence" of social condition.

Second, by comparing the results of Models 1 and 2, we can further rule out a significant direct relationship between sociodemographic characteristics and decision-making type, with only a few exceptions. In fact, once we account for political sophistication, only gender and the geopolitical area of residence still have an independent role in distinguishing between *utilius, amicus,* and *aliens.* These anomalies deserve further consideration.

In general, an individual living in Southern Italy has an increased likelihood of being an *aliens* voter, while living in the Northern regions and, above all, in the Center-North makes people more likely to be *utilius* or *amicus* voters.[13] The more ideologically oriented decision makers tend to reside in the regions of the country with the strongest Catholic and communist political subcultures. As mentioned earlier, at least up until the beginning of the 1990s, the most successful interpretative model of the voting behavior of the Italian electorate was based on the role of territorial subcultures in the process of political socialization of the Italian citizens.

What actually does explain the relatively high concentration of *utilius* and *amicus* voters in these areas? With the advent of the Second Republic, the importance of political subcultures has visibly declined: left-wing voters are still overrepresented in the Center-North and underrepresented in the North, but regional differences are much less marked, and far more volatile. Yet although identification with a subculture and strong partisanship are less important now than they were in the past, the North and Center-North regions remain exceptional for their level of politicization and civic commitment. Facing a changed political system, these citizens, prompted by tradition and culture, still strive for and create ways to structure their political consciousness and beliefs. This need is unknown, however, to an electorate like that of Southern Italy, which has been brought up for decades to accept being excluded and alienated from the political world (La Palombara 1966; Cartocci 1990; 2007; Putnam 1993; Bardi and Pasquino 1995). More important than identifying as "red" or "white," the inhabitants of the North and Center-North regions have maintained a cultural propensity to think about politics in ideological terms, and they are therefore more likely to adopt *utilius* or *amicus* decision-making strategies. This is even more evident in view of the fact that neither the *amicus* nor the *utilius* type

---

13. This factor can also be considered responsible for the overrepresentation of large cities' inhabitants among *utilius* voters.

can be categorized as "red" or "white"; both are made up of individuals who vote for various parties and for both coalitions. This conclusion is further confirmed by the irrelevance of religiosity in dividing subjects into different types.[14]

A second interesting finding relates instead to gender: being male increases the probability of being a *utilius* voter as opposed to both an *aliens* voter and an *amicus* voter, and, also, in 2001, the probability of being an *amicus* voter as opposed to an *aliens* voter. Women, then—assuming an equal level of education, interest, social position, inclination to discuss politics with others, and so on—have a lower propensity than men to approach politics using ideological categories. One way to account for this finding is to argue that politics is the continuation of the war by other means, and thus tends to be a predominantly masculine business. Alternatively, one can hypothesize that being socially marginalized gives women little inclination to capture the complexity of political debate (Milbrath 1965).[15]

Let us now consider age and occupation. These two variables do not affect the probability of belonging to one type or another in any

14. This interpretation of the results needs to be subjected to empirical control through a study of the influence cultural traditions have on the political formation of the individual. How did individuals with the characteristics of the *utilius* voter behave in the years in which the subcultures in question were particularly strong? Did they show a relatively high propensity to acquire information and were they, in general, characterized by cultural habits capable of facilitating the transmission and acquisition of political categories like left and right?

15. Although we cannot provide a satisfactory answer to this conundrum, we notice that there is some support for the second explanation. If we consider the distribution of educational certificates according to gender, we find that among women who are *utilius* voters, college graduates and advanced degree holders are disproportionately represented, whereas among *amicus* voters a disproportionate percent of women have only high school certificates. The possession of advanced educational certificates is thus a factor that influences membership of the *utilius* and *amicus* types to a greater extent for women than it does for men. The question as to why, however, remains basically unanswered, though we ourselves are inclined to interpret the disproportionately high number of women in the *aliens* category as a consequence—and a cause—of the widespread social perception of politics as "men's business" (Burns, Schlozman, and Verba 2001).

way.[16] This result is by no means a foregone conclusion. One might have expected, for example, that younger voters would have different attitudes toward politics—and therefore different decision-making strategies—than their older counterparts, having had different political socialization and generational experiences. Yet this was not the case. Once we account for education, interest, and information, the organization of political beliefs does not differ between young people and older people, between those who have voted for the first time and those who have been doing so for years, between those who experienced the First Republic and those who have only heard (bad things) about it.

Even more interesting are the implications of the irrelevance of occupation. This finding means, for example, that it is not being a housewife in itself that reduces the possibility of making choices according to ideological criteria, but rather the fact that housewives have little interest in politics, low levels of education, and a general tendency to gather information only from television. By contrast, housewives who have high levels of political sophistication are distributed among the different types in the same way as members of any other occupational category.

In conclusion, our analysis suggests that sociodemographic factors do not generally determine the nature of the decision-making process, but rather contribute to defining its preconditions, particularly the individual voter's level of political sophistication. It follows that the influence exerted by social and contextual factors is mediated by an individual's level of political sophistication and active political engagement (and that of their larger communities). In particular, education and interest in politics, along with political discussion, continuity of voting, and timing of decision, are the variables that best explain membership of the different types of voters.

16. The only systematicity of any importance is that being a student increases the probability of being an *amicus* voter or a *utilius* voter as opposed to an *aliens* voter, in particular in 2001. This, however, may be explained by the fact that, as a student, the subject in question is registered as a holder of an educational certificate lower than the one for which she is studying and so the effect that is not fully captured by education manifests itself through occupation.

Chapter 6

Systematic and Effective Voting Heuristics

To what extent are the decision-making strategies of *utilius, amicus,* and *aliens* voters heuristics "that make us smart," i.e., shortcuts that allow voters to be up to the task of dealing with political decision making? As we know, heuristics reduce the complexity of choices, but what are the consequences of this for the accuracy with which decisions are made? In short, what can we say about the quality of voters' choices? Actually, very little. Or, to put it more formally, the recognition that it is not possible to establish a priori a criterion for the goodness of the choice makes it impossible to conduct any type of test on the correctness with which the vote is cast. There is no such thing as a voter "who makes a mistake"—no "false consciousness" to which to appeal. The accuracy of the decision-making process, then, is not open to evaluation.

Our approach to decision making does not make any normative judgments about the outcome. The fast and frugal heuristics approach assumes only that heuristics are inferential processes that make it possible to reach a satisficing choice. It is not the job of social scientists to define what should be considered satisficing for each single individual. In fact, this alternative to rational choice was introduced into the decision-making discourse explicitly to show that a process of sequentially evaluating alternatives may be interrupted, even concluded, well before the best option has even been taken into consideration (Simon 1956; 1990). It is in this light, too, that it has been incorporated into the theoretical approach that we are adopting (Gigerenzer 2001; Selten 2001).

But even though a decision-making process cannot be evaluated as more or less accurate vis-à-vis its outcome, it is nonetheless possible to draw conclusions about the *systematicity* with which a decision-making strategy is used and its *effectiveness*.

We expect heuristic decision making to be adopted every time there is a need or opportunity to do so. It is therefore reasonable to hypothesize that the judgment strategies used by *utilius*, *amicus*, and *aliens* are present and recognizable not just in their voting behavior, but also in other decision-making tasks they undertake (Kuklinski and Quirk 2000). In particular, we expect that voters adopt the same inferential processes in situations similar to those that we have used to construct the typology. In other words, we expect them to make use of—or not make use of—the categories of left and right or to apply—or not apply—the *amicus/hostis* criterion even when they express opinions about other political objects, such as, policy issues, their future voting preferences, or the performance of the government. Similarly, we expect *aliens* voters to systematically despise politics and evaluate political objects through negative lenses.

We speak in this case of how systematcally a heuristic is used, aiming to capture the degree of coherence with which voters apply judgment criteria. Concretely, we test for this systematicity by considering sets of questions that are different from those used in constructing the typology. In particular, we analyze: (a) issue preferences and (b) future voting propensity to evaluate the level of ideological coherence; and, (c) the expectations voters have about the capacity of the two coalitions to govern, to evaluate how systematically they either use the *amicus/hostis* judgment logic, or, alternatively, whether they systematically distrust politics tout court. Data for these analyses are available only in the 2001 Itanes survey.

The second criterion for evaluating our classification system is how effectively it captures specific decision-making processes, particularly compared to traditional measures of political sophistication. Still referring to voters' opinions about political issues, their future voting preferences, and evaluations of government capacity, we will compare the coherence of *utilius, amicus,* and *aliens* voters with that of voters with high levels of education and interest in politics. By effectiveness, then, we mean the capacity of our classification to distinguish between voters in terms of how coherently they organize their political preferences.

Systematic application of the heuristics and effective division of voters based on their levels of ideological coherence are the two ways in which we will evaluate the validity of our voting heuristics typology. In both cases the typology is "put to the test" with decision-making tasks that involve objects of judgment different from those originally used to classify respondents into different groups. The test is based on the hypothesis that voters use decision-making strategies consistently. As we will see, the validity of the typology is clearly confirmed with respect to both criteria, so much so as to prompt us to argue that our typology is capable of capturing differences in decision-making performance better than the traditional measures of political sophistication.

Ideological Coherence in Issue Preferences

In Western democracies, political and policy issues are a constitutive part of the political landscape—they are one of the principle short-term factors—and they play a role in both consolidating opinions and motivating the undecided. Issue-voting and the importance of the issues in the organization of public opinion are traditional themes of interest in the study of political behavior (Converse 1964; Sniderman 1991; Hinich and Munger 1994; Venturino 2000; Bellucci 1997; 2002); however, issue preferences have had very little importance in the Italian political scenario, vis-à-vis ideology, parties, leaders, and coalitions, and for this reason they have not been used to classify respondents into different types.

In this section, we ask how *utilius, amicus, aliens,* and *medians* voters organize their opinions on taxation, immigration, education, health care, and other issues. We will not focus our attention on individual preferences in themselves but rather on specific modes of organizing opinions, with the aim of inferring from them the judgment criteria by which voters formulate their preferences.

Political issues play a central role in Downs' voting model: he assumes that placement along the left-right axis is the synthesis of a large number of specific issue positions. The capacity of the ideological dimension to condense an array of different opinions into a single position constitutes a perfect example of heuristic reasoning (Downs 1957). The *utilius* voter's cognitive shortcut is, in fact, to use a reduced, one-dimensional ideological space instead of systematically comparing his own position with those of the parties' on a plurality of issues. Accordingly, we expect the *utilius* voter's opinions on individual issues to conform to the position he takes up on the left-right continuum. Our principle hypothesis, then, will be of consistency between opinions on issues and ideological position. For the *utilius* type in particular, ideological coherence on issue preferences represents a necessary condition in order to confirm the validity of the heuristic. For the other types of voters, however, this coherence is not a constitutive element of their heuristics. Nonetheless, it is also possible to formulate some hypotheses for *amicus* and *aliens* voters.

The heuristic of the *amicus* voter manifests itself in a dichotomous perception of political objects; she simplifies reality by reducing it to a contraposition. This logic, encountered in her judgment on political leaders, could easily serve to coherently organize her position on the issues as well. Indeed, the *amicus/hostis* criterion, in this respect, could lead to a certain degree of coherence between positions on policy issues and placement on the left-right ideological continuum. Note that this is not the same as arguing that the issues are an integral part of the process by which the *amicus* voter chooses. We simply hypothesize that her policy opinions will reflect the framework of ideological contraposition inherent to the political competition, thus generating a coherent arrangement of issue positions and ideology.

Notions of left and right have very limited salience in the case of the *aliens* voter, and it is therefore natural to expect that the coherence between positions on the issues and ideological placement will also be very limited, perhaps even nonexistent. This does not exclude, however, the possibility that *aliens* voters might rely on issues. A quite plausible hypothesis, in line with a one-reason decision-making philosophy, is that the *aliens* voter is especially sensitive to a particular issue of the campaign. His pragmatic nature, his propensity to choose whom to vote for just a short time before the elections or even at the moment of voting, and the ease with which he modifies his choice could well be signs of this. However, the hypothesis that a particular issue is the determining factor in a voting choice is very difficult to capture given the procedures we have so far used to construct our typology, and, moreover, the limitations of survey data. We do, in fact, observe differences in the distribution of opinions among the various types. For example, *aliens* voters are on average much more favorable than others toward restrictive immigration policies. But this observation does not provide us with anything more than an association between a specific opinion and a particular type of voter, from which we cannot infer any systematic algorithms of judgment.

It would be quite another thing, on the other hand, to observe that *aliens* voters were organizing issue preferences based on a criterion wholly different from the concept of a left-right continuum. If this were the case, one could in fact argue for the existence of a judgment heuristic based on ideological categories different from the traditional ones. But this is not the case. A factor analysis of issue opinions limited to the *aliens* group reveals an organization that is analogous to that of the other types and that can be traced back to the traditional left-right axis. In other words, even *aliens* voters organize their opinions on the issues according to the traditional ideological dimension, albeit with a much lower level of coherence than the other types of voters (Baldassarri and Schadee 2006).

Accordingly, we will test the hypothesis of ideological coherence in organizing policy preferences by studying the extent to which an individual's positions on policy issues correspond to his placement on the left-right axis.[1] Having established that all voters organize their issue preferences according to the left-right spectrum, we expect *utilius* and, to a lesser extent, *amicus*, to have a higher degree of coherence than *aliens* and *medians*.

Starting out from a factorial analysis of a wide range of issues, conducted both on the entire sample and separately on each of the types, we selected the six sentences that can most clearly be associated with the left-right scale:

1. It is necessary to reduce taxes even if this leads to a reduction in public services;
2. The state should finance private schools as well as public schools;
3. Health-care services should be entrusted to the private sector;
4. Companies should be given more freedom to hire and fire employees;
5. In politics today, it is better to have a single person who makes decisions rapidly than to follow all of the parliamentary procedures;
6. Italy today needs a strong leader.

For each of these statements the respondent was asked whether she was "very much," "pretty much," "not really," or "not at all" in agreement. Responses were then summed into a numerical score and, through a linear transformation, we built an synthetic index of policy issues position that goes from 1 to 10, where 1 corresponds to the extreme left, 10 to the extreme right, and 5 to a central position. This policy position index was then correlated with self-placement

---

1. The number of *aliens* voters considered here is quite small. This is because only a limited number of these voters place themselves and of these, there is a consistent number of individuals who do not have any opinion on the issues.

on the left-right continuum. The ideological constraint of voters is a function of the degree of correlation between issue position and position on the left-right axis. Obviously, the higher the correlation is, the greater the consistency of the voter type.

Table 6.1 (Model 1) shows the results of linear regression models with self-placement on the left-right continuum as the dependent variable and position on policy issues as the independent variable. All of the correlation coefficients are clearly positive. There are, however, a number of marked differences between the types in terms of the strength of the relationship. In the case of *utilius* and *amicus*, the correspondence between the two measures is very high, with estimated coefficients of 0.75 and 0.63, respectively. Moreover, the coefficient of determination (R^2) for *utilius* voters is 0.47. This means that about half of the variability in the *utilius* voters' placements along the left-right axis is explained by opinions they express on the issues, while the explained variability for *amicus* voters is more than one third.

For the *aliens* voter, the correlation coefficient is, by contrast, very low (0.12) and has limited significance, with an explained variability of around 1 percent. As expected, then, the difference between the ideological coherence of *utilius* and *amicus*, on the one hand, and that of *aliens*, on the other, is very pronounced. The category *medians* is in an intermediate position, with a coefficient of 0.41, which makes it, in certain respects, much more similar to *utilius* and *amicus* than to *aliens*. This accentuates even further the incoherence of the *aliens* voter's use of traditional ideological categories and highlights once more the importance of our assumption of voter heterogeneity. In fact, if we were to consider only the entire sample's level of consistency, we would report a correlation coefficient of 0.50, and speculate about an "average" voter who was relatively coherent in his use of ideological categories, if not completely able to master them. In actual fact, though, we know that this average level is the product of the overlap of very distinct figures representing very distinct groups. Indeed, on the one hand, there is a

TABLE 6.1 Ideological coherence in issue preferences. Linear regression models. Dependent variable: self-placement on the left-right ideological continuum; independent variables: position on issue preferences, judgment on Berlusconi and judgment on Rutelli. Estimates and determination coefficients.

| | Model 1 | | | Model 2 | | | | | | | |
	Issue preferences		R^2	Issue preferences		Berlusconi		Rutelli		R^2	N
Utilius	.750*	(.047)	0.474	.307*	(.045)	.454*	(.040)	-.220*	(.042)	.713	293
Amicus	.633*	(.036)	0.344	.141*	(.031)	.382*	(.033)	-.274*	(.034)	.708	589
Aliens	.123	(.057)	0.014	.010	(.053)	.260*	(.033)	-.150*	(.035)	.201	335
Medians	.415*	(.027)	0.136	.184*	(.025)	.336*	(.018)	.-.230*	(.021)	.358	1430
All	.497*	(.019)	.209	.185*	(.017)	.357*	(.014)	-.242*	(.014)	.483	2647

*Standard errors in parentheses. * p <.000*

Source: Itanes 2001.

block of voters who have at their disposal a very good under-standing of ideological categories, while, on the other, we find a substantial group of people who are almost entirely oblivious of their meaning.

The relationship between positions on the issues and placement on the left-right axis continues to be significant for *utilius, amicus,* and *medians* even when we introduce two control variables into the regression model: their judgment of Berlusconi and judgment of Rutelli (each valued from 1 to 10). When we introduce other ex-planatory elements, the estimated coefficient for the issue position index clearly diminishes in value (Table 6.1, Model 2) both for *utilius* (0.31) and *amicus* voters (0.14). In both cases, however, the esti-mated coefficient remains significant, while the explained variability increases to about 70 percent. By contrast, controlling for the prime-ministerial candidates renders issue preferences totally irrelevant for predicting *aliens* voters' placement.

In conclusion, then, our first test of the systematicity in the use of heuristics has produced uncontroversial findings. While *utilius* and *amicus* have opinions on the issues that are coherent with their own ideological position, *aliens* voters do not organize their opin-ions on the issues according to the categories of left and right, nor do they seem to have at their disposal other criteria capable of giving coherence to their judgments. This obviously does not allow us to rule out the possibility that an individual *aliens* voter is able to make use of a *rationale* of his own. What is certain, however, is that there are no collectively shared criteria for organizing issue prefer-ences other than the categories of left and right. Another thing that needs to be noted is that only the *aliens* voter, i.e., the one who most actively refuses to take an interest in political life, does not organize issue preferences with any form of coherence, whereas, by contrast, even the *medians* voter has a certain level of ideological coherence.

These results also confirm the centrality of policy issues for *utilius* voters. In keeping with what we hypothesized, these voters have, in absolute terms, the highest correlation coefficient and its weight remains substantial when other predictive factors are introduced. Even among *amicus* voters, however, the coherence between issues and ideology is very high, suggesting that the *amicus/hostis* logic, when applied to political issues, performs well. The ideological consistency of the *amicus* voter is a further sign of her marked need for integration (Sniderman, Brody, and Tetlock 1991), i.e., of her need to make her system of political beliefs both coherent and homogenous.

Ideological Coherence in Organizing Future Voting Preferences

The opportunity for another test of ideological coherence is provided by the following question:

> I will now read out to you a list of parties. For each one can you tell me whether or not it is possible that you will vote for it in the future? Say whether you will definitely vote for it, whether you might vote for it or whether you would never vote for it. (Itanes 2001)

The question was followed by a list of twelve parties. In this way the respondents were asked to make pronouncements about their future voting propensity by selecting degrees of probability ranging from certainty ("I will vote for it") to possibility ("I might vote for it") to exclusion ("I would never vote for it"). This situation is comparable to the one in which our survey respondents found themselves when deciding which party to vote for, but offers more information than simply their voting choice. The way in which future voting propensity was ascertained in this case does not limit the choice to a single party. Instead, the information available is much richer, because each respondent is able to report more than one preference.

Reporting their preferences on a set of parties, our respondents provide us with precious information about the judgment criteria underlying the choice. We can do this by comparing the set of parties one subject indicates with the sets chosen by other subjects who use the same heuristic. In particular, if a group of voters all use the same decision-making process, they should rank their preferences following very similar principles. We use a scaling technique to analyze the voting preferences.

The procedure of scaling that we use here, called multiple unidimensional unfolding, was introduced by Van Schuur (1984) as a probabilistic application of Coombs's unfolding model (Schadee 1995; Corbetta 1999, 269–72). This technique is based on the assumption that every subject (for example, the voter) and every stimulus (for example, every party that the voter is willing to vote for) can be positioned along the same underlying dimension. The smaller the distance that separates subject and stimulus, the greater will be the subject's preference for the stimulus (Van Schuur and Post 1990, 1). The analysis is oriented at identifying the one-dimensional arrangement of the stimuli that better reproduces subjects' preferences.

Starting with the distribution of the individual preferences, the scaling technique will assess whether a single order of stimuli common to all respondents exist. In our case, the preferences are the parties that a voter is willing to vote for, indicated by both the response "I will vote for it" and the response "I might vote for it."

We begin by investigating the scalability of the parties along a unidimensional order. Scalability is a measure of the level of intersubjectivity in a sequence of preferences, i.e., a measure of the extent to which the preferences expressed by each respondent are compatible with a hypothetical general order of the parties. The more a given order is shared by the respondents, the more each individual's hierarchy of party preference will be in agreement with it. If we assume one correct ordering, only a certain number of sequences of responses are permitted, while the others are considered as erroneous. For example, if three parties are in the sequential order ABC, an individual who says that he/she might vote for A and C should also declare that he/she might vote for B; if that does not happen, it means that the judgment she has expressed does not conform the hypothetical order's underlying judgment criteria and therefore her response is counted as an error (Schadee 1995, 93–94). Any order, then, can be broken down into the sequence of triplets that composes it, and the number of errors is calculated with respect to every triplet.

The strength of an order—aka its scalability—will be measured using Loevinger's H coefficient. This index of scalability is a function of the number of observed errors over the number of predicted errors, where the latter is calculated on the basis of a model of independence (i.e., according to a model that takes account exclusively of the different marginal distribution of the objects).[2] The H coefficient equals 1 when the data perfectly reproduce an unfolding scale, while it is 0 when the data are statistically independent.

An analogous coefficient can be calculated both for each subject and for each of the stimuli (Post 1992). In short, the scalability of the responses is indicative of the existence of an intersubjective judgment criterion, while the actual order that arises out of the scaling procedure gives us information about the content of that criterion. Scaling the voting predispositions for each voter type will enable us to compare both the orders obtained and their general scalability, the latter being a measure of the consistency of the order within the type considered.[3]

---

2. The scalability coefficient H is calculated as:

$$H = 1 - (\text{observed errors}/\text{predicted errors})$$

And is based on the sum of the observed errors and the sum of the expected errors—calculated on the basis of a hypothesis of independence—for each of the triplets that make up the scale (Van Schuur and Post 1990, 12). For further information on the multiple unidimensional unfolding method and its implementation, see also Post (1992).

3. The program MUDFOLD has been used to implement the multiple unidimensional unfolding analysis (see van Schuur and Post, 1990).

In particular, we hypothesize that the *utilius* and *amicus* voters will have a certain consistency in their criteria for judging and selecting parties, consistent with their strategies of choice: the criterion of spatial proximity for *utilius* voters and that of the contraposition of coalitions for *amicus* voters. It is natural to expect *utilius* to order the parties using the left-right axis, while *amicus*, given that their decision-making strategy focuses principally on the coalition, might be expected to have some minor inversions vis-à-vis the left-right continuum when they sequence the parties, retaining a clear distinction, however, between the parties of the center-left coalition and those of the center-right coalition. When it comes to *aliens* and *medians*, on the other hand, we cannot automatically assume that the way they order parties will conform to the categories of left and right. We hypothesize, in fact, that the index of scalability will be much lower than for either *utilius* or *amicus*, especially in the case of *aliens* voters.

The first important result is, without doubt, the existence of a single order common to all the types considered and that this order includes the entire set of parties, with only one exception, the Lista Bonino, a libertarian party with an anticlerical agenda, which has been particularly active on humanitarian and civil rights issues, such as abortion, divorce, euthanasia, and the legalization of soft drugs. The sequence is as follows:

CI RC DS Verdi Demo PPI CDU CCD FI AN LN

The sequence clearly reproduces the left-right continuum. What is striking is the clarity with which this criterion for organizing preferences emerges not just among *utilius* and *amicus* voters but also among *medians* and *aliens* voters. It is important to underline, moreover, that the question about future voting propensity did not in itself contain any reference to the categories of left and right.

There are, however, two peculiarities that need to be addressed: the placement of the Comunisti Italiani (CI) in the extreme left position and the exclusion of the Lista Bonino. Namely, the sequence

CI-RC-DS needs to be explained because Rifondazione Comunista (RC), not CI, is usually placed at the extreme left of the order. This inversion can be explained by the fact that RC voters are quite unwilling to vote CI. Both RC voters and CI voters have a propensity to vote for the DS, but while CI voters are prepared to vote RC, allowing for the sequence CI-RC-DS, a large number of RC voters are not willing to vote CI, even though they would consider the possibility of voting for the DS. This apparent contradiction is due to the fact that the CI originated from a prior split in RC, and RC voters still retain a kind of bitterness toward the CI and its "betrayal."

The second peculiarity is the exclusion of the Lista Bonino. It would be possible to introduce this party into the order in a central position only by excluding the CCD and the CDU from the sequence. This is an interesting indicator of the state of reciprocal mutual preclusion that exists between the positions of Catholic conservatism and liberalism. Since both could reasonably be located in the center, it is inevitable that the presence of one excludes the other and vice versa.

Let us now consider the differences between the types in detail. The various types differ, first, in terms of the number of preferences expressed, and, second, in the consistency of the ordering. Both results clearly support our hypothesis that judgment heuristics are used systematically. Let us first consider the number of preferences expressed. The question is structured so that each respondent is free to indicate more than one party—even all the parties—to choose only one, or not to choose any at all. Now, about a third of *aliens* voters do not identify even one party toward which they think that they might direct their future vote, while another 16 percent indicate just one party. These voters reject politics and seek it out as little as possible. By contrast, only a quarter of *utilius* voters limit their preferences to a single party, while about 10 percent of *amicus* and *medians* voters choose a single party or none at all. This is an important indicator of the modes of evaluation involved in the decision-making process. *Aliens* voters adopt a "minimalist" approach to the problem of voting choice, both by postponing the choice and by maximally reducing the range of possible options. By contrast, *utilius, amicus,* and *medians* voters all usually have more than one preference. This confirms the validity of our initial definition of voting as actual choice and not just a simple expression of identity, membership, or mere habit.

These observations about the number of options the respondents indicated play a preliminary role in defining the pool of respondents that are actually considered in the unfolding analysis. We consider only those respondents who indicate at least two parties, since those who express none or a sole preference do not provide any information about the ordering of the parties. In fact, by definition these voters do not commit any error and as a consequence, if they were introduced into the analysis, they would inflate the scalability coefficients. Moreover, we are still interested in the manner of organizing the preferences and not in the individual preferences in themselves.

Given these premises, the scalability coefficient H can be considered a measure of the degree of agreement between the respondents. Normally, an H value between 0.3 and 0.4 is an indication of limited scalability, while values higher than 0.5 indicate a consistency among the obtained ordering that should be considered quite significant. Table 6.2 illustrates both the scalability coefficients of the individual parties and the coefficient for the entire scale.

For *utilius* and *amicus* the H value for the entire scale is surprisingly high (0.8). Almost 80 percent of the voting propensities expressed by *utilius* and *amicus* voters are perfectly reproducible from the order. In particular, this means that those who declare that they are willing to vote for two parties (for example, RC and Democratici) are also disposed to vote for the parties situated between them (DS and Verdi) with a frequency greater than what would occur by chance, obviously taking into account the marginal distribution of preferences. The preferences expressed by *utilius* and *amicus* voters, then, can clearly be traced back to the categories

TABLE 6.2 Ideological coherence in voting preferences. Results from the multiple unidimensional unfolding analysis of voting predispositions. Scalability coefficients H for the entire scale and each individual party.

	Scale	*CI*	*RC*	*DS*	*Ver*	*Dem*	*PPI*	*Cdu*	*Ccd*	*FI*	*AN*	*LN*	*N*
Utilius	**.78**	.84	.75	.81	.71	.76	.76	.76	.78	.81	.80	.76	275
Amicus	**.77**	.79	.75	.77	.69	.73	.74	.79	.80	.81	.84	.80	549
Aliens	**.33**	.41	.33	.34	.25	.31	.32	.33	.38	.32	.34	.27	456
Medians	**.51**	.65	.54	.52	.44	.49	.50	.50	.55	.51	.53	.37	1267
All	**.58**	.67	.57	.58	.50	.55	.56	.57	.61	.58	.60	.55	2547

Source: Itanes 2001.

of left and right or, at the very least, to a principle of ideological proximity.

By contrast, for *aliens* voters the H coefficient is only 0.3 and for *medians* voters 0.5. Once again, the *aliens* voter stands out for the limited organization of his opinions. In fact, half of *aliens* voters either do not declare any preference or indicate only one possible party, while for those who do indicate at least two parties, it is very difficult to understand the criteria according to which these choices come about. The results in Table 6.2 confirm the ideological coherence of *utilius* and *amicus* as well as the fickleness of *aliens*, while the level of scalability of the individual parties is more or less homogenous within each type.

Univocal Evaluations of Governmental Capacity

Up until this point, we have pointed out how the categories of left and right constitute a valid yardstick in a variety of contexts not only for *utilius*, but also for *amicus* and *medians* voters. The absence of these two ideological categories, moreover, has been seen to be just as systematic in *aliens* voters. No evidence has yet been furnished, however, in relation to a systematic application of the *amicus/hostis* judgment criterion, apart from—obviously enough—our analysis of voters' judgments on political leaders from which it derives. Similarly, we do not have any independent verification of the fact that the *aliens* voter systematically despises politics and avoids it as much as possible, besides the fact that he clearly does not rely on ideological categories. To this end, we now consider the evaluations that voters make of the governmental capacities of the two competing coalitions. The 2001 Itanes survey asked:

> I would like to know who in your opinion is able to deal with the following problems better: a center-left government or a center-right government? (Itanes 2001)

This question was followed by a set of nine items related to the management of the health-care system, legal system, public administration, and relations with Europe, and to themes such as immigration, primary and secondary education, taxation, unemployment, and crime. Each of these items was accompanied by the following response options: "a center-left government," "a center-right government," "no difference between the coalitions," and "no government is able to resolve it."

In general, these questions are designed to ascertain the respondent's opinion about the capacity of the two coalitions to take positive action, i.e., the ability of each of the two line-ups to confront each particular problem and their capacity to resolve it. Thus, the respondent is not asked to express an opinion on the salience of the problems but rather on which of the two coalitions could make a more effective contribution to resolving them. Some of these are *position* issues, namely those with respect to which the two coalitions have different agendas and intend to pursue alternative policies, while others are *valence* issues, those for which the coalitions have the same goals, but might be perceived of as more or less capable of actually achieving them. The respondents' opinions are influenced in part by their own political orientation—indeed it could hardly be otherwise—but are at the same time also based on the perceived efficacy of the coalitions on specific issues. In fact, as shown in Table 6.3, the judgments in favor of a center-left government or center-right government are distributed differently depending on the issue considered. In 2001 the center-right alliance was expected to do better, on average, than the center-left alliance on each of the nine issues, though with important variations. On issues such as immigration and the fight against crime,

TABLE 6.3 Distribution of judgements on the governmental capacity of the center-left and center right coalitions. Percentage values (3,187 ≤ N ≤ 3,193).

	Center-right coalition	Center-left coalition	No difference/no coalition can solve the problem	Total
Immigration	44.3	18.8	36.9	100%
Crime	43.0	16.5	40.5	100%
Unemployment	39.1	22.9	38.0	100%
Public administration	39.1	18.2	42.7	100%
Justice system	37.1	22.9	40.0	100%
Taxation	36.3	24.4	39.3	100%
Education	34.4	23.3	42.2	100%
Healthcare	33.9	24.4	41.7	100%
Relations with EU	31.9	24.1	44.0	100%
Mean	37.7	21.7	40.6	100%

Source: Itanes 2001.

more than 40 percent of respondents thought that a center-right government would have been better able to deal with such problems—confirming, by the way, the well-known argument about issue ownership—while only a third of voters thought that a center-right government would have been better able to manage relations with Europe and guarantee an effective health-care service.

Our focus, however, is not on specific responses to single issues, but on how systematically respondents perceive the future performance of the two coalitions. Having established that there are differences, in aggregate terms, in the ways in which voters judge the efficacy of the coalitions' governmental action, it is reasonable to expect differences in the way in which they formulate such judgments.

The *amicus* voter is characterized by a simplified vision of politics in which her decision making focuses on the two alternative coalitions. Given such a perspective, it is reasonable to expect that this type of voter will show a higher degree of coherence in evaluating the coalitions' future performance, and judging them independently of the particular issues. The *amicus* voter's heuristic, because it emphasizes both her closeness to her own coalition and her antipathy toward its opponent, should lead her to express judgments about governmental capacity that are invariably in support of the same coalition regardless of the issue. Indeed, the distribution of respondents who always indicate that a single coalition will be best able to confront all nine problems varies across the voter types. While more than half of *amicus* voters[4] were completely in support of the same coalition (52 percent), little more than a third of *utilius* voters, only 15 percent of *aliens* voters, and 27 percent of medians voters made such one-sided judgments about the governmental capacities of the coalitions (Table 6.4).

---

4. In this analysis the category *amicus* includes all the respondents who satisfy the *amicus/hostis* judgment criterion, thereby including a component of respondents usually categorized as belonging to the *utilius* type.

TABLE 6.4 Coherence in coalitional preferences. Distribution of respondents according to the level of homogeneity in their evaluations of future governmental performance. Percentage values.

	Only Utilius	*Amicus +*	*Aliens*	*Medians*	*All*
9/9 preferences for the same coalition	37.2	**51.6**	14.8	27.0	29.9
9/9 no difference or no coalition can solve problem	3.4	4.6	**24.0**	10.5	12.4
Other combination of responses	59.4	43.8	61.2	62.5	57.7
Total	100%	100%	100%	100%	100%
N	145	752	880	1432	3209

Source: Itanes (2001)

We can conclude, then, that the *amicus/hostis* judgment criterion is generally applied systematically in evaluation tasks that involve the coalitions. The observation is clear: *amicus* voters conceive of governmental capacity as a monolithic talent inherent exclusively to one coalition or the other. This leads them to make a single judgment enveloping all of the issues instead of a set of judgments each separately formulated on particular issues. Just as there was no room to evaluate every single individual when judging leaders, here, too, the problems in themselves receive no attention. What counts is the coalition.

The *aliens* voter, by contrast, is expected to be quite skeptical toward the future performance of both coalitions and to show very little hope that politics can actually solve the problems of the country. Indeed, this expectation is confirmed by our analysis of how systematic the *aliens* evaluations of government performance are (Table 6.4). A surprising one-fourth of *aliens* voters respond to all nine questions saying that there is no difference between coalitions or that no government can actually solve these problems. This figure is much lower among *utlilius* and *amicus* (around 4 percent), and in the entire sample (12 percent). This confirms our intuition that the *aliens* voter is not simply less interested in politics, but in fact has no trust in the political system and no hope that politics will bring anything positive to himself or the country. The cynic realism with which one in four *aliens* systematically respond to our questions on the future performance of the government is a clear sign that a refusal of all-things-political organizes their belief system. In this sense, and in this sense only, the *aliens* voter does in fact show a good deal of coherence.

The Effectiveness of the Voting Typology

In the preceding sections, we offered some evidence of the systematic use of decision-making strategies. Voters use the same cognitive shortcuts every time there is a need and opportunity to do so. It is possible, however, to object that the high degree of coherence in *utilius* and *amicus* voters' responses, just like the ideological inconsistency in those of *aliens*, is simply a product of different levels of political sophistication. In other words, it has not yet been demonstrated that ideological or coalitional coherence is actually attributable to the use of heuristics themselves instead of simply higher levels of cognitive sophistication. Indeed, as we know, the various types of voters have different levels of political sophistication and it is therefore necessary to consider the possibility that it is the level of education and interest in politics as opposed to the heuristics themselves that produce such consistently organized opinions. We focus here on education and interest in politics because, as emerged from the analysis in Chapter 5, they are the most effective and stable indicators of cognitive sophistication.

If ideological coherence on policy issues and preference organization based on left-right axis were functions only of educational attainment or interest in politics, individuals with high levels of political sophistication would have the highest levels of coherence, while those with limited education and little interest in politics would have the lowest. If the level of sophistication, not the heuristic, determined the consistency of responses, the differences between more and less sophisticated voters would be much starker than the differences between heuristic types. A similar argument can be made for the systematic evaluation of the coalitions' expected performance. High levels of education and political interest might explain the systematic consistency of the *amicus* voter's judgments, while low education and scarce interest in politics might drive the pessimism or apathy of the *aliens* voters.

In general, our analysis confirms that policy preferences and future voting preferences are indeed more coherently organized among individuals with high levels of education and political interest. Similarly, mistrust in coalitions is more likely to emerge among less educated and interested voters, while systematic reliance on the same coalition is higher among more interested voters. However, as we shall see, our classification based on the actual decision-making strategies is more effective than the traditional measures of political sophistication in distinguishing between respondents on all four indicators of coherence that we have identified. This result is an important piece of evidence in support of the effectiveness of our proposed typology and of the principles of heuristic reasoning that have inspired it. But let us examine the results in detail.

First, we consider the level of ideological coherence as measured by the correlation between issue position and self-placement on the left-right continuum (Figure 6.1). As expected, the correlation coefficients are higher among more sophisticated respondents. For the noninterested, the estimate of the coefficient (Model 1) is 0.40; for

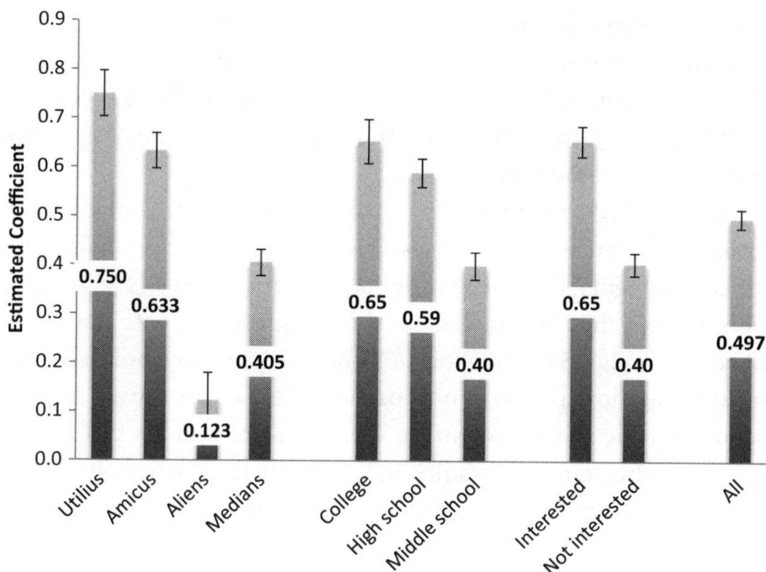

FIGURE 6.1 Ideological coherence in issue preferences. Estimated coefficients for the relationship between self-placement on the left-right continuum and issue preferences by type of decision making, education, and interest in politics.

Source: Itanes 2001.

the interested, on the other hand, it is 0.65. The same pattern exists for levels of education, with increasingly higher values of 0.40, 0.59, and 0.65. However, the range of these values is not any wider than the one between *utilius* and *amicus,* on the one hand, and *aliens,* on the other. On the contrary, the differences captured by the measures of sophistication are less pronounced than those that the typological division reveals. Recall that the correlation coefficient was 0.75 for *utilius* voters, 0.63 for *amicus* voters, 0.41 for *medians* voters, and 0.12 for *aliens* voters.

A very similar result is obtained when we consider the coherence with which future voting preferences are organized. Scaling future voting preferences for different levels of education and interest in politics, we find that in this case too the data confirms the existence of a single order of voting predispositions common to all the categories considered. Moreover, the parties are rank ordered according to the left-right continuum and the sequence is analogous to that obtained in our previous analysis.

As expected, with increasing levels of education and interest, the level of coherence also increases. The gaps between the coefficients for each category, however, are not particularly marked (Figure 6.2). For example, the H coefficient for those respondents with low levels of education is 0.54, while it is 0.71 for college degree holders. This means that more than half of those who hold at the most a middle school certificate express future voting choice options that correspond to the standard/traditional order of the parties, while for college graduates the corresponding proportion is about two thirds.

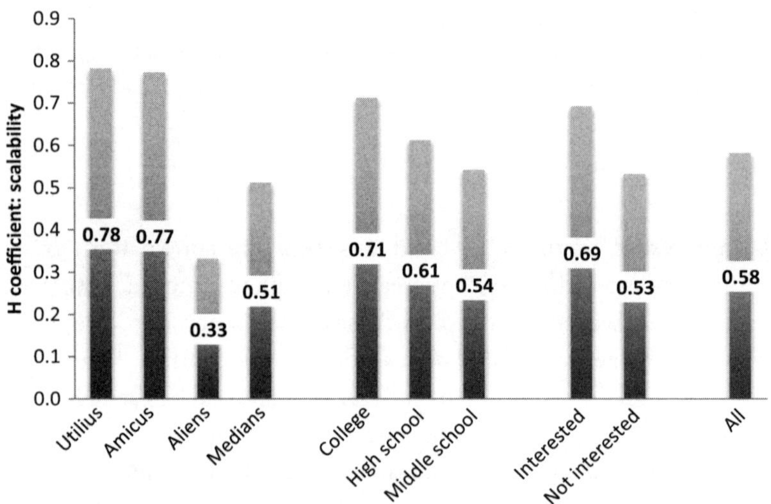

FIGURE 6.2 Ideological coherence in voting preferences. Coefficient H for the scalability of future party choices by type of decision making, education, and interest in politics.

Source: Itanes 2001.

The difference between the noninterested and the interested is roughly the same.

More importantly, we find no support for the hypothesis that more educated and more interested voters have levels of coherence superior to those who use the *utilius* and *amicus* heuristics. In fact, the H coefficient for the most highly educated and the interested is lower than for *utilius* and *amicus*: 0.71 as opposed to 0.78 for *utilius* and 0.77 for *amicus*; and at the same time, the value of 0.33 that we found for *aliens* voters is the lowest of all. There is little use trying to weigh the significance of a difference of 0.1 in the scalability coefficient; the crucial point is that high levels of education or interest are not in themselves sufficient for attaining the level of coherence shown by *utilius* and *amicus*.

In general, *utilius* and *amicus* show a coherence in organizing their opinions on the issues that is higher than that of both *aliens* voters and the sample as a whole. They also systematically organize their future voting intentions more than do the other voters. As we have seen, this fact cannot be attributed simply to these voters' higher level of political sophistication. High levels of education and interest certainly facilitate the formation of coherent opinions as well as voting preferences consistent with a standard order of the parties on the left-right axis, but *utilius* and *amicus* voters are characterized by a higher level of coherence than that observed among the most sophisticated individuals while, conversely, *aliens* voters are less coherent than the least sophisticated.

The importance of this finding should be appreciated in light of the fact that the categories of *utilius* and *amicus* comprise a large part of the sample, and most of the people in these categories do not have high school or college diplomas. Similarly, *utilius* and *amicus* voters do not necessary have a lot of interest in politics. However, by relying on simplifying decision-making strategies, they manage to achieve levels of coherence in the organization of their political preferences that are similar or even superior to those of the most educated and interested part of the population.

A similar argument can be made when comparing *amicus* voters' level of coalitional coherence of and *aliens* voters' systematic mistrust of future governments to those of voters with high and low levels of political cognition, respectively. Figure 6.3 graphs the proportion of voters who name the same coalition as better able to solve all of the nine policy problems about which they were asked. While educational attainment does not differentiate respondents, interest in politics does: 41 percent of people interested in politics express systematic support for either one or the other coalition, whereas only 21 percent of those who are not interested in politics show the same level of coalitional coherence. However, this figure is 52 percent among *amicus* voters, and, on the other hand, only 15 percent among *aliens*. The *amicus/hostis* logic is therefore successfully applied by *amicus* voters more effectively than the most politically sophisticated voter.

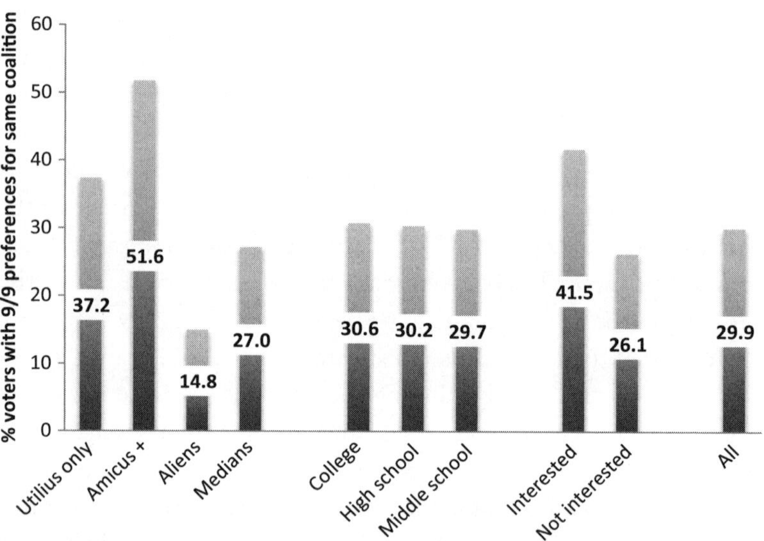

FIGURE 6.3 Coalitional coherence. Proportion of voters who expect a better the same coalition on all nine issues by type of decision making, education, and interest in politics.

Source: Itanes 2001.

Finally, Figure 6.4 supports our claim that *aliens'* negative take on politics is indeed more pronounced than that of the less interested or educated citizens. The proportion of voters who see no differences between the coalitions on all nine issues, or have no hope that any coalition can solve any problem is 14 percent among those who have only a middle school degree, or are not interested in politics. The figure for *aliens* voter is 10 percent higher.

If we define the validity of a decision-making strategy as its capacity to organize the political belief system in a way that will lead to a satisficing choice, and if we assume that ideological or coalitional coherence are valid indicators of a political judgment's cogency, we

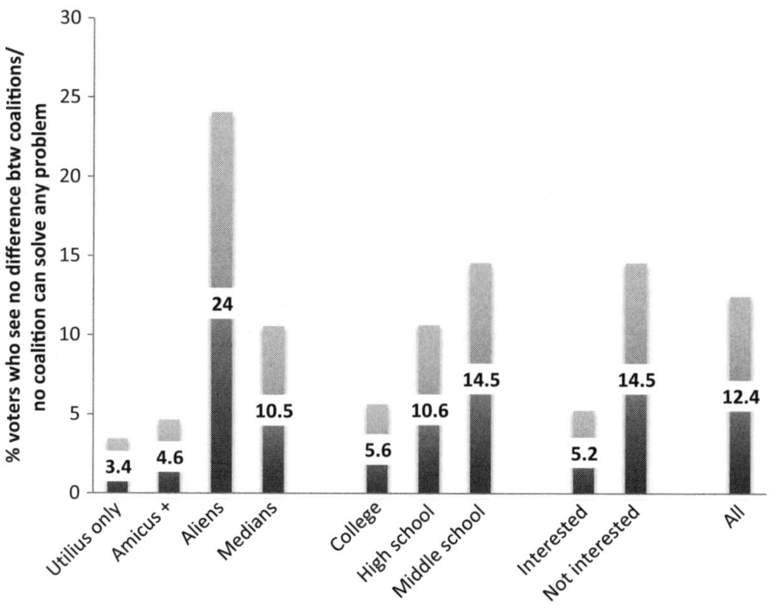

FIGURE 6.4 Coalitional mistrust. Proportion of voters who see no differences between the coalitions on all nine issues, or have no hope any coalition can solve any problem by type of decision making, education, and interest in politics.

Source: Itanes 2001.

can conclude that effective decision making is not exclusively tied to educational attainment or interest in politics. The effectiveness of *utilius* and *amicus* decision-making strategies, coupled with the extremely poor ideological performance of *aliens'*, make sense if we assume that these types of voters rely on decision-making shortcuts—heuristics—that inform how they structure their preferences in significantly different ways.

The division of voters into the *utilius*, *amicus*, and *aliens* types captures "something more" than just sophistication. The heuristics employed by the *utilius* and *amicus* types give them a "competitive advantage" in the appropriate use of the left-right criterion for party choice, while the *aliens* type, which expressly rejects the decision-making mechanisms employed by *utilius* and *amicus*, is much less capable of using the same criterion to organize the parties and his own opinions on the issues, even compared to the least educated and interested voters. However, even the *aliens* voter is not bereft of an organizing principle. He seems to be guided by a cynic realism, or pessimism, that systematically comes into play when he is required to evaluate political objects.

Up until now we have spoken of heuristics "in the plural," implicitly assuming that the cognitive shortcuts of *utilius*, *amicus*, and *aliens* are different. In the next chapter, we will provide additional evidence to support this claim.

Chapter 7

Heterogeneity of the Decision-Making Processes

Either people use decision-making heuristics, or they do not. In this chapter we ask whether the *utilius, amicus,* and *aliens* forms of political reasoning have a continuous or discrete nature: is the left-right dimension, for example, a conceptualization accessible to all citizens, albeit with different levels of detail, or are there some citizens who know its coordinates and others who do not? And what about the *amicus/hostis* logic? Finally, does a rejection of politics necessarily mean a rejection of all its conceptual categories, or is it possible to be mistrustful of politics and yet at the same time still use conventional "yardsticks of evaluation" when judging it? While the traditional *modus operandi* of most studies of political sophistication tend to quantify the level of coherence along a continuum, an approach based on heuristic decision-making processes should lead to a categorical differentiation of the respondents.

Asserting that the forms of reasoning in question are discrete means affirming that individuals were divided by these decision-making strategies in reality even before they were identified by the researcher's analysis. In other words, the classification in question is not based on arbitrary "cuts," dividing up a continuous spectrum for the sake of having convenient divisions; rather, it aims to capture natural divisions inherent in the population. This position dismisses any notion of the typology as an ideal type, i.e., a conceptual construct "in which reality has to be subsumed as an example" (Weber 1904, 112), and instead invites an interpretation of the types as natural kinds, not analytical types (Duprè 1993).

The empirical analysis presented in this chapter will not provide a definite answer to the quasi-philosophical question of whether the distinction between *utilius, amicus,* or *aliens* voters pertains to reality or is instead simply the byproduct of an analytical effort. However, in this chapter we will move one step in this direction, examining more deeply the nature of the decision-making strategies of the various types and providing further evidence of their heterogeneity. Proving the actual heterogeneity of the types is rendered very difficult, first of all, by the nature of the data at our disposal. As discussed in Chapter 4, survey data do not allow for a careful mapping of information processing, but give us only a static snapshot of respondents' political views. Given this constraint, we will rely on two types of empirical evidence: (a) the organization of choice elements and how they map into the actual voting decision, and (b) the extent to which certain decision-making criteria, such as the *amicus/hostis* logic, are distributed across the population, albeit with different concentration, or are instead part of the cognitive baggage of only a portion of the population, and completely absent among others.

The Organization of the Elements of Choice

A decision-making process is, in essence, comprised of the way in which information is gathered and opinions are formed, and moreover, how they come together to identify one particular option amongst a set of other possibilities. To explain how a choice is made, then, it is not sufficient to consider just its outcome—in our case the party that a given person votes for. Instead, it is necessary to take into account the elements of choice that are very close to the choice itself, such as information, opinions, and beliefs, and the way in which these exert influence on the decision-making process and are in their turn conditioned by it. Although we cannot trace the processes of information gathering and opinion formation used by the Italian voters in the context of the 1996 and 2001 general election campaigns, it is nonetheless possible to rely on the snapshot depicted by our surveys, and look at how, at the end of the political campaign, our respondents organized various elements of choice.

By elements of choice we mean those factors, quite proximate to voting behavior, that are likely to have had an important role in defining people's choices. Namely, we rely on three elements that have great predictive capacity vis-à-vis the voting behavior of Italian citizens: self-placement of the left-right ideological continuum, evaluation of the two PM candidates, and the television broadcaster most watched by the voter. The latter element of choice is easily explained. In Italy, two television networks have 95 percent of the of audience share: the public service RAI, and Berlusconi's commercial network, Mediaset. Unsurprisingly, one of the stronger predictors of voting behavior is which television network respondents watch (Diamanti and Mannheimer 1994; Pisati 2000; Sani 2001; Ricolfi 1994).

We are not interested, however, in dealing with the relationship, often obvious, between each of these factors and a voter's actual choice. To affirm that a positive evaluation of Silvio Berlusconi is strongly correlated with a vote for the Casa delle Libertà or that 90 percent of those who place themselves on the left side of the political spectrum vote for the Ulivo certainly has great significance from a statistical point of view but is of little substantive interest. Moreover, these factors are often intertwined in a tangle of causal relations that are difficult to tease out. Each one can be considered at once a cause and a consequence.

The goal of investigating the relationship between elements of choice and voting behavior is to test whether voters make use of certain political objects and overlook others according to the cognitive shortcuts they use, with the result that the interdependence between elements of choice varies depending on the type of voter. We expect that both the composition of the various elements of choice and their relationship with voting behavior depend on the type of voter. In addition, we also expect that the interdependencies between elements of choice will be the same in both election years considered. This latter hypothesis tests the overall consistency of the heuristics, but it is important to notice that it does not test whether the behavior of individuals is stable over time, i.e., whether individual voters always use the same heuristic or rather change from one election to the next.

In order to study the interdependence between elements of choice we use log-linear models. Particularly suitable for the multivariate analysis of contingency tables (Agresti 1990; Corbetta 1992), these models make it possible to represent the structure of relationships among multiple categorical variables at an adequate level of complexity, selecting only the interactions necessary to reproduce the frequency distributions of the contingency table. The purpose of the exercise is to study the interdependencies between the variables under observation, making no distinction in this case between dependent and independent variables.

If there is no relationship between the variables, the log-linear model that best fits the data will be a model of independence that takes into account only the marginal distribution of each variable. In standard notation, this model is represented as the sum of all the variables. Any type of actual association, on the other hand—be it two-way, three-way or of a higher order—is expressed in the model by way of a multiplication sign (*) between the variables (Wilkinson and Rogers 1973).

In this analysis we consider the interdependencies between six variables: **V**oting behavior (Ulivo; Polo / Casa delle Libertà), **T**ype (*utilius; amicus; aliens*),[1] **Y**ear (1996; 2001) and three elements of choice, which capture the variegated nature of the elements that mostly contribute to the construction of Italian voters' image of the world of politics: (1) a long-term factor, **S**elf-placement[2] along the ideological

---

1. In some interactions the variable Type takes on a reduced, dichotomous form: T2 (*utilius; amicus + aliens*).

2. In some interactions the variable Self-placement takes on a reduced, dichotomous form: S2 (left; right + center).

continuum (left; right; center; or not collocated), (2) a short-term feature of the competition, the evaluation of the two PM **C**andidates[3] (comparison in favor of Berlusconi; comparison in favor of Prodi/ Rutelli; balanced comparison); and (3) mass media consumption, voter's preferred TV network **B**roadcaster (Mediaset; RAI + other).

The log-linear modeling strategy will serve two purposes. First of all, we will investigate the results of a general model in which we consider simultaneously all the possible associations between variables for all the types and both years. This model, although extremely complicated, provides useful hints concerning the relative weight of different elements of judgment and a convincing confirmation of the stability of our classifications over time. Second, we will investigate the results of three different models, one for each type, to get a better sense of their peculiarities. This latter analysis will confirm the existence of profound differences between *utilius* and *amicus* voters on the one hand, and *aliens* voters on the other and will lead to an interesting finding concerning the effect of television broadcast network on *aliens* voters.

To avoid getting distracted by a long discussion of the details of selecting the model, let us pass on immediately to its substantive significance (Table 7.1 provides all the necessary information for the selection of the best general log-linear model for interested readers).

The general log-linear model that best reproduces the interdependencies between the elements of choice for all the types and both years is the following (5.a in Table 7.1):

$$\mu + Y + T + S + C + B + V + S^*P + S^*B + C^*B + T^*V^*$$
$$(S + C + B) + Y^*V^*(S2 + C2) + Y^*T2^*(S + C2 + B + V)^4$$

and is made up of:

3. In some interactions the variable Candidates takes on a reduced, dichotomous form: C2 (comparison in favor of Berlusconi; comparison in favor of Prodi-Rutelli + balanced comparison)

4. In its extended form, the model is: $\mu + Y + T + C + P + B + V + C^*P + C^*B + P^*B + T^*C^*V + T^*P^*V + T^*B^*V + Y^*C2^*V + Y^*P2^*V + Y^*T2^*C + Y^*T2^*P2 + Y^*T2^*B + Y^*T2^*V$.

TABLE 7.1 General log-linear model: Year, Type, Self-placement, Candidates, Broadcaster, and Voting preference.

		χ^2	*df*	*p.*
M1) Model of independence	$\mu + Y + T + S + C + B + V$	6360.0	194	.000
M2) Margins * Year	$M1 + Y * (T + S + C + B + V)$	6026.0	186	.000
M3) Four-variable interactions	$M2 + Y * T * V * (S + C + B)$	158.8	134	.071
M4) Three-variable interactions	M3-Y. T. V. $(S + C + B)$	175.2	143	.035
M4a)–Interaction btw year, vote, and TV	M4-Y. B. V	175.3	144	.040
M4b) Type in dychotomous form	M4a + Y. T2. $(S + C + B + V)$	177.5	149	.055
M5) + Interactions between elements of choice	M4b + S * C + S * B + C * B	141.4	141	.475
M5a) Self-placement and leaders dychotomous	M5–Y.C2.(T2+S +B) +Y.V. S2	144.9	145	.487
M5b)–Interaction btw year TV and type	M5a–Y. B.T2	147.2	146	.457

Wilkinson and Rogers' notation (1973): (*) including lower order effects; and (.) = relating exclusively to higher order effects.

Source: Itanes (1996; 2001).

1. a constant (the μ parameter) that depends on the size of the sample;
2. estimates of the parameters for each individual variable;
3. all the possible two-variable associations between year, type, voting preference, and the three elements of choice;

4. all the three-variable associations that involve type, voting preference, and each element of choice (T*S*V, T*C*V, T*B*V)

5. the three-variable associations between year, voting preference, and self-placement (Y*S2*V) and year, voting preference, and candidates (Y*P2*V);

6. finally, the associations between year, type, and each of the elements of choice includes only the distinction between the *utilius* group and the other two groups (Y*T2*S, Y*T2*C2, Y*T2*B, Y*T2*V).

The presence of an association indicates that the variables in question combine in systematic ways not attributable to chance. For example, the interaction S*C suggests that ideological self-placement and evaluation of the PM candidates are linked: e.g., there are more people who combine a right-wing self-placement and positive evaluation of Berlusconi than expected by chance. Another example: the interaction between TV broadcaster and voting preference (B*V) testifies to the existence of a positive relationship between watching Mediaset TV channels and voting for the center-right coalition or, correspondingly, between watching RAI TV programs and voting for the center-left coalition. Obviously—and this is the advantage of using log-linear modeling—these effects are net of any other factor considered in the model.

There are two major findings from this model that should be highlighted. The first is that each element of choice occurs in a three-variable association with type and voting preference (T*S*V, T*C*V, T*B*V): voting preference invariably enters into the model in interaction with two other variables: each element of choice and the typology. This means that voting preference is associated with ideology, candidate evaluations, and the TV network, as is to be expected, but that this influence is systematically mediated by the decision-making strategy that the voters adopt. In fact, if an element of choice always influenced voting preference in the same way, this would be reproduced by a simple interaction between the element in question and voting preference. For example, the hypothesis that self-placement on the left-right dimension had a similar relationship with vote preference for each voter would be confirmed by the simple presence of an interaction between self-placement and voting preference (S*V). In contrast, all the choice factors enter into relation with voting behavior in a specific manner depending on the type of decision-making strategy involved. If indeed the elements of choice have a causal effect on voting behavior, we will conclude that voters differ from one another in terms of the effect of these factors on their choice, thus suggesting that our typology is capable of capturing the diverse array of effects.

The parameter estimates for the three-variable associations (Baldassarri 2002, Appendix Table 30) highlights a few interesting facts. There being in general a strong relationship between self-placement and voting preference, the estimated effect for the three-variable association T*C*V suggests that the relationship between self-placement and voting preference is much stronger for *utilius* voters than for *aliens* voters. This means, for example, that the relationship between being to the left and voting Ulivo is much stronger in members of the *utilius* category than it is in members of the *aliens* category. The intensity of the relationship also distinguishes *utilius* voters from *amicus* voters, albeit to a lesser extent.

The relationship between evaluation of the PM candidates and voting preference reveals a higher level of coherence in *amicus* than in *utilius* voters. So far, what emerges is entirely consistent with our description of the mechanisms of choice. *Utilius* stand out as voters who pay a great deal of attention to the use of ideology and therefore to positioning along the left-right axis. Likewise, *amicus* voters appear to make effective use of the dichotomous nature of the objects at their disposal: the candidates. *Aliens* voters, on the other hand, show the highest degree of incoherence both in the use of ideology and judgments on leadership, thereby remaining true to their image as voters who are inattentive, uninterested, and therefore hardly inclined to coordinate opinions, judgments, and voting behavior.

Viewed from a more causal perspective—which is, however, not completely justified given the nature of the data at our disposal— these results could also be read as a measure of the influence exerted by ideology, the PM candidates, and TV broadcasters on voters' choices. From this point of view, *utilius* voters, being more sophisticated, above all from a cognitive point of view, are principally susceptible to ideological messages, while *amicus* voters, whose sophistication is of a less cognitive and more affective nature, are more susceptible to the candidates' image. *Aliens* voters, on the other hand, being removed from politics and its forms of communication, are not easily reached by any type of message and are certainly less subject to the influences of ideology and leaders.

The second of our findings concerns the stability of the typology. The model fully corroborates our hypothesis that the association between voting behavior and the elements of choice will be essentially unaltered over two consecutive elections: the associations between type, elements of choice, and voting preference turn out to be the same in both the elections (T^*S^*V, T^*C^*V, T^*B^*V). This is also the case for the two-variable association between the components of the belief system (S^*C, S^*B, C^*B). In fact, the election year does not appear in any of these associations and this means that the way in which the type of heuristic conditions the relationship between elements of choice and voting preference does not significantly vary between the given years.

The fact that the division of voters into *utilius*, *amicus*, and *aliens* is reproducible in different years further legitimizes our classification. Given that what is at stake are decision-making strategies, it is particularly important to verify that the mechanisms identified recur stably and consistently over time and are not dictated exclusively by contingent factors. The only differences between the two elections are an increased coherence in the relationship between ideological self-placement and voting preference and between evaluation of the candidates and voting preference. Compared to 1996, in 2001, self-placement to the right or to the center increased the tendency to vote for the Casa delle Libertà just as, again in 2001, preferring Rutelli to Berlusconi further increased the probability of voting for the Ulivo.

Utilius, *amicus*, and *aliens* are different—this much is clear. We now need to understand *how* different they are and whether this difference is attributable exclusively to how coherently they structure their political beliefs or whether the differences are inherent to the very nature of the cognitive frameworks that guide their reasoning.

Utilius vs *Aliens*: Ideology *Versus* the "TV Remote" Effect

To determine more directly whether the differences between the types are merely a product of the strength and coherence with which given individuals arrange political objects or whether they actually indicate alternative modes of organizing various elements of choice themselves, we created a log-linear model for each of the types under consideration. This will allow us to capture their similarities and differences easily. In Table 7.2 we illustrate the models selected for the types *utilius*, *aliens*, and *medians*. We will focus in the rest of this section, however, on the differences between just two types, *utilius* and *aliens*. No reference will be made to *amicus* because the variables taken under consideration are, for this type of voter, so closely correlated that they render the estimate of the parameters unstable and highly unreliable. For example, of the *amicus* voters that vote Ulivo, as many as 80 percent place themselves to the left of the political spectrum, prefer Prodi or Rutelli to Berlusconi, and watch RAI TV network. The Polo/Casa delle Libertà electorate behaves in a similar way. This is obviously not a substantive problem; on the contrary, it is a further confirmation of the high level of consistency and congruity with which this type of voter structures his attitudes.

For the *utilius* category of voters, the interaction effects between five variables (voting preference, year, self-placement, PM candidates, and TV network broadcaster)[5] are the following:[6]

$$Y^*(C + V) + V^* (S + C) + S^*C + S^*B + C^*B$$

TABLE 7.2 Log-linear models by type: Year, Self-placement, Candidates, Broadcaster and Voting preference.

	Year	Self-placement —Candidates —Vote	TV Broadcast	$\chi2$	df	p
utilius	$Y^*(S + V)$	$S * C + S *$ $V + C * V$	$B * (S + C)$	49.4	49	.457
aliens	$Y^*(S * V$ $+ C * V)$	$S * C * V$	$B * V$	47.5	44	.332
medians[1]	$Y^*(S + C + B)$	$S * C + S *$ $V + C * V$	$B * C * V$	70.8	45	.008

1. *For the medians model, we needed to introduce a cell-specific parameter that models the combination of self-placement on the center, favor for Berlusconi, watch RAI TV network and vote for the center-right coalition. The alternative would have been a saturated model [Baldassarri, Schadee 2003, 30].*

Wilkinson and Rogers' notation (1973): (*) including lower order effects.

Source: Itanes (1996; 2001).

---

5. Here we use the same variables and methods that we used in the construction of the general model discussed above.

6. $X^2 = 49.4$; df = 49; p = 0.457.

First of all, it should be noted that the year of the elections appears in the model only in relation to candidate judgments and voting preference (Y*C, Y*V). The other factors remain exactly the same for both years, thereby confirming the *utilius* decision-making mechanism's high degree of consistency. There are two-way associations between elements of choice (S*C + S*B + C*B) but, in contrast to what was observed in the general model, there is no relationship between TV network and voting preference, suggesting that the *utilius* voter's choice is not directly influenced by his use of the media. Of course, even among *utilius* voters, those who watch Mediaset TV channels form a disproportionately large number of Polo/Casa delle Libertà voters and vice versa. However, in the *utilius* electorate in general, the relationship between voting preference and TV network is completely mediated by other factors. In keeping with the image of a particularly sophisticated voter, *utilius* does not base his voting choice directly on the messages emanating from the media. Rather, he chooses in accordance with his ideology and assessment of the leaders.

In stark contrast, let us now examine the interdependence between the same five variables for the *aliens* voter.[7] The log-linear model that best fits the data is the following:

$$Y^* V^* (S + C) + V^* S^* C2 + Y(V + S + C) V^* (S+C) + S^*C + V^* B$$

The contrast with the model of the *utilius* voter is striking. There are no particular analogies between the two types. Moreover, given the *aliens* model's high level of complexity, it makes no sense to try to undertake a systematic comparison between the two. In fact, the *aliens* voter type is characterized by procedures for organizing political notions that are quite confused. There must certainly be more than just one model of judgment involved here. The relationships between variables are so complex that in this study we cannot even

---

7. $X^2 = 47.5$; df = 44; p = 0.332.

hope to offer an adequate account of them, much less hazard an interpretation.

Amidst the substantial heterogeneity of the *aliens* voters, there is one meaningful association that stands out: the TV network broadcaster interacts with voting preference in the model, without any association with the other variables and without any variation by year. Thus, while the interdependence between ideology, evaluation of the candidates, and voting preference is fairly complex and strongly subject to contingent variations, the simple relationship between TV broadcaster and voting preference does distinguish and define the *aliens* voter, to an extent that makes us hypothesize a 'TV remote' effect. In fact, TV seems to be an autonomous instrument, capable of influencing voting choice on par with self-placement along the left-right axis or evaluation of the leaders. Thus, one could hypothesize that *aliens* voters use television as a cognitive and information-related shortcut that resolves voting choice, without necessarily requiring traditional political attitudes structured in a coherent manner. We are not simply claiming that exposure to the RAI or Fininvest news programs influences public opinion (Diamanti and Mannheimer 1994; Pisati 2000; ITANES 2001). What we are suggesting, rather, is that the relationship between TV and voting preference is direct, i.e., that it is not mediated by political attitudes. Our hypothesis, then, is that TV is an autonomous factor in explaining the electoral behavior of *aliens* voters.

To test for the actual presence of a "TV remote" effect among *aliens* voters, we ran multinomial logistic regression models with voting preference as the dependent variable (Ulivo; Polo/Casa delle Libertà; other), and as independent variables a set of political attitudes predictive of voting behavior: self-placement on the left-right axis (left; right; center or not collocated), evaluation of the prime-ministerial candidates (a mark from 1 to 10), measures of party[8] and

---

8. A continuous variable (1 – 4), based on the following question: "Among the various political parties is there one that you feel closer to than the others?" "Not close" "Sympathetic" "Fairly close" "Very close".

coalition[9] identification, opinions on a range of political and policy issues[10] and, finally, TV broadcaster (Mediaset; RAI or other).

This model, reproduced for both *utilius* voters and *aliens* voters as well as for the entire sample, confirms our expectations. Controlling for the influence of all the other factors listed above, the variable relating to TV broadcaster is significant ($p < 0.05$) in the category of *aliens* voters (and in the entire sample), thus suggesting that the TV network broadcaster is an autonomous explanatory factor in voting behavior on par with collocation, leaders, and issues for a substantial proportion of voters (*aliens*), though not at all for a sizeable portion of the rest (*utilius*).

This result confirms both the interpretation of "TV as an organizational resource that is an alternative to the party" (Segatti 1995, 172) and, in general, the importance of television in influencing voting choice (Sartori 1989), but it also adds an important specification about the type of voter that is susceptible to this form of influence. If the "TV remote" effect had been examined only for the entire sample, we would have completely overlooked key information about what characteristics distinguish voters who are actually influenced by television from those who are more discerning in their intake and use of the media. Television influences the voting decision, but not in the same way for all voters.

Thus, the distinction between *utilius* and *aliens* takes on substance. The *utilius* voter's decision-making process is influenced by ideological position, judgments on political leaders, and, to a lesser extent, the issues. Television does not play any major role in his decision-making process. This is not to say that he cannot be influenced by it. Rather, it simply means that any influence that the media

---

9. A continuous variable (0 -16 in the 1996 Itanes sample and 0–9 in the 2001 Itanes sample) based on the count of comparisons between leaders structured according to a coalition-oriented logic:

| # compariesons in favor of polo (CdL) − # compariesons in favor of Ulivo |

10. A score (1–10) based on opinion on political issues (see Chapter 6).

does exert is on the process of judgment and not directly on the choice itself. By contrast, while the *aliens* voter's choice is certainly conditioned—albeit to a lesser degree than the *utilius* voter's—by ideology and leader evaluations, his decision is primarily directly affected by the television network he watches. In sum, for *aliens* voters, the 'TV remote' effect acts independently of all other variables. It does not create coherence between political opinions and voting preference but rather imposes itself directly on the voting choice.

Although we have interpreted these results in causal terms, there remains the question of whether the selection of a TV channel is a deliberate choice or an everyday habit, and whether for some of these voters the causal arrow might actually go in the opposite direction. Many years ago, Phil Stark designed a TV remote for Thomson in the form of a scepter, inspired by the idea of a flow of power between viewer and television screen. Considerable uncertainty still remains, however, about in which direction this power might actually be flowing. Is power wielded by the armchair over the screen or is it the screen that influences the armchair and its occupant? In general, the question of the degree to which the use of the means of mass communication is truly voluntary or deliberate remains largely unanswered. However, from what we know about the two types of voter in question, it seems plausible to argue that, when it comes to political information, *utilius* (and *amicus*) voters might exercise more control over their television network choice, while *aliens* voters are more likely to absorb political information passively while they go about their everyday lives.

In this section, the different roles TV network broadcasts play has served to exemplify the marked differences between the *utilius* and *aliens* types, not only in their cognitive capacities or access to the means of ideological representation, but also in terms of how they actually organize the various elements of choice. The next section will provide similar evidence regarding *amicus* voters.

Amicus/Hostis: A Zero-Sum Game

We hypothesized that *utilius* and *amicus* are distinguished by two different judgment strategies: the criterion of spatial proximity and the *amicus/hostis* logic. The two types differ from one another in terms of a number of factors, both cognitive and motivational (Chapter 5), but, at the same time, they both show high levels of coherence in organizing their issue and future voting preferences according to the left-right ideological axis (Chapter 6). In general, both *utilius* and *amicus* voters can systematically organize a range of political objects in terms of left and right. This fact might lead to the hypothesis that the two types could in actual fact be reduced to the same judgment heuristic, i.e., that they are guided by a single mechanism of simplification.

How is it possible for us to argue, then, that *utilius* and *amicus* voters actually use fundamentally different cognitive shortcuts? The question can be posed in the following terms: *utilius* and *amicus* were originally identified by their different modes of representing political debate, even though the classification criteria used were not mutually exclusive. These two types were distinguished in a systematic manner from the rest of the electorate by both their sociodemographic profiles and their levels of political sophistication. They were also both found to use the categories of left and right. This form of ideological representation, however, was theorized as a heuristic only for one of the two, *utilius*, and so the fact that the categories of left and right are present in such a marked manner in *amicus* voters could give rise to the hypothesis that *amicus* are in fact guided by the same heuristic as *utilius* voters, with the *amicus/hostis* judgment criterion little more than another way of projecting the representation of political space onto the left-right axis.

It is fitting, then, for us now to investigate how widespread the use of the *amicus/hostis* judgment criterion is in each of the types. If this criterion were in fact present among *utilius* voters, although less prevalently than among *amicus* voters, the hypothesis of difference between *utilius* and *amicus* would be weakened, lending support to its alternative, i.e., that the two types in fact capture the same cognitive shortcut. If, on the other hand, the *amicus/hostis* evaluation criterion turns out to be a characteristic peculiar to *amicus* voters, it makes sense to argue that *utilius* and *amicus* use different heuristics. In the following analysis, then, we will investigate how prevalent the *amicus/hostis* criterion is among the different types, seeking to understand whether it can be regarded as a cognitive mechanism inherent exclusively to a specific subset of voters or a more widely used mode of evaluation.

To capture the uniqueness of each of the judgment shortcuts it is first of all necessary to overcome the problem of the nonexclusiveness of the categories we have considered up to now. As we know, about half of the voters classified in the *utilius* category also possess the characteristics of the *amicus* voter and, conversely, a substantial component of *amicus* voters are "potential" *utilius* voters (given that 30 percent of *amicus* voters in 1996 and 20 percent in 2001 show that they are capable of correctly ordering the parties even though they do not vote for the parties closest to themselves). In order to investigate the similarities and differences between these two groups with respect to the singular or multiple nature of their underlying decision-making mechanisms, we need to make a finer distinction, one that allows us to avoid any overlap between the two hypothesized heuristics.

In particular, let us distinguish within the *utilius* group those voters who are at one and the same time both *utilius* and *amicus*—we call these *utilius&amicus*—from those who are *utilius only*. Likewise, let us subdivide the *amicus* voters into those who are capable of correctly placing the parties along the left-right dimension but do not actually vote for the party closest to them, identifying them as "*amicus* potential *utilius*," or in shorthand *amicus~utilius*, and the rest, the *amicus only*.

To investigate how extensively present the *amicus/hostis* judgment strategy is, we analyze the way in which voters' evaluations of leaders are structured by considering the entire set of bivariate correlations of judgments on leaders. As we know from Chapter 4 (Tables 4.3 and 4.4), judgments on leaders are not distributed in a random manner, nor is each leader evaluated exclusively for himself or for the party that he represents. On the contrary, the coalition to which political leaders belong influences how they are assessed. This occurs among more than a quarter of voters systematically enough to have inspired the criterion for defining the *amicus* heuristic. But is this judgment criterion shared, albeit to a lesser degree, by the rest of the voters? To anticipate our main result, the analysis of bivariate correlations clearly demonstrates that the *amicus/hostis* style of judgment is confined to the *amicus* type of voters, and there is no trace of such a reasoning strategy among *utilius only*, *aliens*, or *medians* voters. To illustrate this, however, we must briefly discuss how correlation coefficients are computed, and, in particular, how the use of ipsative measures makes it possible to bypass the problem of respondents' systematic differences in the use of evaluation scales.

The analysis of correlation between responses is complicated by a few difficulties with the comparability of the responses. As is well known, the use of evaluation scales is subject to systematic differences between respondents as well as individual idiosyncrasies. In our case, these relate in particular to (a) the overall respect and esteem that individual respondents have for politicians in general, and, (b) how different respondents record their opinions on the same scale, i.e., the mark from 1 to 10.

The evaluations respondents make of leaders is, first of all, influenced by the level of esteem they have toward politics "as a profession," i.e., by the level of respect they have for the category of politicians as a whole. Respondents who consider politicians a dishonorable bunch will evaluate any leader negatively, possibly denying a passing mark to all party representatives. On the other hand, those who think that political activity is a worthy pursuit will be inclined to evaluate all politicians positively. But taking into account voters' general level of respect for politics does not have implications just for the average level of leader evaluation. It also has repercussions for the second element of differentiation between respondents, i.e., the use of the evaluation scale. In fact, both the voter who rejects politics and the citizen who has great faith in politicians end up using a limited section of the evaluation scale (for example, marks only from 1 to 5 or from 6 to 10). Consequently, the differences between the pairs of politicians are more limited than they would be for respondents who use the entire range of marks. Because the estimation of the coefficients draws on the cardinal character of the evaluations, these differences in judgment variance make it impossible to compare inter-individual judgments directly.

In order to eliminate the effects both of individuals' general level of respect for politics and of individual idiosyncrasies in the use of the evaluation scale, the evaluation of leaders is standardized for every individual respondent and the correlation coefficients are computed using these standardized variables. In other words, we "stretched" the judgment yardstick of those who only use a reduced range of the scale in order to make it comparable to that of those who have used the entire scale to express their opinions. In this way, it is possible to study the structure of respondents' judgments and to analyze the similarities and differences between the members of each particular type, freed from the distortions of individual idiosyncrasies.

Pearson's correlation coefficients provide information about the direction, indicated by the coefficient's sign, and strength, indicated by the coefficient's absolute value, of the relationships between each pair of leaders. A positive sign indicates that the two leaders tend to be judged similarly, whereas a negative sign points to inversely correlated judgments. The values go from -1 to 1: coefficients very close to 1 or -1 signify a strong correlation (positive or negative) between variables while values close to 0 indicate complete independence between the two judgments. For the *amicus/hostis* logic of judgment we should observe positive coefficients close to 1 in case of judgments on leaders within a coalition and negative coefficients close to -1 in judgments on leaders of opposing coalitions.

Table 7.3 shows the bivariate correlations with standardized variables for each pair of leaders. These correlations allow us to study the organization of the evaluations of three leaders of the

TABLE 7.3 Pearson's correlation coefficients of judgments on political leaders. Judgments are standardized at the individual level.

		Amato	D'Alema	Rutelli	Belusconi	Fini
Utilius &Amicus	D'Alema	.76				
Amicus ~ Utilius		.76				
Amicus only		.73				
Utilius only		.05				
Aliens		.09				
Medians		.04				
All		.30				
Utilius &Amicus	Rutelli	.81	.82			
Amicus ~ Utilius		.80	.76			
Amicus only		.76	.80			
Utilius only		.15	.25			
Aliens		.05	.15			
Medians		.02	.19			
All		.29	.42			
Utilius &Amicus	Berlusconi	-.85	-.88	-.90		
Amicus ~ Utilius		-.88	-.87	-.88		
Amicus only		-.84	-.87	-.89		
Utilius only		-.44	-.53	-.53		
Aliens		-.36	-.44	-.50		
Medians		-.39	-.49	-.46		
All		-.53	-.62	-.62		
Utilius &Amicus	Fini	-.82	-.87	-.89	.82	
Amicus ~ Utilius		-.81	-.81	-.83	.81	
Amicus only		-.79	-.85	-.86	.82	
Utilius only		-.40	-.28	-.43	.16	
Aliens		-.18	-.24	-.30	-.02	
Medians		-.24	-.35	-.45	.10	
All		-.42	-.52	-.58	.35	
Utilius &Amicus	Bossi	-.82	-.80	-.81	.74	.69
Amicus ~ Utilius		-.75	-.75	-.81	.72	.56
Amicus only		-.75	-.76	-.77	.68	.60
Utilius only		-.20	-.32	-.38	.03	-.08
Aliens		-.31	-.30	-.27	-.06	-.22
Medians		-.25	-.28	-.33	.02	-.10
All		-.40	-.40	-.43	.15	.06

Source: Itanes 2001.

Ulivo: Giuliano Amato, Massimo D'Alema, and Francesco Rutelli, and three of the Casa delle Libertà: Silvio Berlusconi, Gianfranco Fini, and Umberto Bossi. In this way, we can discover whether judgment based on coalition is a characteristic shared by all types of voters or whether it is peculiar to *amicus*. The result is easy to gauge. If the same judgment structure existed for all voters, we would observe the same parameter for each of the types. Running down the columns for each pair of leaders, it is immediately apparent that there are only a few substantive differences between the types in the direction of the correlations and very substantial differences in the value of the parameters and therefore in the strength of the correlations.

Let us now consider in particular how widespread the use of the *amicus/hostis* criterion is. This logic of judgment implies positive correlations between leaders of the same political alliance and, conversely, negative coefficients for members of opposing coalitions. Moreover, the absolute value of these coefficients should be high, in that the *amicus/hostis* process of evaluation tends to maximize both unity within the coalition and differences between the coalitions. This expectation is amply confirmed for voters who have the characteristics of *amicus*, i.e., the *utilius&amicus*, the *amicus ~ utilius*, and the *amicus only* voters. All of these groups have strong, positive coefficients for the correlations between leaders of the same coalition, while the coefficients are just as strong but negative for the correlations between opposing leaders. We can confirm, then, that these voters systematically judge leaders based on their coalition. Alongside a highly favorable evaluation for Rutelli there will likely be an analogous appreciation for D'Alema and Amato, just as a negative judgment of Berlusconi is tied to an analogous disapproval of Fini and Bossi and vice versa.

The magnitude (in absolute terms) of the correlation coefficient between opposing leaders gives us an additional piece of information. A unit increase in the value of the evaluation of Berlusconi leads to a practically equivalent reduction in the assessment of Rutelli. What we see is a zero-sum game between the coalitions. The *amicus* voter metes out a "limited quantity of esteem," which is fought over by the leaders of the two coalitions.

Thus, we can confirm our expectation that each type of *amicus* uses a marked *amicus/hostis* logic structure. This, however, is a result that to some extent is only to be expected given the criterion used to construct the *amicus* type. What is striking, instead, is the clear and unmistakable distinction between the *amicus* voters and all the other voter types. In fact, *utilius only* voters stand out for extremely low, almost nonexistent, correlation coefficients for evaluations of leaders of the same coalition. This means that the coalition does not influence the judgment expressed on its individual components, aka parties and leaders. A *utilius* voter's evaluation of D'Alema, for example, is independent of his judgment of Amato or Rutelli. The only correlations with any statistical significance are those comparing opposing leaders, but these are hardly of a strength comparable to those generated by *amicus* voters.

Utilius voters are therefore indifferent toward any consideration based on the coalitions, consistent with the image of a voter who moves within a logic that is prevalently party-oriented. The *utilius only* voters' evaluation of leaders is less structured and more independent than that of *amicus* voters both because they are free from coalition-based logics and because their focus is on an object, the party, that is an autonomous entity with a life on its own, and therefore less dependent on the image of the leader in itself. The evaluation of a leader is for *utilius* voters more a judgment *ad personam* and much less a founding element of their political identity. We therefore conclude that there is a substantial difference between how *amicus* and *utilius only* voters structure their evaluations of leaders.

Even more surprising is the fact that, when it comes to the use of the *amicus/hostis* judgment criterion, *utilius only* voters seem to organize their responses in a way analogous to *aliens* and *medians* voters'. In fact, the latter two also only have significant coefficients, though very weak, for correlations between opposing leaders, while the ties between political leaders of the same coalition are often nonexistent. *Utilius only* and *aliens* are therefore very similar in their noncoalitional organization of judgments, in stark contrast to the highly systematic nature of *amicus* voters' judgments.

In conclusion, the *amicus/hostis* judgment criterion, with its emphasis on the coalition-oriented nature of the competition, can be distinguished from criteria of judgment based solely on the categories of left and right, confirming our hypothesis that *utilius* and *amicus* use different heuristics. The key finding here is that the use of the left-right spatial criterion does not lead to an *amicus/hostis* organization of preferences. The heterogeneity of the evaluation processes becomes clear when we divide the types into sub-groups by using an analytical distinction capable of isolating and highlighting the particular characteristics of one or other of the hypothesized heuristics.

Types of voters: ideal or real?

We opened this chapter asking whether the *utilius, amicus*, and *aliens* forms of political reasoning have a continuous or discrete nature.

As far as the use of the ideological dimension is concerned, we have seen that many respondents, even among the *aliens* voters, tend to place themselves on the left-right continuum. These individuals differ, however, in their capacity to collocate the parties in the same ideological space (Chapter 4). The level of coherence between issue preferences and self-placement, on the other hand, is quite high, and in general, all the voter types follow a criterion of spatial proximity when organizing their voting predispositions for the future (Chapter 6). The representation of political space using the left-right axis, then, is very widespread and deeply rooted. This perspective serves to organize a wide range of political objects and a substantial portion of voters define their individual preferences using its spatial criterion. This criterion, however, is not present in all voters. There are some individuals who do not possess its coordinates and others who refuse to make use of it. Because of this, it is impossible to rule out the possibility that it is a discrete element in the population—i.e., that there are some individuals that are completely bereft of the coordinates of the left-right dimension.

The *amicus/hostis* evaluation criterion does show itself to be a discrete element. Our analysis of the Pearson's correlation coefficients for the evaluation of the leaders (Table 7.3) reveals a clear contrast between those voters who use the *amicus/hostis* logic and those who do not. This confirms the discrete nature of the *amicus/hostis* criterion, which is not a property that is widespread among voters but rather a particular characteristic of some of them. Along the same lines, referring back to our findings in Chapter 6, we can interpret the systematic way in which *aliens* voters dismiss both coalitions as another instance of a heuristic judgment that is either present or absent, and so does not seem to have a continuous nature (cf, Table 6.4).

Although we cannot reach any definitive conclusion, there is substantial evidence pointing to the discrete nature of our decision-making strategies. The types have roots in reality, in concrete forms of problem resolution inhering in people. The strategies of choice are not abstract frameworks of reasoning to which individuals conform in an approximate manner, but rather specific cognitive mechanisms that guide their processes of inference. In other words, the types reveal themselves to have the characteristics of heuristics—cognitive shortcuts based on systematic use of a reasoning algorithm, i.e., a form of calculation that is discrete in nature in the sense that either individuals use it or it is completely absent.

Chapter 8

Conclusions

I pardon the people themselves for their democracy. One must forgive everyone for looking after his own interests. But whoever is not a man of the people and yet prefers to live in a democratic city rather than in an oligarchic one has readied himself to do wrong and has realized that it is easier for an evil man to escape notice in a democratic city than in an oligarchic one.

—XENOPHON

Winston Churchill once famously said: "the best argument against democracy is a five-minute conversation with the average voter." Quotations of this kind often embellish worrisome considerations concerning the distance between the ideal citizen and his or her actual (real-world) counterpart. In contrast, this book started out by questioning the very idea of an "average" voter itself, suggesting that this might not be a valid analytical category for understanding how people make up their minds and choose in the domain of politics. Indeed, our analysis has repeatedly shown that "average" voters are nowhere to be found. Moreover, through the book, we have maintained an agnostic position on which course of action should be considered "good" for democracy. Instead of blaming voters for their poor knowledge of politics, or judging the rationality of their reasoning or the correctness of their choices, we assumed that any political choice is the byproduct of some reflexive process and set out to study the actual mechanism(s) of choice.

Inspired by the decision-making literature and previous works in political cognition, we argued that in performing the common task of voting, citizens use various cognitive shortcuts in accordance with the type of information and the level of cognitive sophistication that they have at their disposal. Indeed, our argument is that by using different strategies of reasoning, voters with varying degrees of interest and types of information are able to make the complex task of evaluating political contests manageably simple, and so to reach a satisficing decision.

In the case of the Italian electorate of the 1990s, we have found that there is a group of voters, the *utilius* voters, who rely systematically on the ideological categories of left and right and use a criterion of spatial proximity to evaluate political parties. A second group, the *amicus* voters, rely instead on a dichotomous understanding of the electoral competition and follow a decision-making strategy based on evaluations of the two front running candidates and their party coalitions. Although less demanding from a cognitive and information perspective, this way of reasoning allows voters to construct a map of the political landscape that is almost as effective as that of the *utilius* voters. Finally, there is a substantial group of voters, the *aliens*, who are distant from politics, refuse or are unwilling to use classical ideological categories, do not like parties and political leaders, and are generally skeptical about all-things-political. These voters do not rely on any discernible voting strategy, and they seem to be easy prey for television broadcasters.

The dramatic differences between these types of voter cannot be captured by analyses that are based on the concept of the average voter. In fact, an analysis of the "average" profile of the Italian electorate might actually be deceptive. By smoothing over the substantial qualitative differences between voters, it will average out to nothing more than a statistical construct. In reality, it seems that the Italian population is divided between citizens who are highly capable of handling the political debate either through classical ideological categories—the *utilius*—or through an effective simplification of the political competition—the *amicus*—, and citizens who are peripheral to politics, and do not possess the instruments necessary for making sense of it—the *aliens*.

Our assumptions of voter heterogeneity, along with ecological rationality, have lead us to create a classification system for Italian voters and to identify different cognitive shortcuts. In the following section we will discuss in greater detail our research's contribution to the theoretical debate over the definition and measurement of political sophistication. Although the goal of the present work is not to assess whether the representation of the Italian electorate that emerges from the analysis is good or bad news for democracy, we will compare our findings to both traditional and more pessimistic representations and discuss the extent to which an approach based on the concept of cognitive heuristics can lead to more optimistic conclusions about citizens' capacity to navigate the field of politics.

Results

We can summarize the theoretical contribution of our study in four points: (1) the stability of the typology of voting heuristics makes it possible to propose it as a general interpretative framework for decision-making strategies in a political environment characterized by a multiplicity of parties and a mixed electoral system; (2) the heterogeneity of cognitive processes makes it necessary to abandon explanatory models of voting based on the assumption of homogeneity of the effects; (3) the proportion of people who have a structured understanding of politics might be larger than has been suggested by prevailing views of the general level of citizens' political competence; and (4) classifying citizens according to factual differences in the way in which they organize political objects is a more effective yardstick for measuring their level of political sophistication than a classification based on their level of education, information, and/or interest in politics.

Stability of the Cognitive Shortcuts

Our typology of voting heuristics is applicable to a large array of electoral events and provides a general interpretative framework capable of elucidating the role of several factors affecting voters' decision-making processes, including cognitive and contextual factors, sociodemographic characteristics, and the structure of the political system.

The typology of voting heuristics we have constructed shows that, in spite of the volatility of Italian politics, it is possible to identify stable and lasting classification criteria. This is possible, however, only if one can resist the temptation of letting oneself be swayed by the exceptional characteristics inherent to any election. In contrast to the numerous analyses that concentrate on the idiosyncrasies of particular elections, our classification is an attempt to capture the nature of the cognitive processes that inform voter decision making, with the objective of revealing those elements that are stable and systematic.

There are three fundamental aspects of our interpretive proposal that allow it to be generally applicable. First, the classificatory criteria are expressed in a way that makes the typology applicable to different elections and even to different nations, granted that they have multiple parties and a mixed electoral system. This is due principally to the fact that the classificatory criteria are based on *structured modalities of representing politics* rather than on single explanatory factors. In fact, the systems in which political objects are organized tend to be stable over time, whereas the evaluation of a single specific object, be it the charisma of a leader or the success of a party slogan, is destined to change considerably from one election to the next.

Second, following the principle that heuristics are domain-specific and should be psychologically plausible, our classificatory criteria are based on *cues that are encrypted in the ecology of the political system*, and that are available to the individual voter, depending on her cognitive and affective dispositions.

Third, our typology classifies voters *independently of the party they vote for*. The cognitive shortcuts are hypothesized as empty containers, as pathways that can be pursued by individuals with different ethical perspectives and expectations, and for this reason they are available to and, as our analysis amply confirms, are actually made use of by voters of different parties and coalitions. An additional advantage of this approach is that it avoids the danger of stereotyping party voters (for example, "Berlusconi's housewives" or the "left-wing intelligentsia"), in that every party counts amongst its own supporters both politically sophisticated people and individuals who are less attuned to the dynamics of politics. At the same time, as we shall see in the last section of this chapter, it also makes it possible to capture how well the parties conquer different segments of the electorate.

Voter Heterogeneity vs. Homogeneity of Effects

Recognizing the actual heterogeneity of decision-making strategies requires acknowledging that the various determinants of voting preference can have different effects on different types of voters. Both researchers and politicians are interested in understanding the effects of the media on voting, the impact that a given prime-ministerial candidate has, the influence exerted by an appeal to certain specific issues, and so on. However, questions like "What effect does TV have on voting?" are badly conceived and lead to inaccurate results. They should be substituted with: "Which voters are influenced by television?" In fact, since voters deploy diverse decision-making strategies, any conclusion about the influence of the media, the charisma of leaders, or the appeal of specific issues that does not take into account the heterogeneity of the electorate would be a potentially misleading simplification. In other words, any consideration of the factors that determine voting must be brought back to the type of voter being discussed. Only by abandoning the assumption of the homogeneity of effects, i.e., the idea that one factor exerts the same influence on all individuals in the same way, is it possible to liberate ourselves from the wrongheaded image of an "average" voter and the sterile claims that are made about him.

The Political Sophistication of the Mass Public

Beginning with the research undertaken by Converse (1964), in which the American electorate was characterized by minimal levels of constraint and consistency, there has been a continuous bolstering of the image of an electorate that is ill-informed, barely interested in politics, ignorant about the workings of institutions, deprived of ideological categories, and furnished with only a very limited capacity to think abstractly. In the case of Italy, this picture has been accompanied by a series of studies that have underlined the limited civic virtue of large sectors of the Italian society (Banfield and Banfield 1958; Almond and Verba 1959; Putnam 1993; Pasquino 2002; Cartocci 2007).

By contrast, our analysis demonstrates that a substantial number of voters—around one third of the population, if we sum *utilius* and *amicus* voters—have a logically structured understanding of politics and can be considered politically "competent," i.e., they are able to interpret the public debate through the conceptual categories that it offers them. Quite apart from any consideration of its desirability, this result certainly appears more realistic than those of competing theories, all too readily disposed to emphasize the inconsistency of citizens but little inclined to investigate the variety of the cognitive frameworks they use. At the same time, we should recognize that not all forms of consistency in political judgment serve citizens well in the task of choosing a party or coalition to vote for: the logic of rejecting all-things-political followed by *aliens* voters makes it easy for this type of voter to evaluate leaders and party agendas (by doling out negative judgments across the board). However, the distance it creates between citizens and politics might also be the basis of the relative ease with which television broadcasts "breach into" the political reasoning of this type of voter.

These considerations are also relevant to the debate over the efficacy of cognitive shortcuts. As discussed in Chapter 2, the concept of heuristic oscillates from being understood as a biased form of reasoning to a valuable strategy that allows individuals with scarce information and time to make good decisions. As is often the case, the truth lies somewhere in between: while the heuristic followed by the *amicus* voters can indeed be considered a fast and frugal strategy that allows citizens to simplify their understanding of the electoral competition by reducing it to the choice between the two major coalitions, thus focusing on the most important cue and bypassing ancillary information, the negative attitude of *aliens* voters does not lead them to focus on political cues that are directly relevant to the voting decision. Although more research is needed, it is reasonable to advance the hypothesis that *aliens* voters might be relying on fast and frugal strategies of a quite generic nature, such as the minimalist, recognition, or the take-the-first heuristics, all of which might be easily based on occasional, biased political messages coming from the television. It is dubious, however, and remains to be ascertained, whether these heuristics can be fully satisficing when applied to the domain of politics.

Measuring Political Sophistication

The concepts of political cognition and sophistication are constantly being redefined, particularly in relation to the problem of their measurement. A certain theoretical consensus and, even more, a widespread empirical practice have resulted in education, information, and/or interest in politics becoming the most frequently used indicators of political sophistication. Consequently, it is by now standard practice to divide voters into different groups according to one or more of these indicators.

We, on the other hand, classified voters based on factual differences in the way they organize political objects and not on their education, information, or interest. Moreover, as demonstrated in

Chapter 6, the political sophistication of the Italian citizen is actually much more closely tied to his capacity to factually organize political information than it is to his level of education, information, or interest in politics. In fact, our division criterion is more effective than the traditional indicators of sophistication are at distinguishing between voters based on the consistency of their political judgments. We thus concluded that levels of education or interest in politics are not particularly adequate or effective gauges for distinguishing between voters in how they understand the political system or how consistent their opinions are. It seems preferable, instead, to experiment with classificatory criteria that capture processes active in the organization of political reasoning.

Note that the advantage of our typological construction lies precisely in the fact that it originates from putative mechanisms of choice and does not divide respondents based on some indicator of the concept of sophistication. Heuristic reasoning is to some extent tied to levels of political cognition and sophistication but not in an exclusive way. In fact, even though *utilius* and *amicus* voters are on average better educated and more interested than the rest of the sample, they nonetheless include a significant number of voters who are completely uninterested, uninformed, and/or poorly educated. Similarly, political cognition is not a trait that is totally absent from *aliens* voters. As we have seen, both in the case of *utilius* and *amicus*, and in that of *aliens* voters, the way in which individual voters relate to forms of ideological representation has a direct impact on how they choose.

Outlines for Future Research

In the course of this book, we have identified forms of political reasoning and formulated hypotheses on how voting heuristics work based on the way in which respondents structure their attitudes and political behavior. Although the analysis of observational data remains an extremely useful instrument of inquiry, especially for understanding how information is encrypted in the political system, to document the actual existence of these cognitive strategies, however, *we cannot rely exclusively on survey interviews*. To prove the existence of heuristic reasoning, it is necessary to capture the relevant algorithms of reasoning at the precise moment at which the decision-making process is taking place. To that end it would be opportune to make use of in-depth interviews and, above all, laboratory experiments, to be able to observe the actual frameworks of reasoning at work (Kuklinski and Quirk 2001). In this section we consider a few specific hypotheses about the workings of each of the types, point to the numerous aspects that still need to be addressed, and sketch the outlines of experimental designs that could help move this research forward.

Utilius

The *utilius* voter uses ideology as a cognitive shortcut. In particular, he makes use of the left-right axis as an ideological representation of the political space and defines his own voting preferences by following a principle of spatial proximity. Experimental research has already tested, through surveys, different theories of spatial voting (the relationship between candidates' policy positions and voters' choices), coming to the conclusion that proximity voting is far more common than both discounting and directional voting (Tomz and Van Houweling 2008). In addition to conducting further research to confirm the workings of the heuristic and its diffusion in the population, it would be useful to investigate the actual content of the concepts of left and right and the precise nature of the ideological discourse underlying them. As far as the debate on the meaning of left and right is concerned, it is possible to recognize two alternative positions (Schadee 1995). One maintains that the left-right distinction has an "intrinsic significance," which can in its turn be related back to the position one takes on the ideal of equality (Bobbio 1999) or, alternatively, to a "synthesis of attitudes" (Sartori 1982,

256) that vary over time. The other denies the existence of any substantive autonomy to the categories in question, considering them just conventional labels deriving from the positioning of the parties and therefore devoid of any semantic independence from the parties themselves.

In the former case, the ideological categories have substantive content and so it is possible to use them to evaluate different political objects independently of any reference to parties. The latter hypothesis, on the other hand, conceives of left and right as empty labels, devoid of substantive meaning and therefore of no use in any judgment exercise when decoupled from references to parties. The construction of an experimental situation in which there is no possibility of referring to parties would make it possible to clarify whether individuals would still use the left-right distinction as a criterion for structuring their belief system.

A second element of interest in the *utilius* voter relates to the motivations behind her voting choice. According to Downs, political behavior is motivated mainly by egoistic goals (Downs 1957), in particular by economic ones. If this were true, voting choice should change with variations in the subject's socioeconomic condition. This hypothesis could be tested by creating an experimental situation in which respondents find themselves subject to the "veil of ignorance" hypothesized by John Rawls (1971) in which "no one knows his place in society, his class position or social status, nor does any one know his fortune in the distribution of natural assets and abilities, his intelligence, strength and the like" (*ibidem*, 11). In these conditions, if individuals were motivated exclusively by self-interest, their ideological position would vary with changes in their perception of their interests. If, on the other hand, their subjective position on the left-right axis were tied to a set of values, to an ethical imperative that is independent of their material interest, their opinion would remain unaltered.

This last distinction between interest and value reference, as well as pointing to a further subtlety in the problem of the meaning of ideology, also suggests a third line of inquiry related to the *utilius* voter: the way in which material interests and values combine. In fact, it is possible that these two factors give rise to tradeoffs, i.e., to situations in which choosing based on material interests goes against choosing according to values (Chubb, Hagen, and Sniderman 1991). The construction of experimental scenarios in which subjects are forced to choose between material and other relevant interests could provide useful information about the motivations that inform the decision-making process.

Amicus

Let us now consider the *amicus* voter. The *amicus/hostis* evaluation criterion calls to mind some of the features of the likeability heuristic described in Chapter 3. Brady and Sniderman (1991) show that many people, even though they cannot define concepts like liberalism and conservatism, are nonetheless able to estimate in a fairly accurate manner the political opinions of liberals and conservatives. This is possible to the extent that these individuals combine their own knowledge about the theme in question with their own feelings toward liberals and conservatives. This is a heuristic used by individuals with a level of political sophistication that allows them to coherently organize both their own beliefs and their own feelings about politics. In fact, by combining their knowledge and their "likes and dislikes" (Brady and Sniderman 1991, 92) these people manage to extract the maximum value from the information at their disposal. A characteristic trait of this heuristic is a bipolar organization of preferences and, in particular, a tendency to maximize the differences between oneself and the opposite side's proponents, and, conversely, to magnify the agreement between oneself and anyone in favor of the same position. There are, then, a certain number of similarities to the judgment mechanism of the *amicus* voter, so much so that the capacity of *amicus* voters to use the concepts of left and right both for the issues and for organizing future voting preferences (Chapter 6) could be interpreted as a "virtuous" combination of the likeability heuristic's affective and cognitive elements.

A second distinguishing feature of the *amicus* voter type is the extreme ideological coherence of the individuals who belong to it. These people are not only systematic in structuring their judgments but are also particularly coherent in organizing their attitudes and behavior. The *amicus* voter's cognitive strategy conforms to the *dominance search model* of decision making advanced by Henry Montgomery (1983; 1989). According to this framework

> the decision-making process is seen as a search for a dominance structure, i.e. a cognitive structure in which one alternative can be seen as dominant over the others. In such a structure, the drawbacks, if any, of the to-be-chosen alternative are neutralized or counterbalanced in one way or another and because of this the final choice will follow in a self-evident way from the given structure (Montgomery 1989, 23).

This process of choice, described in four phases, begins with a preliminary selection of the options that have the greatest probability of becoming dominant. It then continues with the selection of the most attractive option and more or less systematically and exhaustively evaluating it against the rejected options. The final step, defined as the dominance structuring phase, is specifically aimed at reinforcing the belief system by confirming the "goodness" of the option selected. This step involves various information structuring mechanisms for neutralizing or counterbalancing any information that would be inconsonant with the chosen option. For example, any disadvantages tied to the chosen alternative are deemphasized, counterbalanced, or even cancelled out by accentuating its attendant advantages. In general, the dominance search model explains how an individual constructs an intrinsically coherent belief system. It also suggests an algorithm of choice, based on the selection of an alternative and on the verification of its qualities, that could actually conform to the *amicus* voter's characteristic "reduction to a dichotomy" mechanism. This algorithm can be tested using Lau and Redlawsk's dynamic process tracing methodology.

While this model accounts for the high coherence with which the *amicus* voter organizes his political preferences, it remains to be fully determined whether the primary object of choice is indeed party coalitions, rather than political leaders, issues, or single parties. Our analysis has shown that *amicus* voters systematically structure their evaluations of political leaders, parties, and government performance on various issues in coalitional terms. In particular, the fact that *amicus* voters reorganize the empathetic task of judging political figures in terms of a criterion (the coalition) that is extraneous to the candidates' individual qualities is a notably strong mark of the incisiveness of the *amicus/hostis* criterion.

Nevertheless, the coalition-oriented nature of the judgment should be further tested. This could be done, for example, by studying how subjects evaluate political figures and issues that cannot be traced back to a contraposition between line-ups, in particular by placing them in a situation in which they have to evaluate certain political objects in the absence of the information necessary to reduce them to a dichotomy.

Finally, it is necessary to examine in greater detail what significance the concepts of left and right have for *amicus* voters. *Amicus* voters actually do seem to use these concepts—even though less systematically than *utilius* voters do—and so the framework of analysis sketched out above for *utilius* voters could also be useful in evaluating how *amicus* voters make sense of them. Do left and right have an autonomous substantive value or are they simply a set of labels interchangeable with those of the coalitions?

Aliens

Let us now turn to the *aliens* voter. We did not formulate any specific strategy of reasoning in advance for this type of voter, aside from his refusal of politics. Through the analysis, we collected a few pieces of evidence about his susceptibility to the TV remote effect and his sensitivity to short-term factors. We did not, however, identify any specific organization of beliefs that could lead to identifying his decision-making strategy.

Aliens voters are not without a systematic representation of politics, though. On the contrary, they have a clear image of politics as something negative—something that should be rejected, with which it is better not to have any contact, and that cannot be trusted. In Chapter 6, we showed how this is reflected in the cynic realism with which they believe there are no differences between the party coalitions, and expect no politician to be able to solve the problems of the country. This, too, is a systematic representation, and in keeping with it the *aliens* voter is not interested in politics, acquires information almost exclusively from TV, and does not define himself according to the categories of left and right.

Nevertheless, these voters, too, make choices, and our hypothesis is that they adopt a decision-making process suited to a task that they do not like performing, thus making limited use of information and time. Nothing in their distaste for politics would prompt them to acquire elaborate knowledge of political objects. We expect these voters' choice process to be based on a single, good reason and to adopt either the minimalist, recognition, or take-the-first heuristics. In fact, these are reasoning processes that are general, valid, useful in different contexts, and accessible to people who do not have much time (and patience) for politics. These strategies do not require any organization of political beliefs; the only objective is to find a convincing argument without making any further effort to confer consistency on one's beliefs. The randomness or the accessibility of the point of departure makes it possible, moreover, to explain the role television plays in orienting the voting preference of *aliens* voters. Inference and choice are based on a single, good reason. There is no gesture toward comparing options, or entertaining alternative arguments.

To test these three possible heuristics, *aliens* voters should be presented in an experimental setting with different combinations of campaign stimuli and choice options, varying both the type of stimuli and the order in which the options are presented. While the minimalist heuristic entails a random selection of the cue, the recognition heuristics would combine campaign stimuli with the corresponding option. Finally, the take-the-first heuristic should be particularly sensitive to the order in which the options are presented.

As for the actual content of the cues, on the other hand, there is no reason to believe that *aliens* voters take into account factors that are all that different from those considered by *utilius* and *amicus*. For *aliens* voters, too, the political objects are the parties, leaders, coalitions, and issue positions. In contrast to the other types of voters, however, *aliens'* one-reason decision-making strategy does not lead to a coherent organization of these objects, which makes their choice extremely volatile.

FAQ: "Who Do They Vote For in the End?"

Voting heuristics have been conceived as empty boxes: as pathways that can be freely pursued by individuals with contrasting ethical frameworks and diverse political preferences. The fact that classification into types is based on formal criteria—and is thereby free of value judgments—allows us to interpret choice as the outcome of a decision-making algorithm. Moreover, as has been shown, conceiving of choice as a procedure does not in itself entail imposing any form of rationality on the actor. Implicit to our analytical strategy is the assumption that there is no relationship between voters' decision-making strategy and the parties for which they vote. The moment has now arrived, however, to satisfy a legitimate curiosity on the part of the reader: how do *utilius, amicus, medians,* and *aliens* vote?

Answering this question will also allow us to assess how capable of persuasion the parties involved in the electoral competition were. To win, it is not enough to have a good record or good arguments;

candidates also need to offer voters "good reasons." What is at issue, then, is the art of persuasion, which has to come to terms with the different ways in which voters understand the political world. In fact, because the judgment processes of *utilius*, *amicus*, and *aliens* are subject to different kinds of solicitations, persuasion too needs to be considered in terms of the electorate's heterogeneity. Such is the art of political marketing: differentiating communicative strategies according to the type of citizens to which they are directed (Diamanti and Mannheimer 1994; Rodriguez 1994).

Figure 8.1 reports the distribution of votes for the majority voting system (first-past-the-post) component of the elections, while Tables 8.1 and 8.2 report the distribution of party preferences in the proportional voting system component of the elections. First, it should be noted that each type is made up of an electorate that encompasses the whole set of the parties, thus corroborating our original decision not to divide voters in terms of the vote they cast but rather to consider at a theoretical level that the same heuristics were applicable to different parties and coalitions.

There are, however, a few peculiarities worth considering. As far as the voting preferences in the majority voting system component of the elections are concerned, the *amicus* category is made up of a disproportionately high number of Ulivo voters and a correspondingly low number of Polo/Casa delle Libertà voters. By contrast, especially in 2001, there was a remarkably large proportion of center-right voters within the *aliens* category. Along similar lines, in the proportional voting system component of the election, there was a strikingly large number of Forza Italia voters among *aliens* constituents. They make up about one third of Forza Italia voters in 1996 and more than half in 2001. On the other hand, PDS /DS voters are overrepresented in the *amicus* category (Tables 8.1 and 8.2).

In general, then, the most significant results are the pro-Ulivo character of *amicus* voters and the strong orientation toward the center-right, in particular toward Forza Italia, of *aliens* voters. In

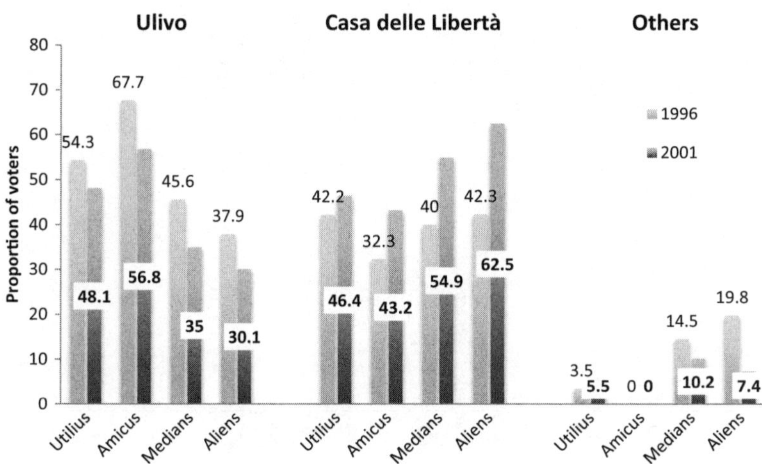

FIGURE 8.1 Vote for the Coalition. Proportion of votes in the majority voting system component of the 1996 and 2001 elections by type of voter. Number on top of the columns report the proportion of voters in 1996, while the numbers at the center of the columns report values for 2001.

Source: Itanes 1996 and 2001.

particular, Berlusconi's party managed to reach and conquer the component of the electorate that is most averse to having anything to do with politics, furnishing precisely the less motivated voters with the "good reasons" necessary for making a voting choice. The hypothesis, advanced in Chapter 7, that television exercised a determining influence on exactly this group of voters is now reinforced by observing their disproportionate support for Berlusconi's party.

There are two different ways to interpret this result. On the one hand, one can discuss the efficacy of the strategies of communication adopted by the Polo/Casa delle Libertà or, conversely, the Ulivo's weakness in reaching out to and obtaining the support of voters who are more skeptical about politics. On the other hand, one can indulge in gloomy analyses of the negative role television plays in democratic life. Giovanni Sartori, for instance, has repeatedly voiced this view, at times adopting quite scathing imagery:

TABLE 8.1 Vote for the Party. Proportion of votes in the proportional voting system component of the 1996 election for the major parties by type of voter. N=1904.

	Partito della Rifondazione Comunista (PRC)	Partito Democratico di Sinistra (PDS)	Partito Popolare Italiano (PPI)	Other center-left parties	Forza Italia (FI)	Alleanza Nazionale (AN)	Other center-right parties	Other parties	Total
utilius	11.8	29.9	11.3	2.5	19.4	17.1	4.9	3.0	100.0
amicus	7.0	**39.3**	8.0	7.9	14.6	13.2	3.4	6.6	100.0
medians	9.0	23.5	4.8	7.7	14.7	18.1	7.2	14.8	100.0
aliens	8.5	11.7	5.4	5.0	**33.2**	15.2	5.4	15.7	100.0
all	9.1	28.6	7.4	6.4	18.2	16.4	5.6	8.2	100.0

Source: Itanes 1996.

TABLE 8.2 Vote for the Party. Proportion of votes in the proportional voting system component of the 2001 election for the major parties by type of voter. N=2274.

	Partito della Rifondazione Comunista (PRC)	Democratici di Sinistra (DS)	Democrazia é Libertà- Margherita (Dem)	Other center-left parties	Forza Italia (FI)	Alleanza Nazionale (AN)	Other center-right parties	Other parties	Total
utilius	11.3	28.3	9.9		27.0	17.1	3.1	3.4	100.0
amicus	5.5	**30.5**	14.2	5.4	26.0	11.8	5.4	1.2	100.0
medians	6.1	14.7	10.9	2.7	36.4	15.9	4.8	8.6	100.0
aliens	4.5	10.1	9.3	2.2	**52.0**	9.0	4.8	8.1	100.0
all	6.4	19.7	11.3	2.9	35.0	13.9	4.7	6.0	100.0

Source: Itanes 2001.

the euphoria of post-communism has already passed and the premonitions of imminent dangers have grown. Amongst these, those mollycoddled numbskulls brought up on television and full of nonsense (Sartori 1993, 329).

Television, however, is just a medium of communication, whereas the capacity to communicate remains a virtue that belongs—or does not belong—to those who make use of it (Guizzardi 1994). Silvio Berlusconi's success with the media and above all his victory in the 2001 election campaign can easily be explained by examining the magnitude and the multiplicity of the means of communication—and persuasion—of which he disposes. But the disparity in means is only part of the story.

In this book, we have attempted to explain how individuals receive and organize information coming from the world of politics, which political objects they reference, and what their strategies of choice are. Asking what forms voters use to represent politics also means clarifying and identifying the channels through which politics is communicated. The left-right dimension and the contraposition between the coalitions are two frameworks that allow individuals to conceive of politics and to organize new information about it. The rejection of politics, or at least of its traditional forms of representation, is a third framework. All three, even the last, come into action at the very moment at which a political message is received; even an aversion to politics is a representation of it. The choice open to the researcher, then, is either to remain immobile in the face of the "mollycoddled numbskulls full of nonsense" or, as others have already done, carry on in the job of trying to make sense of how ordinary citizens make sense of politics.

REFERENCES

Agosta, A. 1994. "Maggioritario e proporzionale." In *Milano a Roma. Guida all'Italia elettorale del 1994*, edited by I. Diamanti, R. Mannheimer, 15–28. Roma: Donzelli.

Agresti, A. 1990. *Categorical Data Analysis*. Wiley: New York.

Almond, G. A. and S. Verba. 1963. *The Civic Culture: Political Attitudes and Democracy in five Nations*. Princeton: Princeton University Press.

Anderson, J. R. 1991. "Is human cognition adaptive?" *Behavioral and Brain Sciences* 14:471–517.

Anolli, L. and P. Legrenzi. 2001. *Psicologia generale*. Bologna: Il Mulino.

Arceneaux, K. and R. Kolodny. 2009. "Educating the Least Informed: Group EndLorsements in a Grassroots Campaign." *American Journal of Political Science*. 53(4): 755–770.

Arkes, H. R. and K. R Hammond. 1986. *Judgement and decision making: An interdisciplinary reader*. New York: Cambridge University Press.

Aronson, E. and T. Wilson, R. Aker. 2010 (7th edition). *Social Psychology*. Upper Saddle River, NJ: Prentice Hall.

Arrow, K. J. 1951. *Social Choice and Individual Values*. New York: Wiley.

Baldassarri, D. 2002. "La decisione di voto. Le elezioni politiche italiane del 1996 e 2001." Tesi di Laurea in Sociologia, Università degli Studi di Trento.

Baldassarri, D. 2003. "Il voto ideologico esiste? L'utilizzo delle categorie di sinistra e destra nell'elettorato italiano." *Quaderni dell'Osservatorio Elettorale* 49:5–35.

Baldassarri, D. and Peter B. 2007. "Dynamics of Political Polarization." *American Sociological Review*. 72: 784–811.

Baldassarri, D. and H. M. A. Schadee. 2004. "Il fascino della coalizione." *Rivista Italiana di Scienza Politica* 2:249–276.

Baldassarri, D. and H. M. A. Schadee. 2006. "Voter Heuristics and Political Cognition in Italy: An Empirical Typology," *Electoral Studies,* 25: 448–466.

Baldini, G., M. Bucchi, T. Fava. 2001. "Comunicazione politica e decisione di voto: una ricerca sulle elezioni comunali del 1999." In *Mass Media ed elezioni,* edited by G. Sani, 225–274. Bologna: Il Mulino.

Banfield, E. C. and L. Fasano Banfield. 1967 [1958]. *Moral Basis of a Backward Society.* New York: Free Press.

Bardi, L. and G. Pasquino. 1995. "Politicizzati e alienati." In *Sulla soglia del cambiamento. Elettori e partiti alla fine della prima Repubblica,* edited by A. Parisi, H. M. Schadee, 17–42. Bologna: Il Mulino.

Barlucchi, M. C. 1998. "Il tipo ideale weberiano: una definizione operativa." *Sociologia e ricerca sociale* 55:59–91.

Bartels, L. M. 1996. "Uninformed Votes: Information Effects in Presidential Elections." *American Journal of Political Science* 2:194–230.

Bartolini, S. and R. D'Alimonte. 1995. *Maggioritario ma non troppo. Le elezioni politiche del 1994, la campagna elettorale, l'offerta politica, il voto: un'analisi dettagliata per comprendere l'evoluzione del sistema politico in Italia.* Bologna: Il Mulino.

Bartolini, S., and P. Mair. 1990. *Identity, Competition, and Electoral Availability: The Stabilization of European Electorates: 1885–1985.* Cambridge: Cambridge University Press.

Bazerman, M. H. and M. A. Neale. 1983. "Heuristics in negotiation: Limitation to dispute resolution effectiveness." In *Negotiating in organizations,* edited by M. H. Bazerman, R. J. Lewicki, 51–67. Beverly Hills: Sage.

Bearman, P. 1993. *Relations into Rhetorics: Local Elite Social Structure in Norfolk, England: 1540–1640.* New Brunswick, NJ: Rutgers University Press.

Bellucci, P. 1997. "Classi, identità politiche e interessi." In *A domanda risponde. Il cambiamento del voto degli italiani nelle elezioni del 1994 e del 1996,* edited by P, Corbetta, A. M. L. Parisi, 261–316. Bologna: Il Mulino.

Bellucci, P. 2002. "L'elettore che ragiona: offerta di politiche e scelte di voto." In *Le ragioni dell'elettore,* edited by M. Caciagli, P. Corbetta, 371–406. Bologna: Il Mulino.

Bellucci, P., P. Segatti. 2010. *Votare in Italia: 1964–2008.* Bologna: Il Mulino.

Berelson, B., P. Lazarsfeld, W. McPhee. 1954. *Voting: A Study of Opinion Formation in a Presidential Election.* Chicago: University of Chicago Press.

Biorcio, R. and I. Diamanti. 1987. "La scelta di voto: dal risultato all'attore sociale. Appunti per una rilettura del comportamento elettorale in Italia." *Quaderni dell'Osservatorio Elettorale* 19:43–85.

Biorcio, R. and P. Natale. 1989. "La mobilità elettorale degli anni '80." *Quaderni dell'Osservatorio elettorale* 8:41–88.

Bobbio, N. 1999. *Destra e sinistra. Ragioni e significati di una distinzione politica.* Roma: Donzelli.

Boudon, R. 1995. *Le juste et le vrai,* Paris: Fayard.

Boudon, R. 1996. "The 'Cognitivist Model': a generalized 'Rational Choice' Model." *Rationality and Society* 8:123–150.

Boudon, R. 1998. "Social Mechanisms Without Black Boxes." In *Social Mechanisms,* edited by P. Hedström, R. Swedberg. Cambridge: Cambridge University Press.

Boudon, R. 2003. *Raison, bonnes raisons.* Paris: Presses Universitaires de France.

Brady, H. E. and P. M. Sniderman. 1991. "The likability heuristic." In *Reasoning and Choice. Exploration in Political Psycology,* edited by P. M. Sniderman, R. A. Brody, P. E. Tetlok, 93–119. Cambridge: Cambridge University Press.

Brandstätter, E., G. Gigerenzer, and R. Hertwig. 2006. "The priority heuristic: Making choices without trade-offs." *Psychological Review.* 113(2): 409–432.

Brody, R. A. 1991. "Stability and change in party identification: presidential to off-years." In *Reasoning and Choice. Exploration in Political Psychology,* edited by P. M. Sniderman, R. A. Brody, P. E. Tetlock, 179–205. Cambridge: Cambridge University Press.

Budge, I., I. Crewe, D. Farlie. 1976. *Party identification and beyond: representations of voting and party competition.* Wiley: London.

Budge, I., D. Robertson, D. Hearl. 1987. *Ideology, Strategy and Party Change: Spatial Analyses of Post-war election Programmes in 19 Democracies.* Cambridge: Cambridge University Press.

Bullock, J. G. 2011. "Elite Influence on Public Opinion in an Informed Electorate." *American Political Science Review* 105: 496–515.

Burns, N., K. Schlozman, S. Verba. 2001. *The Private Roots of Public Action: Gender, Equality and Political Participation.* Cambridge: Harvard University Press.

Caciagli, M. and P. Corbetta. 2002. *Le Ragioni dell'elettore. Perchè ha vinto il centro-destra nelle elezioni italiane del 2001.* Bologna: Il Mulino.

Calhoun, C. 1991. "The Problem of Identity in Collective Action" In *Macro—Micro Linkages in Sociology* edited by Joan Huber 51–75. Newbury Park, CA: Sage.

Camerer, C. and R. Hogarth. 1999. "The effects of financial incentives in experiments: a review and capital-labor-production framework." *Journal of Risk and Uncertainty* 19:7–42.

Campbell, A., P. E. Converse, W. E. Miller, D. E. Stockes. 1960. *The American Voter*. New York: Wiley.

Campus, D. 2000. *L'elettore pigro. Informazione politica e scelte di voto*. Bologna, Il Mulino.

Carmines, E. and R. Huckefeldt. 1996. "Political Behavior: An Overview." In *A New Handbook of Political Science*, edited by R. E. Goodin and H. D. Klingemann, 223–254. Oxford: Oxford University Press.

Carmines, E. and J. Stimson. 1982. "Racial Issues and the Structure of Mass Belief System." *Journal of Politics* 44:2–20.

Cartocci, R. 1990. *Elettori in Italia. Riflessioni sulle vicende elettorali degli anni ottanta*. Bologna: Il Mulino.

Caramani, D. 1997. "La partecipazione elettorale: gli effetti della competizione maggioritaria." In *Maggioritario per caso*, edited by R. D'Alimonte, S. Bartolini. Bologna: Il Mulino.

Caramani, D. 2004. *The Nationalization of Politics*. Cambridge: Cambridge University Press.

Cartocci, R. 2007. *Mappe del Tesoro*. Bologna: Il Mulino.

Chaiken, S., A. Liberman, A. H. Eagly. 1989. "Heuristic and systematic information processing within and beyond the persuasion context." In *Unintended thought*, edited by J. S. Uleman, J. A. Bargh, 212–252. New York: Gulford Press.

Chiaramonte, A. 1994. "Gli effetti distorsivi del nuovo sistema elettorale." *Rivista Italiana di Scienza Politica* 3.

Chierici, C. 1997. "Il nuovo sistema elettorale: formule, collegi, schede." In *A domanda risponde. Il cambiamento del voto degli italiani nelle elezioni del 1994 e del 1996*, edited by A. Corbetta, M. L. Parisi, 81–91. Bologna: Il Mulino.

Chubb, J. E., M. G. Hagen, P. M. Sniderman. 1991. "Ideological reasoning." In *Reasoning and Choice. Exploration in Political Psychology*, edited by P. M. Sniderman, R. A. Brody, P. E. Tetlok, 140–163. Cambridge: Cambridge University Press.

Clarke, H., D. Sanders, M. Stewart, P. Whiteley. 2003. *Political Choice in Britain*. Oxford: Oxford University Press.

Cobalti, A. and A. Schizzerotto. 1994. *La mobilità sociale in Italia. L'influenza dei fattori di diseguaglianza sul destino educativo, professionale e sociale dei singoli nel nostro paese*. Il Mulino: Bologna.

Cob, M. D. and J. Kuklinski. 1997. "Changing Minds: Political Arguments and Political Persuasion." *American Journal of Political Science.* 41(1): 88–121.

Cohen, C. E. 1981. "Person categories and social perception: Testing some boundary conditions of the processing effects of prior knowledge." *Journal of Personality and Social Psychology* 40:441–452.

Conover, P. and S. Feldman. 1981. "The Origins and Meanings of Liberal / Conservative Self identifications." *American Journal of Political Science* 25:617–645.

Conover, P. and S. Feldman. 1984. "How People Organize the Political World: A Schematic Approach." *American Journal of Political Science* 46:760–785.

Converse, P. 1964. "The Nature of Belief Systems in Mass Publics." In *Ideology and Discontent,* edited by D. E. Apter, 206–261. New York: Free Press.

Converse, P. 1990. "Popular Representation and the Distribution of Information." In *Information and Democratic Processes,* edited by J. A. Ferejohn, J. H. Kuklinski. Urbana: University of Illinois Press.

Corbetta, P. 1992. *Metodi di analisi multivariata per le scienze sociali.* Bologna: Il Mulino.

Corbetta, P. 1999. *Metodologia e tecniche della ricerca sociale.* Bologna: Il Mulino.

Corbetta P. and G. Mazzoleni. 1995. "Partiti, media e informazione politica" in *Sulla soglia del cambiamento.* Edited by A. Parisi and H. Schadee. Bologna: Il Mulino.

Corbetta, P. and A. M. L. Parisi. 1997. *A domanda risponde. Il cambiamento del voto degli italiani nelle elezioni del 1994 e del 1996.* Bologna: Il Mulino.

Corbetta, P. and A. M. L. Parisi. 1997. *Cavalieri e fanti. Proposte e proponenti nelle elezioni del 1994 e del 1996.* Bologna: Il Mulino.

Corbetta, P., A. M. L. Parisi, H. M. A. Schadee. 1988. *Elezioni in Italia. Struttura e tipologia delle consultazioni politiche.* Bologna: Il Mulino.

Czerlinski, J., G. Gigerenzer, D. G. Goldstein. 1999. How good are simple heuristics? In *Simple Heuristics That Make Us Smart* edited by Gigerenzer, G., Todd, P.M. & the ABC Research Group. New York: Oxford University Press.

Dalton, R. and M. P. Wattenberg. 2000. *Parties Without Partisans: Political Change in Advanced Industrial Democracies,* Oxford: Oxford University Press.

D'Alimonte, R. and S. Bartolini. 1997. *Maggioritario per caso. Le elezioni politiche del 1994 e del 1996 a confronto: il ruolo del sistema elettorale, le coalizioni, le scelte degli elettori.* Bologna: Il Mulino.

D'Alimonte, R. and S. Bartolini. 2002. *Maggioritario Finalmente. La transizione elettorale 1994–2001*. Bologna: Il Mulino.

Dawes, R. M., D. Faust, P. E. Meehl. 1991. "Clinical versus Actuarial Judgment." *Science* 243: 1668–1673.

DeBond, W. F. and R. H. Thaler. 2002. "Do Analysts Overract?" In *Heuristics and Biases. The Psychology of Intuitive Judgment*, edited by T. Gilovich, D. Griffin, D. Kahneman, 678–685. Cambridge: Cambridge University Press.

Delli Carpini, M. X. and S. Keeter. 1993. "Measuring Political Knowledge. Putting First Things First." *American Journal of Political Science* 37:1179–1206.

Denzau, T. and D. C. North. 2000. "Shared Mental Models: Ideologies and Institutions." In *Elements of Reason. Cognition, Choice, and the Bounds of Rationality*, edited by A. Lupia, M. D. McCubbins, S. L. Popkin. New York: Cambridge University Press.

De Sio, L. 2011. *Competizione e spazio politico. Le elezioni si vincono davvero al centro?* Bologna: Il Mulino.

Diamanti, I. 1996. *Il male del Nord. Lega, localismo, secessione*. Donzelli: Roma.

Diamanti, I. and R. Mannheimer. 1994. "Milano a Roma." *Guida all'Italia elettorale del 1994*, edited by A. Diederich. Roma: Donzelli.

Dieckmann, A. and J. Rieskamp. 2007. "The influence of information redundancy on probabilistic inferences." *Memory & Cognition*, 35, 1801–1813.

DiMaggio, P. 1997. "Culture and Cognition." *Annual Review of Sociology* 23:263–287.

Downs, A. 1957. *An Economic Theory of Democracy*. New York: Harper & Row.

Druckman, J. N. 2004. "Political preference formation: Competition, deliberation, and the (ir)relevance of framing effects." *American Political Science Review* 98:671–686.

Druckman, J. N. and A. Lupia. 2000. "Preference Formation." *Annual Review of Political Science* 3:1–24.

Druckman, J., C. L. Hennessy, K. St. Charles, and J. Webber. 2010. "Competing rhetoric over time: Frames versus cues." *The Journal of Politics* 72:136–148.

Duprè, J. 1993. "The Disorder of Things." In *Metaphysical Foundations of the Disunity of Science*. Cambridge: Harvard University Press.

Edwards, W. 1954. "The theory of decision making." *Psychological Bulletin* 51:380–417.

Edwards, W. 1961. "Behavioral decision theory." *Annual Review of Psychology* 12:473–498.

Einhorn, H. J. and R. M. Hogarth. 1981. "Behavioral decision theory: Processes of judgement and choice." *Annual Review of Psychology* 32:53–88.

Elstein, A. S., L. S. Shulman, S. A. Sprafka. 1978. *Medical problem solving: An analysis of clinical reasoning*. Cambridge: Harvard University Press.

Elster, J. 1979. *Ulysses and the Sirens*. Cambridge: Cambridge University Press.

Elster, J. 1999. *Strong Feelings. Emotion, Addiction and Human behavior*, edited by A. Bradford. London-Cambridge: The MIT Press.

Elster, J. 2007. *Explaining Social Behavior*. Cambridge: Cambridge University Press.

Enelow, J. and M. Hinich. 1984. *The Spatial Theory of Voting. An Introduction.* Cambridge: Cambridge University Press.

Enelow, J. and M. Hinich. 1990. *Advances in the Spatial Theory of Voting.* Cambridge: Cambridge University Press.

Fabbrini, S. 1998. *Quale democrazia. L'Italia e gli altri.* 2 ed. Bari: Laterza.

Fabbrini, S. 2000. *Tra pressioni e veti: il cambiamento politico in Italia.* Bari: Laterza.

Fiorina, M. 1981. *Retrospective Voting in American National Elections.* New Haven: Yale University Press.

Fiorina, M. 1990. "Information and Rationality in Elections." In *Information and Democratic Process*, edited by J. A. Ferejohn, J. H. Kuklinski. Chicago: University of Illinois Press.

Fischhoff, B. 2002. "Heuristics and Biases in Application." In *Heuristics and Biases. The Psychology of Intuitive Judgment*, edited by T. Gilovich, D. Griffin, D. Kahneman, 730–748. Cambridge: Cambridge University Press.

Fiske, S. T. and D. R. Kinder. 1981. "Involvement, Expertise, and Schema Use: Evidence from Political Cognition." In *Personality, Cognition, and Social Interaction*, edited by N. Cantor, J. F. Kihlstrom, 171–190. Hillsdale: L. Erlbaum Associates.

Fiske, S. T., D. R. Kinder, W. M. Larter. 1983. "The Novice and the Expert: Knowledge-Based Strategies in Political Cognition." *Journal of Experimental and Social Psychology* 19:381–400.

Fiske, S. T. and P. W. Linville. 1980. "What does the Schema concept buy us?" *Personality and Social Psychology Bulletin* 6:543–557.

Fiske, S. T., R. R. Lau, R. A. Smith. 1990. "On the Varieties and Utilities of Political Expertise." *Social Cognition* 8:31–48.

Fiske, S. T. and S. E. Taylor. 1991. *Social Cognition*. New York: McGraw Hill.

Franklin, M. N., T. T. Mackie, H. Valen. 1992. *Electoral change. Responses to evolving social and attitudinal structures in Western countries*, Cambridge: Cambridge University Press.

Frederick, S. 2002. "Automated Choice Heuristics." In *Heuristics and Biases. The Psychology of Intuitive Judgment*, edited by T. Gilovich, D. Griffin, D. Kahneman, 548–558. Cambridge: Cambridge University Press.

Galli, G., V. Capecchi, V. Cioni Polacchini, G. Sivini. 1968. *Il comportamento elettorale in Italia*. Bologna: Il Mulino.

Gamson, W. A. 1990. *The Strategy of Social Protest*. Homewood, IL: Dorsey.

Gigerenzer, G. 2000. *Adaptive thinking: rationality in the real world*. New York: Oxford University Press.

Gigerenzer, G. 2010. "Moral Satisficing: Rethinking Moral Behavior as Bounded Rationality." *Topics in Cognitive Science*, 2: 528–554.

Gigerenzer, G., and H. J. Brighton. 2009. "Homo heuristicus: Why biased minds make better inferences." *Topics in Cognitive Science*, 1, 107–143.

Gigerenzer, G. and D. G. Goldstein. 1996. "Reasoning the fast and frugal way: Models of bounded rationality." *Psychological Review* 103:650–669.

Gigerenzer, G. and D. G. Goldstein. 1999. "Betting on One Good Reason: The Take the Best Heuristic." In *Simple Heuristics That Make Us Smart*, 75–96. New York: Oxford University Press.

Gigerenzer, G., J. Czerlinski, L. Martignon. 2002. "How Good Are Fast and Frugal Heuristics?" In *Common Sense, Reasoning and Rationality*, edited by R. Elio, 149–173. New York: Oxford University Press.

Gigerenzer, G., Hertwig, R., Pachur, T. 2011. *Heuristics: The foundations of adaptive behavior*. New York: Oxford University Press.

Gigerenzer, G. and R. Selten. 2001. *Bounded Rationality. The Adaptive Toolbox*, edited by G. Gigerenzer, R. Selten. Cambridge: MIT Press.

Gigerenzer, G., P. Todd, Abc Research Group. 1999. *Simple Heuristics That Make Us Smart*. New York: Oxford University Press.

Gilbert, M. 1994. *The Italian Revolution. The End of Politics Italian-Style?* Boulder: Westview Press.

Gilens, M. 2001. "Political Ignorance and collective policy preferences." *American Political Science Review* 95:379–396.

Gilovich, T. 1991. *How we know what isn't so: The fallibility of human judgment in everyday life*. New York: Free Press.

Gilovich, T. and D. Griffin. 2002. "Introduction—Heuristics and Biases: Then and Now." In *Heuristics and Biases. The Psychology of Intuitive Judgment*, edited by T. Gilovich, D. Griffin, D. Kahneman, 1–18. Cambridge: Cambridge University Press.

Gilovich, T., D. Griffin, D. Kahneman. 2002. *Heuristics and Biases. The Psychology of Intuitive Judgment*. Cambridge: Cambridge University Press.

Girotto, V. 1996. "Introduzione alla teoria del prospetto e alle sue applicazioni in ambito politico." In *Psicologia e Politica*, edited by P. Legrenzi, V. Girotto, 19–42. Milano: Raffaello Cortina.

Goldberg, A. 2012. *Where Do Social Categories Come From? A Comparative Analysis of Online Interaction and Categorical Emergence in Music and Finance*. Dissertation.

Goldstein, D. G. and Gigerenzer, G. 1999. "The Recognition Heuristic: How Ignorance Makes Us Smart." In *Simple Heuristics That Make Us Smart*, edited by G. Gigerenzer, P. Todd, ABC Research Group, 75–96. New York: Oxford University Press.

Goldstein, D. G. and G. Gigerenzer. 2002. "Models of ecological rationality: The recognition heuristic." *Psychological Review*, 109, 75–90.

Goldthorpe, J. H. 2000. *On Sociology. Numbers, Narratives, and the Integration of Research and Theory*. Oxford: Oxford University Press.

Gordon, S. B. and G. M. Segura. 1997. "Cross-National Variation in the Political Sophistication of Individuals: Capability or Choice?" *The Journal of Politics* 59:126–147.

Gould, R. V. 1995. *Insurgent Identities: Class, Community, and Protest in Paris from 1948 to the Commune*. Chicago, IL: University of Chicago Press.

Green, D. P., and A. S. Gerber. 2008. *Get Out The Vote: How to Increase Voter Turnout*, Second Edition. Washington, DC: Brookings Institution Press.

Guizzardi, G. 1994. "Messaggi e immagini." In *Milano a Roma. Guida all'Italia elettorale del 1994*, edited by I. Diamanti, R. Mannheimer, 143–150. Roma: Donzelli.

Hamill, R., M. Lodge, F. Blake. 1985. "The Breadth, Depth, and Utility of Class, Partisan, and Ideological Schemata." *American Journal of Political Science* 29:850–870.

Hamill, R. and M. Lodge. 1986. "Cognitive consequences of Political Sophistication." In *Political Cognition*, edited by R. Lau, D. O. Sears, 69–93. Hillsdale, NJ: Laurence Erlbaum Associates.

Hedström, P. 2005. *Dissecting the Social: On the Principles of Analytical Sociology*. Cambridge: Cambridge University Press.

Henrion, M. and B. Fischoff. 2002. "Assessing Uncertainty in Physical Constants." In *Heuristics and Biases. The Psychology of Intuitive Judgment*, edited by T. Gilovich, D. Griffin, D. Kahneman, 666–677. Cambridge: Cambridge University Press.

Hinich, M. and M. Munger. 1994. *Ideology and the Theory of Political Choice*. Ann Arbor: University of Michigan Press.

Hinich, M. and W. Pollard. 1981. "A New Approach to the Spatial Theory of Electoral Competition." *American Journal of Political Science* 25: 323–341.

Hirschmann, A. O. 1970. *Exit, voice and loyalty: responses to decline in firms, organizations and states*. Cambridge: Harvard University Press.

Huckfeld, R., Sprague, J. 1995. *Citizens, Politics and Social Communication: Information and Influence in an Election Campaign*. New York: Cambridge University Press.

Inglehart, R. and H. D. Klingemann. 1976. "Party identification, Ideological Preference and the Left-right Dimension among Western Mass Publics." In *Party Identification and beyond: Representations of Voting and Party Competition*, edited by I. Budge, I. Crewe, D. Farlie, 243–273. London: Wiley.

Itanes. 1997. "Itanes 1990–1996." *Italian National Election Studies, in Misure. Materiali di ricerca dell'Istituto Cattaneo*.

Itanes. 2001. *Perché ha vinto il centro-destra. Oltre la mera conta dei voti: chi, come, dove, perché*. Bologna: Il Mulino.

Johnson, P. E. 1998. *Social Choice: Theory and Research*. Thousand Oaks, California: Sage.

Kahneman, D. and A. Tversky. 1972. "Subjective probability: A judgment of representativeness, in." *Journal of Behavioral Decision Making* 5:187–200.

Kahneman, D. and A. Tversky. 1973. "On the psychology of prediction." *Psychological Review* 80:237–251.

Kahneman, D. and A. Tversky. 1979. "Prospect theory: An analysis of decision under risk." *Econometrica* 47:263–291.

Kahneman, D. and S. Frederick. 2002. "Representativeness Revisited: Attribute Substitution in Intuitive Judgment." In *Heuristics and Biases. The Psychology of Intuitive Judgment*, edited by T. Gilovich, D. Griffin, D. Kahneman, 49–81. Cambridge: Cambridge University Press.

Kahneman, D., P. Slovic, A. Tversky. 1982. *Judgment under Uncertainty: Heuristics and Biases*. Cambridge: Cambridge University Press.

Katsikopoulos, K.V., and L. Martignon. 2006. "Naïve heuristics for paired comparisons: Some results on their relative accuracy," *Journal of Mathematical Psychology*, 50, 3, 488–494.

Kinder, D and D. Sears. 1985. "Public Opinion and Political Action." In *Handbook of Political Science*, edited by G. Lindzey, E. Aronson, 625–741. Vol. 2. Boston: Addison-Wesley.

Klayman, J. and Y. W. Ha, 1987. "Confirmation, disconfirmation, and information in hypothesis testing." *Psychological Review* 94:211–228.

Kleinnijenhuis, J. and P. Pennings. 2001. "Measurement of Party Positions on the basis of Party Programs, Media Coverage and Voter Perceptions." In *Estimating the Policy Position of Political Actors*, edited by M. Laver, 162–182. London: Routledge.

Krosnick, J. A. 1990a. "Expertise and Political Psychology." *Social Cognition* 8:1–8.

Krosnick, J. A. 1990b. "Lessons learned: A Review and Integration of Our Findings." *Social Cognition* 8:154–158.

Kuklinski, J. 2001. *Citizens and Politics*. Cambridge: Cambridge University Press.

Kuklinski, J. and P. J. Quirk. 2000. "Reconsidering the Rational Public: Cognition, Heuristics, and Mass Opinion." In *Elements of Reason. Cognition, Choice, and the Bounds of Rationality*, edited by A. Lupia, M. D. McCubbins, S. L. Popkin, 153–182. New York: Cambridge University Press.

Kuklinski, J. H., P. J. Quirk, J. Jerit, R. F. Rich. 2001. "The Political Environment and Citizen Competence." *American Journal of Political Science* 45:410–424.

Kuklinski, J., R. C. Luskin, J. Bolland. 1991. "Where is The Schema? Going Beyond the "S" Word in Political Psychology." *American Political Science Review* 85:1341–1356.

La Palombara, J. 1966. "Italy: Fragmentation, Isolation, Alienation." In *Political Culture and Political Development*, edited by L. W. Pye, S. Verba. Princeton: Princeton University Press.

Laland, K. N. 2001. "Imitation, Social Learning, and Preparedness as Mechanisms." In *Bounded rationality. The adaptive toolbox*, edited by G. Gigerenzer, R. Selten, 233–247. Cambridge: MIT Press.

Laponce, J. A. 1981. *Left and Right: The Topography of Political Perceptions*. Toronto: University of Toronto.

Lau R. and D. Redlawsk. 2007. *How Voters Decide: Information Processing During Election Campaigns*. Cambridge: Cambridge University Press.

Lau, R. and D. O. Sears. 1986. *Political Cognition*. Hillsdale, New York: Erlbaum.

Laver, M. and B. Hunt. 1992. *Policy and Party Competition*. New York: Routledge.

Lawrence, C. N. 2003. "The Concept of Political Sophistication." *The Impact of Political Sophistication on the Decision-Making Processes of Voters*, PhD dissertation, The University of Mississippi.

LeDuc, L., R. G. Niemi, P. Norris. 2002. *Comparing Democracies 2. New Challenges in the Study of Elections and Voting*. Sage: London.

Legnante, G. 1998. "Le tipologie del comportamento elettorale in Italia." *Quaderni di Scienza Politica* 5:111–172.

Legnante, G. and G. Sani. 2002. "La campagna più lunga" In *Maggioritario Finalmente. La transizione elettorale 1994–2001*. Edited by D'Alimonte, R. and S. Bartolini. Bologna: Il Mulino. 41–78.

Levin, I. P., S. L. Schneider, G. J. Gaeth. 1998. "All frames are not created equal: a typology and critical analysis of framing effects." In *Organizational Behavior and Human Decision Processes*, 76:149–188.

Lijphart, A. 1968. "Typologies of Democratic Systems." *Comparative Political Studies*. 1:3–44.

Lipset, S. M. and S. Rokkan. 1967. "Cleavage Structures, Party System and Voter Alignments. An Introduction." In *Party System and Voter Alignments*, edited by S. M. Lipset, S. Rokkan, 1–64. New York: Free Press.

Lodge, M. G. and R. Hamill. 1986. "A Partisan Schema for Political Information Processing." *American Political Science Review* 80:505–519.

Lodge M. G., K. McGrawn, P. J. Conover, S. Feldman, A. Miller. 1991. "Where Is the Schema? Critiques." *American Political Science Review* 85:1357–1383.

Lopes, L. L. 1991. "The rhetoric of irrationality." *Theory and Psychology* 1:65–82.

Luce, R. D. and H. Raiffa. 1957. *Games and Decisions*. New York: Wiley.

Lupia, A. 1994. "Shortcuts Versus Encyclopedias: Information and Voting Behavior in California Insurance Reform Elections." *American Political Science Review* 89:63–76.

Lupia A. and M. D. McCubbins. 1998. *The Democratic Dilemma: Can Citizens Learn What They Need to Know?* New York: Cambridge University Press.

Lupia, A., M. D. McCubbins, S. L. Popkin. 2000. *Elements of Reason. Cognition, Choice, and the Bounds of Rationality*. New York: Cambridge University Press.

Luskin, R. C. 1987. "Measuring Political Sophistication." *American Journal of Political Science*. 4:856–899.

Luskin, R. C. 1990. "Explaining Political Sophistication." *Political Behavior* 12:331–361.

Luskin, R. C. 2002. "Political Psychology, Political Behavior, and Politics: Questions of Aggregation, Causal Distance, and Taste." In *Thinking about Political Psychology*, edited by J. H. Kuklinski, 217–250. New York: Cambridge University Press.

Mannheimer, R. 1989. *Capire il voto. Contributi per l'analisi del comportamento elettorale Italia*. Milano: Franco Angeli.

Mannheimer, R. and G. Sani. 1987. *Il mercato elettorale. Identikit dell'elettore italiano*. Bologna: Il Mulino.

Mannheimer, R. and G. Sani. 1994. *La rivoluzione elettorale. L'Italia tra la prima e la seconda repubblica*. Milano: Anabasi.

Maraffi, M. 2007. *Gli Italiani e la politica*. Bologna: Il Mulino.

Markus, G. E. 2000 "Emotions in Politics" *Annual Review of Political Science*. 3:221–250.

Marradi, A. 1998. "Termometri con vincolo di ordinalità: il gioco della torre consente di aggirare la tendenza alla desiderabilità sociale?" *Sociologia e ricerca sociale* 57:49–59.

Martignon, L. 2001. "Comparing Fast and Frugal Heuristics and Optimal Models." In *Bounded rationality. The adaptive toolbox*, edited by G. Gigerenzer, R. Selten, 147–172. Cambridge: MIT Press.

Martignon, L., and U. Hoffrage 2002. "Fast, frugal and fit: simple heuristics for paired comparison." *Theory and Decision*, 52, 29–71.

Martignon, L., U. Hoffrage, N. Kriegeskorte. 1997. *Lexicographic comparison under uncertainty: A satisficing cognitive algorithm*. Manuscript, Max Planck Institute for Psychological Research, Munich.

Martin, J. L. 2011. *The Explanation of Social Action*, New York: Oxford University Press.

Mavrogordatos, G. T. 1987. "Downs Revisited: Spatial Models of Party Competition and Left-Right Measurement." *International Political Science Review* 4:333–342.

McAdam, D. 1982 (1999). *Political Process and the Development of Black Insurgency: 1930–1970*. Chicago, IL: University of Chicago Press.

McFadden, D. 1999. "Rationality for economists?" *Journal of Risk and Uncertainty* 19:73–105.

McIver, J. P. and E. G. Carmines. 1981. "Unidimensional Scaling." Sage University Papers Series on Quantitative Applications in the Social Sciences, 7–24. Beverly Hills, California: Sage.

McKelvey, R. D. and P. C. Ordeshook. 1985. "Elections with Limited Information: A Fulfilled Expectations Model Using Contemporaneous Poll and Endorsement Data as Information Sources." *Journal of Economic Theory* 36:55–85.

McKelvey, R. D. and P. C. Ordeshook. 1990. "Information and Elections: Retrospective Voting and Rational Expectations." In *Information and Democratic Processes*, edited by J. A. Ferejohn, J. H. Kuklinski. Chicago: University of Illinois Press.

McKenzie, C. R. 2003a. "Judgment and Decision Making." In *Handbook of Cognition*, edited by K. Lamberts, R. L. Goldstone. London: Sage.

McKenzie, C.R. 2003b. "Rational models as theories—not standards—of behavior." *Trends in Cognitive Sciences* 7:403–406.

Merton, R. K. 1936. "The Unanticipated Consequences of Purposive Social Action." *American Sociological Review* 1(6):894–904.

Milbrath, L. W. 1965. *Political Participation. How and Why Do People Get involved in Politics.* Chicago: Rand McNally & Co.

Miller, N. R. 1986. "Information, Electorates and Democracy: Some Extensions and Interpretations of the Condorcet Jury Theorem." In *Information Pooling and Group Decision Making*, edited by B. Grofman, G. Owen. Greenwich, CT: JAI Press.

Mohr, John W. 1998. "Measuring Meaning Structures." *Annual Review of Sociology* 24:345–370.

Montgomery, H. 1989. "From Cognition to Action." In *Process and Structure in Human Decision Making*, edited by H. Montgomery, O. Svenson. New York: Wiley.

Müller, W. and Y. Shavit. 1998. *From School to Work. A comparative study of educational qualification and occupational destinations.* Oxford: Clarendon Press.

Mutz, D. 2006. *Hearing the Other Side: Deliberative vs. Participatory Democracy.* Cambridge: Cambridge University Press.

Newell, A., J. C. Shaw, H. A. Simon. 1962. "The Process of Creative Thinking." In *Contemporary approaches to creative thinking*, edited by H. E. Gruber, G. Terrel, M. Wertheimer, 93–119. New York: Atherton Press.

Nie, N. H. and W. Andersen. 1974. "Mass Belief Systems Revisited: Political Change and Attitude Structure." *Journal of Politics* 36:541–591.

Nie, N. H., S. Verba, R. Petrocik. 1976. *The Changing American Voter.* Cambridge: Harvard University Press.

Olson, M. 1965. *The Logic of Collective Action.* Cambridge: Harvard University Press.

Page, B. and R. Shapiro. 1992. *The Rational Public: Fifty Years of Trends in American's Policy Preferences.* Chicago: University Chicago Press.

Pais, A. 1982. "Subtile is the Lord. . . ." *The Science and the Life of Albert Einstein.* Oxford: Oxford University Press.

Pareto, V. 1916. *Trattato di Sociologia Generale.* Firenze: G. Barbéra.

Parisi, A. 1995. "Appartenenza, opinione e scambio." In *Sulla soglia del cambiamento. Elettori e partiti alla fine della prima Repubblica*, edited by A. Parisi, H. M. A. Schadee, 359–392. Bologna: Il Mulino.

Parisi, A. and G. Pasquino. 1977. *Continuità e mutamento elettorale in Italia.* Bologna: Il Mulino.

Parisi, A. and G. Pasquino. 1977. "Relazioni partiti-elettori e tipi di voto." In *Continuità e mutamento elettoral in Italia*, edited by A. Parisi, G. Pasquino, 215–259. Bologna: Il Mulino.

Parisi, A. and H. M. A. Schadee. 1995. *Sulla soglia del cambiamento. Elettori e partiti alla fine della prima Repubblica*. Bologna: Il Mulino.

Pennings, P. and H. Keman. 2002. "Towards a new methodology of estimating party policy positions." *Quality & Quantity* 36:55–79.

Peterson, C. R. and L. R. Beach. 1967. "Man as an intuitive statistician." *Psychological Bulletin* 68:29–46.

Petty, R. and J. T. Cacioppo. 1986. *Communication and Persuasion. Central and Peripheral Routes to Attitude Change*. New York: Springer-Verlag.

Pierce, J. C. and P. R. Hagner. 1982. "Conceptualization and Party Identification: 1956–1976." *American Journal of Political Science* 26:377–387.

Pisati, M. 1997. "Chi ha votato chi. Omogeneità e differenze fra gli elettorati dei diversi schieramenti politici." In *A domanda risponde. Il cambiamento del voto degli italiani nelle elezioni del 1994 e del 1996*, edited by P. Corbetta, A. M. L. Parisi, 91–139. Bologna: Il Mulino.

Pisati, M. 2000. "Il video e il voto. Gli effetti dell'informazione politica televisiva sulle elezioni del 1996." *Rivista Italiana di Scienza Politica* 2:329–353.

Pizzorno, A. 1983. "Sulla razionalità della scelta democratica." *Stato e Mercato* 7:3–45.

Pizzorno, A. 1989. "Individualismo metodologico: prediche e ragionamenti." In *Il soggetto dell'azione. Paradigmi sociologici e immagini dell'attore sociale*, edited by L. Sciolla, L. Ricolfi. Milano: Franco Angeli.

Pizzorno, A. 2001. "Natura della diseguaglianza, potere politico e potere privato nella società in via di globalizzazione." *Stato e Mercato* 62:201–236.

Poggi, G. 1968. *Le preferenze politiche degli italiani. Analisi di alcuni sondaggi pre-elettorali, Qaderni dell'Istituto di studi e ricerche 2*, edited by Carlo Cattaneo. Bologna: Il Mulino.

Polya, G. 1945. *How To Solve It: A New Aspect of Mathematical Method*. Princeton: Princeton University Press.

Popkin, S. L. 1991. *The Reasoning Voter*. Chicago: University of Chicago Press.

Popkin, S. L. and M. A. Dimoch. 1996. "Le conoscenze dei cittadini, le scorciatoie informative ed il ragionamento politico." In *Comunicazione politica nel sistema dei media*, edited by S. Bentivegna. Genoa: Costa & Nolan.

Popkin, S. L. and M. A. Dimoch. 1999. "Political knowledge and Citizens Competence." In *Citizens Competence and Democratic Institutions*, edited by S. Elkin, K. Soltan, 119–146. University Park: Pennsylvania State University Press.

Popper, K. R. 1957. *The Poverty of Historicism*. London: Routledge.

Post, W. 1992. *Non parametric unfolding models, a latent structure approach*. Leiden: DSWO Press.

Prelec, D. 2000. "Compound invariant weighting functions in prospect theory." In *Choices, Values and Frame*, edited by A. Tversky, D. Kahneman, 67–92. Cambridge: Cambridge University Press.

Putnam, R. 1993. *Making Democracy Work*. Princeton: Princeton University Press.

Rahn, W. M. 1993. "The Role of Partisan Stereotypes in Information Processing about Political Candidates." *American Journal of Political Science* 37: 472–496.

Rahn, W. M. 2000. "Affect as Information: The Role of Public Mood in Political Reasoning." In *Elements of Reason*, edited by A. Lupia, Mathew D. McCubbins, S. L. Popkin, 130–151. Cambridge: Cambridge University Press.

Rawls, J. 1971. *A Theory of Justice*. 4 ed. Cambridge: Harvard University Press.

Ricolfi, L. 1984. *Modelli dell'attore e analisi dei dati. Utilitarismo e sociologia*. Torino: Giappichelli.

Ricolfi, L. 1994. *Elezioni e mass-media. Quanti voti ha spostato la tv*, 6:1031–1046. Bologna: Il Mulino.

Ricolfi, L. 1999. *Destra e sinistra? Studi sulla geometria dello spazio elettorale*. Torino: Omega.

Rieskamp, J., and P. E. Otto. 2006. "SSL: A theory of how people learn to select strategies." *Journal of Experimental Psychology*. 135, 207–236.

Rodriguez, M. 1994. "La comunicazione politica." In *Milano a Roma. Guida all'Italia elettorale del 1994*, edited by I. Diamanti, R. Mannheimer, 135–142. Roma: Donzelli.

Rottenstreich, Y. and A. Tversky. 1997. "Unpacking, repacking, and anchoring: Advances in support theory." *Psychological Review* 104:406–415.

Saks, M. J. and R. F. Kidd. "1980–81 Human information processing and adjudication: Trials by heuristics." *Law and Society Review* 15:123–160.

Sani, G. 1973. "Fattori determinanti delle preferenze partitiche in Italia." *Rivista Italiana di Scienza politica* 1:129–144.

Sani, G. 1994. "Modelli di cittadino e comportamenti di massa." In *La rivoluzione elettorale. L'Italia tra la prima e la seconda republica*, edited by R. Mannheimer, G. Sani, 15–36. Milano: Anabasi.

Sani, G. 2001. *Mass media ed elezioni*. Bologna: Il Mulino.

Sani, G. and G. Legnante. 2001. "La comunicazione politica in tv." In *Mass media ed elezioni*, edited by G. Sani. Bologna: Il Mulino.

Sani, G. and G. Sartori. 1978. "Frammentazione, polarizzazione e cleavages: democrazie facili e difficili." *Rivista Italiana di Scienza politica* 3:339–362.

Sani, G. and G. Sartori. 1983. "Polarization, Fragmentation and Competition in Western Democracies." In *Western European Party Systems*, edited by H. Daalder, P. Mair, 307–340. London: Sage.

Sartori, G. 1976. *Parties and Party Systems*. Cambridge: Cambridge University Press.

Sartori, G. 1982. *Teoria dei partiti e caso italiano*. Milano: Sugarco.

Sartori, G. 1982. "Il pluralismo polarizzato: critiche e repliche." *Rivista Italiana di Scienza Politica* 12:3–44.

Sartori, G. 1989. "Videopotere." *Rivista Italiana di Scienza Politica* 2:289–242.

Sartori, G. 1993. *La democrazia. Cosa è*. Milano: Rizzoli.

Sartori, G. 1995. "Ideologia." *Elementi di teoria politica*. Bologna: Il Mulino.

Schadee, H. M. A. 1995. "Destra, sinistra, centro: etichette partitiche e contenuti politici." In *Sulla soglia del cambiamento. Elettori e partiti alla fine della prima Repubblica*, edited by A. Parisi, H. M.A. Schadee, 75–103. Bologna: Il Mulino.

Schmitt, C. 1927. *Der Begriff des Politischen*. Berlin: Duncker & Humbolt. English translation:

Schmitt, C. 2007. *The Concept of the Political*. Translated by George D. Schwab. Chicago: University of Chicago Press.

Segatti, P. 1997. "Un centro instabile eppure fermo. Mutamento e continuità nel movimento elettorale." In *A domanda risponde. Il cambiamento del voto degli italiani nelle elezioni del 1994 e del 1996*, edited by P. Corbetta, A. M. L. Parisi, 215–260. Bologna: Il Mulino.

Segatti, P. and H. M. A. Schadee. 2003. "Gli Effetti di una campagna lunga e Flussi informativi, spazio politico e movimento elettorale" In *Le ragioni dell'elettore*. Edited by M. Caciagli e P. Corbetta. Bologna: Il Mulino.

Segatti P. and C. Vezzoni 2007. "Quanto conta la gente come me? Il senso di efficacia politica. In *Gli Italiani e la politica*. Edited by Maraffi, M. Bologna: Il Mulino. 73–104.

Selten, R. 2001. "What is Bounded Rationality?" In *Bounded Rationality. The Adaptive Toolbox*, edited by G. Gigerenzer, R. Selten, 13–36. Cambridge: MIT Press.

Sharif, E. 1999. "Belief and Decision: the Continuing Legacy of Amos Tversky." *Cognitive Psychology* 38:3–15.

Sharif, E. and R. A. LeBoeuf. 2002. "Rationality." *Annual Review of Psychology* 53:491–517.

Simon, H. 1956. "Rational choice and the structure of environments." *Psychological Review* 63:129–138.

Simon, H. 1957. *Models of Man: Social and Rational*. New York: Wiley.

Simon, H. 1982. *Models of Bounded Rationality*. Vol. 2. Cambridge, MIT Press.

Simon, H. 1985. "Human Nature in Politics: The Dialogue in Psychology with Political Science." *American Political Science Review* 79:293–304.

Simon, H. 1990. "Invariants in human behavior." *Annual Review of Psychology* 41:1–19.

Simon, H. 2000. "Bounded Rationality in social science: today and tomorrow." *Mind and Society* 1:25–39.

Sloman, S. A. 2002. "Two Systems of Reasoning." In *Heuristics and Biases. The Psychology of Intuitive Judgement*, edited by T. Gilovich, D. Griffin, D. Kahneman, 379–396. Cambridge: Cambridge University Press.

Slovic, P. and S. Lichtenstein. 1983. "Preference reversals: A broader perspective." *American Economic Review* 73:596–605.

Smith, E. R. A. N. 1980. "The Levels of Conceptualisation: False Measures of Ideological Sophistication." *American Political Science Review* 74:685–696.

Sniderman, P. M., J. M. Glaser, R. Griffin. 1991. "Information and electoral choice." In *Reasoning and Choice. Exploration in Political Psychology*, edited by P. M. Sniderman, R. A. Brody, P. E. Tetlok, 164–178. Cambridge: Cambridge University Press.

Sniderman, P. M., R. A. Brody, P. E. Tetlok. 1991. *Reasoning and Choice. Exploration in Political Psychology*. New York: Cambridge University Press.

Sniderman, P. M. 1993. "The New Look in Public Opinion Research." In *Political Science: The State of the Discipline II*, edited by A. W. Finifter, 219–245. Washington: American Political Science Association.

Sniderman, P. M. 2000. "Taking Sides: A Fixed Choice Theory of Political Reasoning." In *Elements of Reason. Cognition, Choice, and the Bounds of Rationality*, edited by A. Lupia, M. D. McCubbins, S. L. Popkin, 67–84. New York: Cambridge University Press.

Stille, A. 2006. *The Sack of Rome: How a Beautiful European Country with a Fabled History and a Storied Culture Was Taken Over by a Man Named Silvio Berlusconi*. New York: Penguin Books.

Strack, F., N. J. Smelser, P. B Baltes. 2001. "Heuristics in Social Cognition." In *International Encyclopedia of the Social and Behavioral Sciences*, 6679–6683. Pergamon

Tetlock, P. E. 2002. "Theory-Driven Reasoning about Plausible Pasts and Probable Futures in World Politics." In *Heuristics and Biases. The Psychology of Intuitive Judgment*, edited by T. Gilovich, D. Griffin, D. Kahneman, 749–762. Cambridge: Cambridge University Press.

Todd, P. 2001. "Fast and Frugal Heuristics for Environmentally Bounded Minds." In *Bounded Rationality. The Adaptive Toolbox*, edited by G. Gigerenzer, R. Selten, 51–70. Cambridge: MIT Press.

Tomz, M. and R. P. Van Houweling. 2008. "Candidate Positioning and Voter Choice." *American Political Science Review* 102:303–318.

Tversky, A. and D. Kahneman. 1973. "Availability: A heuristic for judging frequency and probability." *Cognitive Psychology* 54:207–232.

Tversky, A. and D. Kahneman. 1974. "Judgment under uncertainty: Heuristics and biases." *Science* 185:1124–1131.

Tversky, A. and D. Kahneman. 1981. "The framing of decision and the psychology of choice." *Science* 211:453–458.

Tversky, A. and D. Kahneman. 1987. "Rational Choice and the framing of decision." In *Rational Choice: The Contrast between Economics and Psychology*, edited by R. M. Hogarth, M. W. Reder, 295–310. Chicago: University Chicago Press.

Tversky, A. and D. Kahneman. 1992. "Advances in prospect theory: cumulative representation of uncertainty." *Journal of Risk and Uncertainty* 5:297–323.

Tversky, A. and D. Kahneman. 2000. *Choices, Values and Frame.* Cambridge: Cambridge University Press.

Tversky, A., D. J. Koehler. 1994. "Support theory: A nonextensional representation of subjective probability." *Psychological Review* 101: 547–567.

Udéhn L. 2002. "The Changing Face of Methodological Individualism." *Annual Review of Sociology*, 28:479–507.

Van Dijk, T. A. 1998. *Ideology. A Multidisciplinary Approach.* Towbridge: Cromwell Press.

Van Schuur, H. 1984. *Structure in Political Beliefs.* Amsterdam: CT Press.

Van Schuur, H. and W. Post. 1990. *Mudfold. A program for Multiple Unidimensional Unfolding, Progamma.* Groningen.

Van Schuur, W. H. 1992. "Nonparametric unfolding models for multicategory data." *Political Analysis* 4:41–74.

Von Neumann, J. and O. Morgenstern. 1944. *Theory of Games and Economic Behavior.* Princeton: Princeton University Press.

Weber, M. 1904. "Die Objectivität sozialwissenschaftlicher und sozialpolitiscer Erkenntnis." In *Archiv für Sozialwissenschaft und Sozialpolitik*, XIX.

Weber, M. 1922. *Wirtschaft und Gesellschaft.* Mohr: Tübingen.

Wilkinson, G. and C. E. Rogers. 1973. "Symbolic Description of Factorial Models for Analysis of Variance." *Journal of the royal statistical society; Applied Statistics Series C*, 22:392–399.

Zaller, J. 1991. "Information, Values and Opinion." *American Political Science Review* 85:1215–1237.

Zaller, J. 1992. *The Nature and the Origins of Mass Opinion*. Cambridge: Cambridge University Press.

Zuckerman, A. S. 2005 (ed). *The Social Logic of Politics. Personal Networks as Contexts for Political Behavior*. Philadelphia, PA: Temple University Press.

INDEX

ABC Research Group, 33, 48

affectivity, ideological reasoning, 70

age

    multinomial logistic regressions, 145, 147, 149, 151

    profile by voter type, 136, 137

aliens voter, 7, 10–11, 94

    classification criteria, 114–115, 129–130

    decision-making strategy, 11, 116–117, 161

    sociodemographic profile, 127, 131–133, 134–139

    future research, 221–223

    ideological coherence and issue preferences, 12, 161, 163, 164, 165, 172, 192, 193

    judgments on political leaders, 204

    political participation, 142, 144

    political sophistication/cognitive profile, 127, 128, 129, 130

    cynic realism / skepticism about government capacity, 176–177

    "TV remote" effect, 194–199

    vote for coalition, 225

    vote for party, 226, 227

    voter "innocent of ideology," 112–117

    voters per type and overlap with other types, 119–121

Alleanza Nazionale (AN), 87, 103, 226, 227

Amato, Giuliano, 109, 204, 205

America

    electorate, 64, 214–215

    two-party system, 6, 90–91

The American Voter, 17

amicus voter, 7, 10, 94, 155n15

    candidates and voting preference, 192–193

    classification criteria, 110–112

    decision-making strategy, 11, 126, 160, 169, 184

    sociodemographic profile, 127, 131–133, 134–139

    future research, 219–221

    ideological coherence and issue preferences, 163, 164, 165, 192

    judgments on political leaders, 204

    political participation, 140–143

amicus voter (*continued*)
    political sophistication / cognitive profile, 125–126, 128, 129, 130
    sympathetic voter, 105–112
    vote for coalition, 225
    vote for party, 226, 227
    voters per type and overlap with other types, 119–121
amicus/hostis logic, 158, 166, 182, 185, 186, 205, 206
    decision-making strategy, 158
    ideological coherence, 160
    strategy of judgment, 173, 201, 202, 206–207
    zero-sum game, 200–208
anchoring and adjustment heuristic, 39
artificial intelligence, 74
associational membership, 140n12
    multinomial logistic regressions, 146, 148, 150, 152
    participation by voter type, 141, 142, 143
availability heuristic, 39

Beach, Lee Roy, 36
Berlusconi, Silvio, 87, 88, 194
    center-right alliance, 108, 109
    evaluation of political leaders, 204, 205
    positive evaluation, 187, 191
    success with media, 235
Bossi, Umberto, 109, 204, 205
Boudon, Raymond, 29, 30
bounded rationality, 27–28, 27n4
    decision making, 72
    Simon, 48

Cacioppo, John, 44
Casa delle Libertà, 109, 187, 194, 195, 196, 205
    center-right coalition, 88
    victories for leaders of, 109, 111
    voters, 224, 225
Casini, Pierferdinando, 108
Center-North regions
    Italian citizens, 21
    macro-political areas, 135, 136, 137, 138
    voters, 154
Centro Cristiano Democratico and Cristiani Democratici Uniti (CCD–CDU), 88, 103
choice. *See also* elements of choice
    intentionality, 25n3
    non-optimality, 28–29
Christian Democratic Party, 135
Churchill, Winston, 209
citizens, political disaffection, 89
Clean Hands (Mani Pulite), 86
coalitions
    coherence, 182
    governmental capacity, 173–177
    mistrust, 183
    voters, 224, 225
cognitive psychology
    cognitive miser, 43
    decision making, 56
    dual process models, 43–44
    heterogeneity of cognitive processes, 63–67
    research programs, 5
collective action, 24
collective opinion, will of citizens, 67–68
collective rationality, 76

Columbia approach, voting behavior,
17
Communist Party, "Red" zone, 21
Comunisti Italiani (CI), placement,
169–170
correct reasoning, strategy for
citizens, 80–81

D'Alema, Massimo, 108, 109, 204, 205
DBO theory, Hedström, 26
decision makers, voters, 8–9
decision making. *See also* human
decision making
adaptive, 55–56
Bayesian, 46
cognitive psychology, 56
decision-making tree, 35–36
dominance search model, 220
elaboration likelihood model
(ELM), dual model, 44
elements of choice, 186–194
evaluating classification system,
158–159
fast and frugal heuristics, 50, 72, 157
Johnson-Laird's, theory of mental
models (TMM), 74n7
"Man as an Intuitive Statistician," 36
models of individual, 72
prospect theory, 41
rational choice approach, 34–37
research hypotheses, 79–84
theoretical framework, 79–84
voter heterogeneity vs.
homogeneity effects, 213–214
voter heuristics, 157–159
Democratici di Sinistra (DS), 227
Democrazia Cristiana (DC) Democratic Christian party, 86, 87
"White" zone, 21, 135–138

Democrazia é Libertà-Margherita
(Dem), 88, 227
determinants, voting behavior, 18–19
differentiation, belief systems, 65–66
Dini, Lamberto, 108
domain-specific
fast and frugal heuristics, 81
heuristics, 4, 54
dominance search model, decision
making, 220
Downs, Anthony, 18
Downsian model, voter, 72, 160
dynamic process tracing, research
method, 71–73, 221

early socialization model, decision
making, 72
ecological rationality
decision making, 94
fast and frugal heuristics and,
46–56, 80–81
framework, 53
principle of, 82, 83
Simon's concept, 5
ecology, Italian political system,
85–91
economic rationality, 27n4, 36–37
An Economic Theory of Democracy,
Downs, 18
economic voter, Downsian model,
72
education
level of, and voters' judgments,
177–181
multinomial logistic regressions,
146, 148, 150, 152
political sophistication, 124, 128,
129, 130, 153
voter types, 127, 131–133

Edwards, Ward, 34
effectiveness, Italian voters, 84
electoral choice, process and
     outcome, 6
electoral rationale, 15–16
electoral system
     First Republic in Italy, 86
     Second Republic in Italy, 86,
          88–89
electorate, political sophistication,
     214–215
elements of choice
     decision-making process, 186–187
     general log-linear model, 188–191
     interdependence between, 188
     organization of, 186–194
     relationship with voting behavior,
          187–188
Elster, Jon, 30
     decision-making, 26
     economic theory, 23–25
     rational actions, 29
erroneous beliefs, effects of action,
     29
expected utility
     decision tree, 35–36
     possible options and
          consequences, 34–35
     subjective, 34, 54

fast and frugal heuristics
     best choice, 80
     decision making, 50, 72, 157
     domain-specific, 81
     ecological rationality and, 46–56,
          80–81
     research program, 33, 48
     satisficing choice, 9
     sequential procedure, 51

Fini, Gianfranco, 108, 109, 204, 205
Fininvest news programs, 197
First Republic
     Italian voters, 5–6, 21–22, 86
     macro-political areas, 134–135,
          136, 137, 138
     partisan identifications, 89
Forza Italia (FI), 87, 103, 224, 226,
     227

gender
     multinomial logistic regressions,
          145, 147, 149, 151
     profile by voter type, 136, 137,
          138, 155
geopolitical area
     multinomial logistic regressions,
          145, 147, 149, 151
     profile by voter type, 136, 137, 138
Gigerenzer, Gerd, 33, 48
governmental capacity, 173, 174
     evaluations, 172–177

Hedström, Peter, 26
heterogeneity
     assumptions of voter, 211
     cognitive processes, 63–67
     voters, 84, 213–214
heuristics, cognitive shortcuts
     anchoring and adjustment, 39
     art of making it simple, 73–76
     availability, 39
     cognitive shortcuts, 4, 7, 38, 44,
          75–76
     decision-making shortcuts, 184
     definition, 43
     distinct, 11–12
     domain-specific, 4, 54
     imitation, 53

likeability, 70, 106
minimalist, 49
political attitudes and opinions, 69
principle characteristics, 74
representativeness, 38–39
stability of cognitive shortcuts, 212–213
take-the-best, 49–51
take-the-first, 52–53
typology of political, 117–121
voting, 6, 67–71
heuristics and biases
anchoring and adjustment heuristic, 39
availability heuristic, 39
criticisms and future prospects of program, 43–46
dogma of correct reasoning, 37
judgment heuristics, distortions, 11, 40–41
prospect theory, 41
rational choice theory, 40–41
representativeness heuristic, 38–39
research program, 33, 37–42
support theory, 42
heuristics and political sophistication
cognitive profile, 126–133
measurement and hypotheses, 123–126
heuristics and social-contextual factors
hypotheses, 133–134
political participation, 139–141
sociodemographic profile, 134–139
Hinich, Melvin, 106

homo economicus, model of, 23, 33
homo sociologicus, 23
How Voters Decide, Lau and Redlawsk, 71
human action, rationality, 27–28
human rational behavior, Simon, 5

identification, voting phenomenon, 19–20
ideological coherence
issue preferences, 159–166, 179, 180
levels of education and political interest, 177–181
organizing future voting preferences, 166–172
ideological reasoning, affectivity, 70
ideology
aliens voter innocent of, 112–117
political debate, 106–107
types of voters, 207–208
utilius voter, 217–219
imitation heuristic, 53
imitate the majority, 53
imitate the successful, 53
incorrect beliefs, effects of action, 29
individual choice, voting, 15–16, 19, 22–26
information
media and political sophistication, 124
political sophistication, 153
political sophistication by voter types, 128, 129, 130
information processing, 58n1, 65
innocent of ideology
aliens voter, 112–117
American electorate, 64
instrumental rationality, 27n4, 30

integration, belief systems, 65–66
intentionality, choice, 25n3
interactive sophistication, 69
interdependence, variables in
    log-linear model, 196–197
interest
    level of, and voters' judgments,
        177–181
    measure of political, 124n2
    multinomial logistic regressions,
        146, 148, 150, 152
    political sophistication, 124, 128,
        129, 130, 153
    voter types, 127
interviews, public opinion, 81–82
irrationality, judgment, 40
issue preferences
    aliens voters, 161
    amicus voters, 160
    ideological coherence in, 159–166
    linear regression models, 164
    utilius voters, 160
Istituto Cattaneo, 21
Italian democracy, 89
Italian political system
    1996 elections, 102–103, 104
    2001 elections, 103, 104
    ecology of, 85–91
    electoral system, 86–87
    multiparty competition, 90–91
    national elections (1996 and
        2001), 122–123
    typology of voting heuristics,
        212–212
Italian voters, citizens
    average profile, 210–211
    classification, 91–95, 211
    decision making, 31, 82
    electoral system, 86–87

elements of choice, 187
First Republic, 5–6, 21–22
membership networks, 21
national general elections, 5–6
political subcultures, 19
principles, 83–84
rejection of politics, 89–90
Second Republic, 22
typology, 84
voting behavior, 20–21
Itanes (Italian National Election
    Studies), 95

judgment process, integration and
    differentiation, 65–66

Kahneman, Daniel, 33

Lau, Richard, 71–73, 221
left-right ideology
    factorial analysis, 162–163
    placing parties, 97–98, 99n7, 100
    terminology, 98n5
    utilius voter, 95–105
    voting behavior, 11–12
Lega Nord (LN), 87, 88, 103, 114
libertarian party, Lista Bonino,
    169–170
likeability heuristic, 70, 106
Lipset, Seymour, 21
Lista Bonino, libertarian party,
    169–170
log-linear modeling
    general model, 190
    purposes of strategy, 189

majority voting system, 224, 225
Mani Pulite (Clean Hands), 86
Mannheimer, Renato, 92

media
   Berlusconi's success with, 235
   election information, 124–125
   index of exposure, 124n3
   interaction with voting
      preference, 191–192
   multinomial logistic regressions,
      131, 146, 148, 150, 152
   political sophistication, 128, 129,
      130, 153
medians voter, 7, 10, 92, 117
   classification criteria, 117–118
   ideological coherence and issue
      preferences, 163, 164, 165, 179,
      180
   judgments on political leaders,
      204
   political participation, 140–143
   political sophistication / cognitive
      profile, 127, 128, 129, 130
   residual category, 117
   vote for coalition, 225
   vote for party, 226, 227
media partisanship, voting behavior,
   11
membership, voting phenomenon,
   19–20
membership networks, Italian
   citizens, 21
memory and knowledge, 55
Michigan approach, voting behavior,
   17, 72
microeconomic models, preferences,
   40–41
minimalist heuristic, 49
mock election, 80n1
Montgomery, Henry, 220
moral behavior, 55
motivations, voting, 92–93

Movimento Sociale Italiano, fascist
   party, 87, 103
multiple unidimensional unfolding
   H coefficient, 168
   MUDFOLD program, 168n3
   scaling, 167
   voting predispositions, 172
Munger, Michael, 106

national general elections, Italian, 5–6
*The Nature of Belief Systems in Mass
   Publics*, Converse, 64
nomological aspiration, 30n5
nonrandom choice, voting, 15, 16–22
North-east regions
   Italian citizens, 21
   macro-political areas, 135, 136,
      137, 138

occupation
   multinomial logistic regressions,
      145, 147, 149, 151
   profile by voter type, 136, 137, 138
opinion voter, 92n3
optimization algorithms, fast and
   frugal heuristics, 49, 50–51
outcome, electoral choice, 6

Pannella, Marco, 108
Parisi, Arturo, 92
Parliament, 89
parties
   alliances, 107–108
   identification and voting, 17–18
   multiple unidimensional
      unfolding analysis, 172
   placement on life-right
      continuum, 97–98, 99n7, 100,
      122

parties (*continued*)
    utilius voters, 105
    voters ordering, 170–171
    voting for, 226, 227
party ordering, 101–103, 105, 170–171
Partito dei Verdi, 87
Partito della Rifondazione Comunista (PRC), 87, 102, 226, 227
Partito Democratico della Sinistra (PDS), 87, 103, 226
Partito Popolare Italiano (PPI), 88, 103, 226
Partito Socialista Italiano (PSI), 87
Pasquino, Gianfranco, 92
Pearson's correlation coefficients, judgment on leaders, 203, 204
Peterson, Cameron, 36
Petty, Richard, 44
Pizzorno, Alessandro, 116
political activism
    multinomial logistic regressions, 146, 148, 150, 152
    participation by voter type, 139n8, 141, 142, 143
political belief system
    conceptualization, 64
    consistency, 64
    constraint, 64
political choice
political cognition approach, 57–59, 68
    decision making, 81
    experimental studies, 71–73
    human decision making, 9–10
political corruption, judicial investigations, 86

political discussion
    multinomial logistic regressions, 146, 148, 150, 152
    participation by voter type, 139n7, 141, 142, 143, 144
political efficacy, 89
political expertise, 62
political interest. *See* interest
political leaders, judgments on, 204
political psychology, sophistication, 61
political science, political sophistication, 60
political sophistication
    concept of, 59–63
    definitions, 60
    dimensions, 124–125
    education, 124
    expectation, 72–73
    heuristics and, 123–133
    information, 124
    interest, 124
    Italian voters, 84
    mass public, 214–215
    measuring, 215–216
political system, Italian, 5–6, 19, 20–21, 85–91, 212–213
Polo delle Libertà
    alliance, 108–109
    victories for leaders of, 109, 110
    voters, 224, 225
Polya, George, 76
Popper, Karl, 29, 30
predictive error decomposition strategy, 50n4
probability theory, 36
procedural rationality, Simon, 27–28
process of creative thought, heuristic, 74
Prodi, Romano, 88, 108, 189, 194

prospect theory, expectations and
  outcomes, 41
psychological approach, voting, 17
psychological plausibility
  models, 53
  principle of, 82, 83
psychology, political cognition,
  57–59
public administration, 173, 174
public opinion
  decision-making strategy, 6–7
  ideological identification and
    specific opinions, 65
  political cognition, 57

questionnaires, 42n2

RAI TV, 194, 197
randomness, 68
rational behavior, 55
rational choice theory
  application, 18
  decision-making, 4, 26, 34–37, 72
  political involvement, 63n4
  preferences, 40–41
rationale
  electoral, 15–16
  human decision making, 8
rationality
  absolute rationality, 27n4
  adaptation to environmental
    structures, 54
  assumption, 37, 37n1
  collective outcome, 68
  human action, 27–28, 30–31
  model of rational actor, 30, 33
  Olympic rationality, 27n4, 28
Rawls, John, 218
reasoned choice, voting, 16, 26–31

recognition heuristic, 51–52
Redlawsk, David, 71–73, 221
religiosity
  multinomial logistic regressions,
    146, 148, 150, 152
  participation by voter type, 140,
    141, 142, 143, 144
  practicing believers, 140, 140n11
representativeness heuristic, 38–39
Rifondazione Comunista (RC), 170
Rokkan, Stein, 21
Rutelli, Francesco, 109, 189, 194,
    204, 205

salience, 42n2
Sani, Giacomo, 92
Sartori, Giovanni, 92, 225
Scaling, multiple unidimensional
    unfolding, 167
  calculation, 168n2
  ideological coherence by voting
    preference, 179–181
  inter-subjectivity, 167–168
  Loevinger's H coefficient as index
    of, 168
Scalfaro, Oscar Luigi, 108
schemata, 61n3, 61–62
Schmitt, Carl, 105
Second Republic
  Italian voters, 22, 86
  new electoral law, 86, 88–89
  political judgment, 90
  political subcultures, 154
secrecy, voting, 15
self-anchoring scales, 101n8
self-placement
  interaction with voting
    preference, 192
  left-right continuum, 163

Simon, Herbert, 30
    ecological rationality, 5, 47
    human decision making, 81
    procedural rationality, 27–28
    theory of bounded rationality, 48
situational logic, Popper, 29
situation of action, 30
Sniderman, Paul, 57
social science, heuristics, 73–76
sociodemographic and attitudinal
        factors. *See* voting
sociodemographic profiles, 134–139
    utilius, amicus and *aliens,* 134
    voter types for 1996 election, 136
    voter types for 2001 election, 137,
        138
sociologists, decision making, 4–5
sophistication. *See also* political
        sophistication
    definition, 62
    idea of, 123–124
    interactive, 69
Southern Italy
    macro-political areas, 135, 136,
        137, 138
    voters, 154
Stark, Phil, 199
strategy selection learning theory,
        55–56
subjective expected utility (SEU),
        34, 35–36, 54
substantive criteria, voters, 80n1
support theory, preferences and
        judgments, 42
sympathetic voter, *amicus,* 105–112
systematicity
    decision-making strategy, 158
    Italian voters, 84
    use of heuristics, 165–166

take-the-best heuristic, 49–51
take-the-first heuristic, 52–53
taxation, 173, 174
television. *See also* media
    communication, 235
    interaction between media and
        voting preference, 191–192
    media consumption, 189
    utilius vs. *aliens,* 194–199
theory of general equilibrium,
        Walras, 18
true attitudes, Zaller, 42
trust, political parties, 89
Tversky, Amos, 33
TV remote effect, *utilius* vs. *aliens,*
        194–199
two-party system, America, 6,
        90–91

Ulivo, 187, 194
    alliance, 108–109
    center-left coalition, 88, 107
    victories for leaders of, 109, 110,
        111
    voters, 224, 225
unfolding model, Coombs, 167
urbanization
    multinomial logistic regressions,
        145, 147, 149, 151
    profile by voter type, 136,
        137, 138
utilius voter, 7, 10, 94, 155n15
    candidates and voting preference,
        192–193
    capacity of individual to place
        parties, 97–104
    classification criteria, 95–105
    decision-making strategy, 11, 125,
        126, 184, 198–199

future research, 217–219
ideological coherence and issue
preferences, 160, 162, 163, 164,
165, 178–181, 192
ideology vs. "TV remove" effect,
194–199
left-right spectrum, 162–163
political participation,
140–143
political sophistication, 128, 129,
130
self-placement and voting
preference, 192
sociodemographic profile, 127,
131–133, 134–139
spatial voter, 95–105
vote for coalition, 225
vote for party, 226, 227
voters per type and overlap with
other types, 119–121

voters
age, 155–156
aliens, 112–117
amicus, 105–112
classification of Italian, 91–95
complexity of political system,
75–76
gender, 155
heterogeneity, 93
ideological, 207–208
inconsistency and instability of,
64–65
medians, 117–118, 121
occupation, 155–156
opinion, 92n3
overlap between types,
119–121
political choices, 75

profile of Italian electorate,
210–211
self-placement, 122
substantive criteria for judging,
80n1
types, 7, 119–121
utilius, 95–105
voter heterogeneity vs.
homogeneity effects, 213–214
voting
ad personam, 15
art, 3
changes in, orientation, 92n2
complex choice, 3–4
decision makers, 8–9
effectiveness of typology,
177–184
final choice, 223–228
heuristics, 67–71, 223–228
individual choice, 15–16,
22–26
nonrandom choice, 15,
16–22
reasoned choice, 16, 26–31
typology of, motivations,
92–93
voting behavior
interpretative model, 20–21
Italy, 21n2
multinomial logistic regressions,
146, 148, 150, 152
participation by voter type, 139,
139n9, 141, 142, 143, 144
relationship between elements of
choice and, 187–188
Weberian sense of action, 20
voting heuristics
cognition and political culture,
142, 144, 153–156

voting heuristics (*continued*)
    decision-making, 157–159
    final voting, 223–228
    future research, 216–223
    stability, 212–213
    validity, 10–11
voting model, Downs', 72,
    160

voting preferences
    interaction of media with, 191–191
    interaction with self-placement, 191
    organizing future, 166–172

Xenophon, 209

Zaller, John, 42